MAN

AND HIS MOTIVES.

BY

GEORGE MOORE, M.D.,

MEMBER OF THE ROYAL COLLEGE OF PHYSICIANS, LONDON, ETC.; AUTHOR OF "THE POWER OF THE SOUL OVER THE BODY," "THE USE OF THE BODY IN RELATION TO THE MIND," ETC.

"I live to move."—*Sir J. Davies*, 1599.

NEW YORK:
HARPER & BROTHERS, PUBLISHERS,
FRANKLIN SQUARE.
1862.

J. H. Brilhard.

PREFACE.

THIS work is somewhat religious; but it is hoped that the reader will not deem an apology necessary on that account, since it is impossible to reflect on the nature and motives of man, without concluding that religion is the end and purpose of reason.

It was formerly the author's ambition to write acceptably on subjects more strictly professional, but circumstances having pressed the higher objects of thought upon his attention, he feels constrained to express his convictions, not because others have not better exhibited those truths which influence his own mind, but because the manner in which he has felt and presented them may suitably meet the state of some other hearts, and induce in them those sympathies, without which life, instead of brightening toward its close, is apt to become dark indeed.

The topics propounded demand and deserve the fullest consideration of every man, but especially of him whose business it is to administer to the relief of mental and physical disorder. The medical practitioner can scarcely be engaged in his duties, with a right feeling of their importance, without discovering that moral influences operate very extensively, both in causing and in curing the majority of maladies. He sees, too, that religious hope enables a patient to bear calmly, and even cheerfully, those evils which therapeutic agents, however important, can neither remove nor ameliorate, while the absence of religion often aggravates disease, and adds terror to death.

The thoughts presented in this volume are such as occurred to the author, while fully occupied in his profession, and are those that his intimacy with sufferers and with suffering leads him to believe are most needed and most neglected.

The sick bed tests a man almost as much as the martyr's pyre; and those who there see something more than bodily disorder, often learn lessons of the greatest practical value, in relation to the spiritual training of man. The physician thus gains instruction for himself, and he who does his best to render such lessons available to others also, ought rather to be deemed worthy of praise than of blame. Those views, which have encouraged the writer's own heart, under appointed and appropriate trial, will probably tend also, in some degree, to improve the faith, feeling, and practice of those who shall peruse, with candor and kindness, what has been writen in patience and hope.

This volume was designed, in connection with two others—"The Power of the Soul over the Body in relation to Health and Morals," and "The Use of the Body, in relation to the Mind"—both of which have been so far favorably received as to warrant the expectation of an equally indulgent reception of this, which, although of rather a different complexion, will probably be thought an appropriate companion to them. Those persons who are disposed to dig deep, will discover indications in these works that they are based upon a substratum of more difficult materials, designedly kept out of sight. We give an architect credit for laying a good foundation, notwithstanding he conceals it under what is intended to be familiar. The suggestion of an argument is usually sufficient for all the practical purpose of persuasion, since those who are reasonable enough to judge of moral truth, readily work out ideas in their own minds, without an elaborate logic, but still in keeping with their self-consciousness and experience. Truth itself is of no advantage to any man, but as it helps to rectify and regulate his desires, by directing his mind to right objects, thus enhancing his hopes as well as his enjoyments, while imparting motives to look further on in the pathway of heaven.

A more philosophical style might easily have been assumed, with the appearance, at least, of greater profundity; but that is not always shallow which appears transparent, not that deep which is dark. The author prefers to express what he feels in such a manner as to seem but superficial truth, provided what he writes excites his readers to look deeper. He would rather invite them to contemplate distinct objects than endeavor to pierce indefinite space, where worlds of light appear but as clouds, because our sight is insufficient for the vastness before it. Man, himself, is the grand wonder, "*mira profunditas, Deus meus, mira profunditas*," a depth of which each one of us may see a little by looking into himself; and another's aid is valuable only but as it may dispose or enable a man to look within. The main object of the writer has been to preserve before the mind tne grand truth, that intelligent love is the only rightful power of government among rational beings. The subject is divided into chapters, which may be read either consecutively or in a detached maner, each receiving illustration from the rest, and yet not requiring that illustration in order to be understood. There is no metaphysi cal evolution attempted, but throughout the work will be found scattered some of the writer's reasons for believing that the Bible is consistent with nature, with the necessities of man, and with all we can conceive of his Maker. Should any injurious error have been introduced, it is sincerely hoped that it may be corrected by reference to the standard of truth, for it is the author's earnest prayer that all his readers may be led to walk in the light of a heavenly life, struggling against all delusion with unfettered soul.

April, 1848.

CONTENTS.

MAN AND HIS MOTIVES.

CHAPTER I.

MAN—PRIMITIVE AND DERIVATIVE.

MAN is not a natural production, and the elements of earth are not sufficient for his completion. He is an embodied spirit, and from the source of his existence he must derive those supplies which may fit him to fulfill the purposes of his creation, and satisfy his capacity for knowledge and happiness.

It is worthy of especial notice that there is scarcely a people to be named which has not among them the tradition or the prophecy of a perfect human nature; and probably every mind imagines some model man, some ideal type or standard of humanity, which all ought to admire and imitate. But earth, as it is, has never been deemed his home. Some suppose him to have existed in a golden era long since departed; others expect him yet to come. Some think that we are his degenerated offspring; others believe that we are progressively improving upon our ancestors, and that, in due time, the progeny of our successors shall be perfect beings, according to an orderly development, "from inherent qualities," by which at length living *monads* become spiritual paragons, under astronomical influences and in virtue of gravitation, and "the modes of action depending solely on organization." We can not exactly calculate how long a period may be necessary for the purpose of converting an infusorial animalcule into a man, such a transformation never having yet been observed in progress; but we are pretty well assured, by the reluctant testimony of infidels, as well as by the careful research of believers, that man can not have been an inhabitant of earth above seven thousand years. Geology, ethnology, and the natural history of our race, bear ample testimony, in this respect at least, to the truth of the book of Genesis, which testimony is itself a fact strongly in evidence of the inspired origin of that book; since to guess at such coincidences in chronology and science is beyond the reach of fancy. This length of time seems not to be quite enough to answer the purposes of the development theory, but we can get no more. We are not ignorant that skulls and other bones of man have been discovered in caves and in stalagmite formations, mixed with those of extinct mammals, both ruminants and carnivora; and that these bones in no respect differ from modern specimens. It is also true that geologists are nearly unanimous in assigning these remains to periods far within the date above named, and all their conclusions on the subject tend to confirm rather than invalidate the statement in the book of Genesis. If, however, man had existed at an earlier period there can be no very evident reason why his fossil remains should not be found imbedded with those of other creatures in the anterior formations.

As it appears from recent theorists that even now man is at best but a paulo-post chimpanzee, he could scarcely have become bimanal and biped at that date, or, at least, monkeys and men ought then to have been mingled in the same family circle.

History, either sacred or profane, has no respect for the theory of development, and does not quite agree with it. Instead of finding mankind brutal and destitute of the arts of social comfort in the early periods of our race, we have reason to believe that they were highly civilized and cultivated; not, it may be, after the complicated manner of the moderns, but still with sufficient decision, in two forms at least, very much as they now present themselves. There were those among the people of most ancient date who took pleasure in exercising power, in tyranny and rapine; while others, impressed by the manifestations of divine wisdom in the wondrous works of creation, or by the tradition of God's covenant with man, took delight in meditating upon his providence, and preserved a life of quiet thoughtfulness and worship. According to moral motives and the state of will, with regard to the revelations of existence, the minds of men appear always to have been actuated to the attainment of ends in keeping with their faith and knowledge. Religion always made the grand difference among mankind. There were always sons of God as well as of Belial. Those who, being instructed concerning righteousness, and believing and loving truth, were looking forward to a future life, occupied their faculties in subserviency to that end, while those who regarded the present life as their only hope, gave themselves to the indulgence of their tastes for sensual pleasures, and to the contrivance of such means as best promised the fulfillment of their unholy desires. This, substantially, is all we learn of the history of mankind up to the deluge.

The anxiety of infidels to dispose of the deluge, and to satisfy themselves that they need not believe the Bible, is most wonderful and deplorable. How eagerly some of the French savans seized upon the zodiacs sculptured on the temples of Dendera and Esneh, with the hope that they had therein discovered a demonstration that the Mosaic statement was a mistake. Their ingenuity would have been amusing had it not been impiously absurd. M. Jomard proved to his own satisfaction that these zodiacs were three thousand, and M. Dupuis that they were, at the very least, four thousand years older than the Christian era, while M. Gori would not abate a week of seventeen thousand years. That their mathematical wits* were racked to little purpose is seen in their discrepancy. But observe how the truth at last prevails. M. Champollion comes forward in the promising manhood of his intellect, and gives his life to the study of Egyptian antiquities, and instead of guessing at the meaning and dates of these zodiacs, learns really to read them, and finds that the zodiac, the date of which M. Dupuis had so clearly demonstrated to have been at least four thousand years before Christ, was actually erected in the reign of Augustus Cæsar, and that which M. Gori had carried back in his imagination seventeen thousand years, had been raised in the time of Antoninus, A.D. 140.

If we may credit the oldest history we possess, the correctness of which none can invalidate, the most difficult arts were not unknown amidst the family of the first man. And there is little doubt that before the flood the imaginations of men were refined enough for the invention of whatever might contribute to heighten the enjoyment of mere outside beauty, and to render evil so indomitable in the heart of man that to allow him to live on would be but to permit the propagation of iniquity in such fascinating forms as to banish the beauties of holiness from the earth. It could not have been mere ignorance that was hardened

* "Mathematics is based upon nothing, and therefore arises out of nothing."—(Oken's Physio-philosophy, p. 5.) These words are not quoted because they are true—we can have no idea of plus or minus, point, limit, form, dimension, or proportion, but from real things; a man born blind knows nothing of a triangle unless he has felt its parts

against the preaching of Noah: ingenuity and unbelief, satisfied with their own substitutes for divine order in the appliances of a proud and perverted reason that delights in its own works, were always the resisters of righteousness. Savages would have been converted. The antediluvians in general, at the time of Noah, must have been skeptical geniuses, rationalists, and despots, who could not believe in especial judgments, abrupt transitions, and miraculous interferences for the punishment of vice. They lived under the reign of violence and terror, and being ingenious in disobedience, invented their own religion, and worshiped a mock reason while they blasphemed God, and polluted his sacred image in the form of man. Their spirits were fit to be imprisoned.

The flood came—need it be proved? All nations acknowledge it. A reserved few replenished the new world. Whence have we the tradition of a deluge if it never happened? It was not a partial event—the world owns it. The Chaldeans, Assyrians, Egyptians, Grecians, Romans, Phœnicians, Syrians, Armenians, Persians, Chinese, Hindoos, Arabians, Turks, Africans, the North and South Americans, the Aborigines of the South Seas, and every stray tribe of man, all hold a tradition of the deluge; and science finds the record written on the earth—the grand catastrophe assuredly occurred, and faith reads its significance. The Almighty altered the face of the world which he had made, because the spirits of men required a judgment co-extensive with their abode, and they were removed to a place adapted to their wickedness. The living earth perished in the great deep; but Noah and his sons were not barbarians—they could enter into covenant with their Maker, for they had obeyed his voice. But the original evil was in their blood, and soon we find their offspring madly desirous of reigning without righteousness. That they were not, however, without skill, the tower of Babel bears them witness. The city of Nineveh was magnificent in works of art, and the ancient Memphis was not mean. But we will pass on a few hundred years. What does the progress of time prove? Not that man was not mentally developed, but that his intellect was ever prone to seek satisfaction without obeying God, and that Almighty interference has always been required to prevent the total apostasy of our race. Was Abraham, the friend of God, less a man than any of us, or more so than the first son of Adam? No; but he had superior motives, and in the largeness of his heart he believed God, and was also fit to associate with kings. In trusting to the absolute power of Jehovah as the sovereignty of mercy, and reaching forward in faith for life beyond death, and for an endless futurity of blessing at the hand of the Omnipotent, he exhibits, in his brief story, all that constitutes the sublimity of a human soul; while yet, in the folly of his fears, we see a perfect picture of man's infirmity and guiltiness. Thus we are taught, as he was, that our recovery from degradation to the true standing of an obedient and a believing spirit is a divine work, accomplished by the intelligent apprehension of God's purpose to oneself, and a growing conformity to his will from a growing confidence in his love.

The men of old were not minors in humanity. If we may judge from what Moses has written, he was as great a man as Newton: he preferred to suffer with the people of God rather than to dwell as a prince among ingenious idolaters; and he has presented us with reasons for trusting in Jehovah. It is true that he has not given us the mathematical elements of the celestial mechanism; but yet Newton could discover such plain indications in the writings of the chosen shepherd that Omniscience was his teacher, that the philosopher would at once have distrusted his own cal culations had they in any instance contradicted the Mosaic statement. Who could credit Moses if he wrote merely like a philosopher? He does not seek for causes, but sees the hand of God; he states facts, explains not physics; he writes history, not theories; he defends no hypothesis; he does not speculate; and instead of doubtful opinions he annunciates positive precepts. The moral law which he first conveyed to men is so perfectly suited to man's social and spiritual relations that to break it in any particular is evidently in spirit to contravene the whole, and it is so intimate and consistent, that, like creation itself, it bears the impress of its Maker, and can be no other than a transcript of the Eternal Mind, humanly expressed.

The present state of the world is a proof that Moses, in describing the distribution of Noah's descendants, stated an anticipated truth. The prediction may be tested now—it is the history of the world in a few lines. Philosophers, in tracing mankind to their origin, are obliged to terminate their researches in Asia, as the center of civilization, and the source of all those streams of light which have flowed over the earth. Both creation and the deluge place man in the central East. From thence Shem, Ham, and Japheth divide the world among their offspring. Europe was peopled by those of Japheth; those of Ham spread over Africa and the south-western parts of Asia; and those of Shem populated the teeming Orient. "By these were the nations of the earth divided after the flood." (Gen. x. 32.) The slight statement given by Moses is sufficient for the purposes for which it was recorded—it effectually serves to prove the truth of prophecy God spake by all the prophets since the world began. Thus we see the fulfillment of Noah's prediction concerning his sons, and that the nation from whom the Deliverer came is not obscure. The providence of God is thus traced with specific relations to the final arrangement of the nations, when in the reign of Heaven it shall be manifest, that from the commencement of history and prophecy to their consummation, the earth and its inhabitants have been held in the hand of their Maker, and regarded by Him in their totality, for glorious purposes ere long to be completed. Who told Moses that Noah knew that the islanders of Europe should colonize the East, or that Africa should be an oppressed land? And so with regard to all he foretells. Did Moses study the doctrine of chances in Egypt, and speak truth by accident? Then chance is no longer a name for incongruous contingencies, but the mistress of sciences, that not only predicts but fulfills the miracles she utters. Avaunt, deceiving spirit! Ascribe not to chance the word and power of God. Trace a raindrop from the ocean through the clouds and back again to the deep, and find it there, and then perhaps you may be able to foretell what should happen among the sons of men thousands of years before their birth. It is this evolution of man's destinies, as foreshown in prophecy, that renders the Bible so marvelous, astounding, and trustworthy a book, possessing in its own testimony its own divine credentials, and proving that none have a right to question its doctrines until they have invalidated its authority.

Physiologists persuade us that they have proved that the Caucasian is the highest variety of man, and that the descending scale from this is Mongolian, American, Malay, Negro. If this be true, does it not follow that man came from his Maker's hand as a Caucasian rather than a Negro? Surely it is more consistent to suppose that man was made in his highest form at first, and that he afterward degenerated in his habits and cranial development, than to suppose that he improved upon his Creator's workmanship, and raised himself from the lowest type to the highest. It would be easy to show how the highest might, by neglect of the means bestowed by providence, have descended from the proper standard and model of man. Physiology, history, and the sacred scriptures agree in showing that human degradation has always resulted from neglecting the knowledge and advantages which God bestowed on man for the preservation of society in due order, under the influence of industry, religion, and law.

The origin of man, the law, the divine covenant with man, and man's incessant failure, all the facts and all the prophecies in the Pentateuch, belong more or less to the fuller developments of providence which we recognize as history, and we must nullify our own knowledge to deny that of Moses; and far more: we must resign our trust in Jehovah's dealings with man as his Saviour and his Sanctifier; for to destroy the Pentateuch is to destroy the foundation on which Christianity, with all our hopes, is built. With such interests at stake, we have reason to be in earnest in our defense of the credibility of the Hebrew foundling. But to question the authenticity of Moses is like endeavoring to prove that God forsook the world as soon as he had made it, and has had no intercourse with man since his creation. We may agitate the question—the result will still be an unavoidable conviction that a written revelation is not less a fact than the world we live in. But our object was to show that the nature of man has not been gradually evolved from an inferior form, and we appeal to the totality of history as summed up in the Bible, in proof of our position.

Were the subject exhibited in its physiological bearings, we should see abundant proof that the creative fiat has fixed specific limits within which all creatures continue to propagate their kind after their own likeness, so far at least as never to approximate to a new order. Distinction is preserved amidst variety; the shades of gradation are separate lines; and however near the resemblance between species may be, yet there is no mixture. To suppose otherwise were to ascribe confusion to the work of omnipotence, and to regard nature as a force beyond rule, operating at random to an infinite enormity. Those who assert that one race of living creatures may be developed from another are required first to show us an instance of the fact; but let them be careful to avoid mistakes, for their business is to contradict the conviction of all ages, and to prove that it is absurd to believe that "God made the beast of earth *after his kind*, and cattle *after their kind*, and every thing that creepeth upon the earth *after his kind*." The greater caution is necessary in endeavoring to falsify these words, since those who have hitherto attempted it have only so far succeeded as to prove that the presumption of man is at least indefinite.

It might be easily demonstrated that as long as man has been known to man he has appeared in the same general form and proportion as at present, wonderfully adapted to his place and occupation on earth; but it is of far more importance to observe that, as a thinking being, man was the same when Moses wrote as he is now; and that though fully capable of considering the wonders of creation with a reasonable discernment of their Author's power and wisdom, yet the true awakening and appetite of reason were proved rather in demand for spiritual light than speculative knowledge, for then, as now, man could not reflect without feeling himself a sinner; nor think of God without asking how he was to be justified with Him; nor hope for an immortality of good without finding an Almighty Saviour.

Humanity was, at least in this respect, as much developed when Job and his friends discoursed concerning the government of Providence as it is among modern philosophers who labor under the disadvantage of not having received the New Testament; and it must be granted that the Hebrew prophets knew the holy character of God, and were remarkable for their insight into coming events, since much that they predicted is now visible to our eyes. But if the prophets with their sublime ideas, Job and his friends with their mysterious discussions, and Moses with his august record of the verified order of creation, are realities, we learn that Omnipotence has always operated in keeping with the morals of men, and that Providence is not the development of a mere physical contrivance, but the direction of a spiritual supremacy over beings capable of spiritual instruction by appeals to their understandings, and their motives as rational agents.

Man, then, is not a ripening organism, but a peculiar being, having relation both to the past and to the future, and an interest both in history and prophecy, because time, eternity, and man belong to God, who uses them all for the manifestation of Himself. Hence there can be no bound to man's capacity for intelligence, nor limit to his life, since both life and intelligence are united in him for the purpose of evincing God himself as the Eternal Reason. From this cause it arises that all men who have looked upon this world of light, with their spiritual eyesight open to perceive its beauties, have in all ages exhibited that degree and standard of intelligence which reach at once to the highest conclusions of science, and induce a man to join heart and soul with Job, Moses, David, and the prophets in celebrating the majesty of the Eternal, who in Himself gives unity to all the varieties of nature, makes the worlds of matter and of minds one universe, and claims our confiding trust in His hand, because unceasing providence is His one continued act.

From the foregoing and many other considerations, both scientific and religious, we shall probably be justified in preferring to believe the statement that man was expressly created in relation to his Maker rather than that he was developed from an inferior creature. We would not, however, question the fact, that Omniscience is at work in all the universe, diffusing life and mind among innumerable beings, none of which stands alone, and among the minutest of which not a feeling is awakened that is indifferent to the heart of the Creator. He regards all his works, in their infinite totality, with a full knowledge of each inscrutable particular. His love is not divided, His mercy is over all, because all is His; but it is through man that the unity of nature is revealed, and the loving kindness of Omnipotence made manifest. And as no other creature on earth is conscious of God's love, so if he fail, through ignorant or malicious motives, to obey that love, he departs from his right place in creation, and bears a curse where he should have conveyed blessing.

Human existence is not an accident—God has a purpose in it; let us, therefore, endeavor to discover what belongs to us, and by learning how we are provided for, learn also what is demanded on our parts, in order to obtain our right position as individual spirits.

If we may judge from the more recently imported specimens of scientific surmise concerning man's derivation, there appears to be no such great improvement in the theory of development, as will serve to account either for our hopes or our fears, The mere fact that we are conscious beings, that can think of the demands of Deity on our consciences, is, however, the *only* omission in the scheme! Polarization and matter being given, make a man, says the physio-theorist. There is the difficulty; the materials may suffice to form a body, all we want is the soul; in short, the theory fails in its working, and gives us the man—all but himself!

"Man is also a child of the warm and shallow parts of the sea," says Oken, the *logical* physio-philosopher, (§ 213, Ray Soc. Transl.) "It is possible that man has only originated on one spot, and that, indeed, the highest mountain in India. It is even possible, that only one favorable moment was granted in which men could arise. A definite mixture of water, definite heat of blood, and definite influence of light, must concur to his production; and this has probably been the case only in a certain spot and at a certain time." "The deluge cast up the first men," (Oken, p. 324.) "They were littoral inhabitants, and, without doubt (!), carnivorous, as savages still are (?). From whence could they have obtained also fruits, cabbage, and turnips?" Whence, indeed—ask Moses. The certain time and the certain place of theory are the most uncertain things in the world, and the assumed definite mixtures necessary to make a man are more undefined than the man in the moon. But there are two or three points in this anthropology which are worthy of remark. The author acknowledges the deluge, and derives man from the East, and traces him, so to say, to one source. Would he have done so if he had not been compelled, in spite of his theory, to yield to the evidences in favor of these facts?

The philosopher ascribes the production of man to sea-mucus, or, to use chemical language, hydrated carbon. From this, he asserts, all organized beings have originated, and, by *self-elevation*, issued forth into higher organisms. Thus creative will is dispensed with; and man, like all the rest of moving things, grew up of his own accord, from the *infusorium* of a putrid sea-mucus. There stands the word, and there, the fact—"Male and female created *He* them." If it could but be proved that there is no personal God, and that he did not create male and female, this theory would not be half so wonderful;

but that, with the definite mixture of heat, light, carbon, and water, in some certain time and certain place, two of each kind, male and female, of all the myriads of animated being, should have sprung up as a natural matter of course, and that only *once*, is very marvelous indeed, since we can see no reason why what has emerged from the shallow and warm sea should not emerge again. Sea-mucus is under as favorable circumstances for forming a man as ever, both in the West and in the East, or otherwise man and mucus could be scarcely existing in the same globe together. Whence can the organic have originated but from the inorganic? asks the philosopher again. We reply, Could not God create both?

It will probably best promote our object, if we look back to the more authentic record of our origin, and learn our Maker's estimate of our existence.

The first man—the man of earth, *e terrâ terrenus*, was, in his outward existence, fashioned and conformed with the materials of this objective world, in bodily keeping with the order of the elements from which he was to derive the sustentation of his physical life, and those impressions which should excite in his soul ideas and experience. Raised erect from the ground, as if by the hand that formed his body of the dust, he stood forth mature and perfect, exquisitely organized to be the fit inhabitant of the Paradise prepared by the Almighty, on purpose to prove the greatness of His goodness to His most august and stupendous creature. The spirit of animation, the very breath of God, kindled every fibre of his frame, and constituted within it a distinct selfhood, a being of thought and will, which thus reflected the mind that made it capable of perceiving and appreciating Divine purpose. In self-consciousness man responded to the movements of his living heart; within himself he felt existence to be a personality. Gradually the life with in him opened the avenues of knowledge, and, as he stirred and felt, motion and sensation seemed one with himself. As a babe, tenderly nestled by its mother's loving heart, finds every thing around it so thoroughly arranged to meet the demands of its awakening mind, that nothing jars upon its senses; so man, by degrees, awoke to the presence of his prepared place, lapped in Paradise, with nothing wanting to the growth of his soul in knowledge and bliss. All things were so consistent with his nature, that surprise entered not amidst the expanding harmony of his enjoyments. The light, attempered in heaven, touched with the gentleness of God's own finger, the fine sensitive nerves of vision, even through his sealed eyelids, so as to cause them, with an involuntary action, to open of themselves, like the petals of a flower, and to admit into the soul, as at one draught, the whole paradise of sight. Thus man seemed united to all he saw, and, as one that dreams of peaceful glories, the scenes around him appeared but as if formed by his own spirit. Perfume blended with beauty in the dewy radiance, and the varied utterances of love and joy from every living thing mingled their music in the balmy air, and passed together so sweetly into his soul, that they became a world of ideas within him, more mighty in their influence, as thoughts, than were the things that caused them. Man began to reason, and then God met him, and that in such a manner, that he needed not to be told who was his Maker. The Almighty met man to command him, and to call upon him to name every animated thing according to his apprehension of its nature. He invested man with authority, and imparted to him power to hold dominion over all that moved in earth, and air, and sea; because he understood, by converse with Divine Intelligence, why and for what ends all were created. Without laborious research and elaborated logic, man saw the meaning of each form and physical attribute, and required no anatomy to prove the benevolence of design; since every creature expressed, in every action, its own happiness, and all nature responded in joy to the benediction of God. The power, the will, and the pleasure of activity were in man united, in tilling the ground and replenishing the fruitful earth with all that might be cultivated by his skillful hand, to administer to his taste for beauty, or his need for aliment; and it was man's appointed business so to direct his knowledge of nature and necessity, as to contribute, by his wise employment of nature's productiveness, to the wants and pleasures of all the sentient creatures over which he held dominion. Thus the life of man was actively engaged in multiplying blessings, and therefore he felt that life was blessed; he loved to live, because he lived in love, and satisfied the demand of every day by daily taking fresh fruit from the tree of life, as if from the hand of his God and Father. But he still needed a reciprocity of affectionate intercourse, and a fellowship in worship and authority. From his own flesh a help was formed for him by the finger of his Maker, for God knew that man required more than to reign alone over a dumb world, in order to the completion of his blessedness; since finite reason, without a corresponding heart, would need no tempter to turn the Garden of Eden into a solitary waste. Jehovah consummated his gifts, and brought to man a being that might lean upon his bosom, and with kindred love claim to speak with his heart. But human nature was intended to be the revelation of Omnipotence, and therefore, with all its duties, came also danger, and with every good, the possibility of evil. But the highest good was the highest test of the will, and therefore, with affection, man entered on that trial by which he proved himself dependent on God for the power of loving with a right spirit. Man chose to partake with woman of the vain hope of living independently of God for knowledge and for wisdom. He loved the best creature that he could love more than he loved the Being who gave him that object of his heart; and woman wished to have something to confer on man besides herself and her love. He forgot that he was bound, by the very terms of his existence, to hold all his affections in the sanctity of obedience to the loftiest love, and she forgot that love was better than knowledge and dearer than life. They were created under law; they felt, they thought, they desired, they acted, they reigned under law; and the happiness of their disposition, of their ideas, of their actions, proved that the law of their creation and well-being was the benevolence and love of the Creator toward them, for God had so ordered Paradise, on purpose to please and to employ them. But there is duty in law, the creature must obey in order to be blest. The power imparted to man must be regulated by his own will to right ends, he must behave like a thinking spirit, and that can only be by limiting his actions in voluntary and intelligent obedience to acknowledged truth. With this necessary condition, the exercise of power leads only to the enjoyment of present realities, and, with ever-coming hopes, to the enlargement of faculty and fuller bliss. The knowledge of facts and objects is but mental chaos, without an understanding of the Divine intention in the order and plan of nature and Providence; and this intention is revealed to us, that we may learn that love is obeyed only by being trusted.

What might have been but for the fall we need not ask. Perhaps the words "might be" mean impossibility, and whatever is could not have been but as it is. At least we know that all events are managed by the Might that reconciles all things to himself. We may still do what Adam did. He doubtless saw more and more clearly as he studied the handiwork of God, that there is a constant coincidence between the lessons taught by physical order and those taught by moral ordinances; because the will of Heaven is expressed in both, and that will is alike wise and good. But in undue creaturely affection Adam lost sight of goodness and wisdom, and yielding to the voice that contradicted God, he neglected the first of all duties, that of self government, and fondly, and in mere sympathy, subordinated the lordship of his soul by giving to a beauteous creature the whole of his heart, and thus converted God's own temple into the house of idolatry and sin. We habitually do the very same thing. Herein we find proof of our fall, and the profundity of that fall. All the qualities which the first man possessed are visibly lapsed into disorder, and we see and feel them to be so in ourselves and in our associates. The fall is a fact in our own experience; we are born into it and can not raise ourselves out of it. Still, however, in some sort we retain those characteristics of mind which must have distinguished the first human being. There is sense, but it is abused; there is the love of life, but it regards not its source; there is the desire for knowledge, but it is naturally a vague curiosity, or, at best, but the love of natural science blended with curious doubts of manifest truth; there is the love of exercising power, but instead of the fostering dominion of a charitable reason devising good for all that it can serve, it is apt to become an assumption of a right to rule, so as to make government a tyranny of terror, and all obedience mere eye-service; there is the love of sociality and of sex, but it is always ready to degenerate into the calculation of comforts, the dalliance of fond souls, or the luxuriance of romance and wantonness. Instead of affianced faith, with hopes sure and certain, there is fancy with her deluding phantasms, and expectations incompatible with Divine government; instead of wisdom learn ing humbly to work with her own hands in cultivating the rooted tribes of earth, while her soul is turned heavenwards, there is self-satisfied conceit, seeming to see something to laugh at in the distortions of humanity, and yet wondering at man's folly. Instead of a conscience open as light to light, there is cringing and cowardice, and creeping behind the trees to hide from God in the twilight; and instead of a free will, refusing to know evil, there is now a crash of opposing volitions and desires too frequently devoted to works of darkness. But we need not search for sin, it is every where—the similitude to God is gone from the soul of man. We acknowledge that we see his likeness in the moral law, but we do not find it in our hearts. If we look at them in the light we discern a substitute there which the grand Deceiver might have furnished. But, nevertheless, we know a way in which the image of God may be indelibly restored in true knowledge, righteous activity, sensible manifestation, unfailing faith, obedient power, love unfeigned, clear conscientiousness, and liberty of will.

The reception of truth in love is the restoration of the perfect man, and God's own spirit is its source.

We must be conscious of what we need before we shall seek for it, and we must know what is essential to a right state of mind before we shall discern our defects and desire their removal. Let us therefore look a little more closely into this subject.

For the purpose of obtaining a succinct and simple view of the prominent peculiarities of our mental and moral constitution, it will probably be sufficient to consider man in relation to his pleasures. In this view we must, in fact, include both his desires and his endowments, since he can desire only what he may believe shall contribute, either directly or indirectly, to his pleasure; and he can attain this end only by such means as are placed within his power. Thus by studying our inclinations and our aims we shall learn what is essential to our happiness, and ascertain whether we are employing our faculties in a manner calculated to secure our ultimate satisfaction. Every faculty is associated with its appropriate desire, and is exercised with an appropriate pleasure.

1st. Man is endowed with senses; hence the desire and the enjoyment of sense.

2d. Man is enabled to exert himself, and he desires to do so, and finds enjoyment in action.

3d. Man possesses the faculty of conceiving and contemplating the mental images of things not present to his senses; hence he possesses the desire, and experiences the pleasure, of exercising imagination, memory, and fancy.

4th. Man has intellect, or the power of thinking on the nature and property of things in relation to each other; hence he desires knowledge, and enjoys reflection and comparison.

5th. Man is capable of crediting statements beyond his actual experience, and he is apt to believe more than he can learn through his own senses; and in believing he finds pleasure.

6th. Man loves certain qualities which he esteems amiable; hence his desire for objects of affection and his pleasure in them.

7th. Man has the capacity of distinguishing good from evil in relation to moral law; he has a conscience, in the right state of which he desires to do his duty, and in so doing receives pleasure in self-approval, and the approbation of God, and the good and goodwill of his neighbor.

Will, in the abstract, may be regarded as characteristic of consciousness: there is no mind without it. As the possibility of any pleasure implies the possibility of its opposite, pain; so there can be no sense of things, either agreeable or otherwise, but because the willing being, or agent, is correspondingly affected. But there is a higher form of will pertaining to rational existence, by which we choose, not merely according to sensation, but also according to moral conviction. We do not always obey our desires, but sometimes deny ourselves a pleasure in consideration of results that may affect our future well-being; hence it evidently appears that we possess the power, if willing, to exert our faculties either to oppose or to encourage any of our natural desires for the purpose of accomplishing some end, in pursuing which all our endowments are modified, both as regards the dispositions and pleasures connected with them.

Desire, power, and pleasure, imply the existence of a selfhood that desires, acts, and is pleased. The existence of these faculties implies the love of life, and this conducts us to the consideration of immortality. The selfhood has relation to an outward consciousness, through the senses, by which images of objects are impressed on the mind. Desire, action, and pleasure, must of course relate to objects either perceived or inferred. We can not see God, but we can believe in his existence, and love him too, if we feel his benevolence through the many proofs which he presents to our senses. The groundwork of all thought is objective. Our Maker teaches us by what he has actually done for us both in body and in spirit: he does not demand our allegiance but on palpable evidence and conviction.

We can in no case see the cause either of action or reaction, motion or rest, either mentally or materially. We witness only the media and vehicles of power, either dynamic or resistant; and whether we study physical forces or moral influences, we find that objects are alike but signs of spiritual existence; so that all we can know of truth is but inference concerning the relation of things ostensible to things beyond the sphere of our senses, or else but the direct communication to our minds of intelligence from some being better informed concerning the secrets of creation in their union and totality. Reason must either infer from effects to causes, or be instructed by revelation. Belief in God is the end in both cases. By inference man forms a notion of Deity according to the extent of his own knowledge of nature, but by revelation he is taught the moral attributes of God, as a being causing himself to be known to man in righteousness and love forever.

It will therefore be but consistent and reasonable to treat our subject with reference both to natural and revealed truths, while still confining our attention, for the most part, to man's inherent love of pleasure, and the means provided for its gratification. Keeping the capacity either for enjoyment or misery always in view, we may distribute our thoughts without regard to any artificial system; still, however, preserving, as far as possible, throughout our disquisitions, the distinction felt by us all between the intellectual, moral, and emotional conditions of our nature.

This plan is a deviation from that indicated by metaphysicians, but we may, notwithstanding, be able to show that it is not the less congruous with what we know of ourselves, and with what the Maker of mind has condescended to teach us. We would not, however, depreciate the labors of those capacious and masculine intellects that have investigated and expounded the science of mind, but would rather freely and thankfully acknowledge our obligation to many of them, who, like men of faith and reason, have met infidelity on its own ground, and there defeated it, by casting in its eyes a new light, and causing it to see the hideousness of its own features, as if reflected in the bright shield of truth.

CHAPTER II.

SELFHOOD—SOUL, MIND, SPIRIT

WHAT IS a soul? It is yourself. Some notorious physiologists tell us they can not discover the soul, and, according to the best of their judgment, that which is moved by the rational will is the same thing as that which wills to move. Bones, muscles, nerves, bloodvessels, and brain, constitute a thinking and feeling machine, say they, working on chemical and mechanical principles—and that this machine is a man when arranged in the form of a wingless biped, and a brute when contrived for walking on four feet. Moses was not enlightened, like a modern philosopher, by feeling his way in the dark. He saw a little further into the mysteries of man's existence than these physiologists, and certainly concluded, by the divinity within him, rather than by inference, that mere machinery is not disposed to think of the personal character of the Deity; but that a being that reflects upon the past, and pries into the future, with a desire to know God, and to resemble him, is really his representative on earth. If man may be in any respect a similitude of his Maker, it can only be in his mental and moral nature, unless, indeed, the Almighty—preposterous thought!—be himself a bodily being, and nothing more. Of course, no one will deny that matter would feel, and think, and worship, if Omnipotence ordained that it should; but then that must be a matter of which we can not conceive the existence, for it must be a matter with a personal will.

Without turning to the Bible, we can discern that understanding and will, in a moral and religious sense, can proceed only from God's own direct impression of truth on the mind of man. We can know nothing but by Divine teaching, the thinking faculty and the object of thought being both created. The apprehension of God as a personal Being, demanding our obedience and adoration, is surely not a property of matter—adoration is mental conformity to God's will. This power, proceeding from the Creator to the creature, and enabling it to think and will with a recognition of himself, can not be organic. Matter exists, indeed, as a medium for manifesting to us the thoughts even of God himself, but this must be to a mind, to a being, that thus perceives the purpose and will of the Creator, and this being, when conformed to that will and purpose by a corresponding will and purpose in his own person or individuality, is the image of God in as far as any creature can resemble Deity, or reflect his character.

It is the man himself that perceives, thinks, and determines; but the power to perceive, think, and determine can not be predicated of the body, or any part of it, therefore the man himself can not be the body, but something occupying and influencing the body so as through it to become acquainted with the objects of sense. Desire, emotion, intellect, result from the operation of the discerning and reasoning power in consequence of sensation, which is itself a mental perception of bodily impression, and which induces the percipient principle to act according to its own nature. That which perceives is the subject of sensation, and therefore can not have been caused by sensation. Without the anterior existence of an agent to receive impressions through the senses, sense could not be. Reason thus seems indubitably to demand our assent to the fact asserted in the common language of mankind as to the existence of a distinct agent as the actuating principle in a living human body.

But a new kind of rationalism has arisen of late, which, while acknowledging the reality of revelation, nevertheless refuses to receive as truth any thing which can not be demonstrated to the senses. Those who addict themselves to the dogmatism of such a sensible faith not being able to see, hear, touch, or taste the soul, nor to test it by any chemical agents, very consistently deny its existence altogether. And yet, yielding somewhat to the fashion of belief in favor of the Bible as an authoritative document, because its historic, internal, and collateral evidences amount to a demonstration of its rightful claims to our credence, these rational believers have succeeded at last in convincing themselves, that in that marvelous Book there is no such thing spoken of as a soul or spirit irrespective of the body, and therefore they conclude that bodily existence, such as we witness, is all we are taught by the words spirit and soul as applied to man, either in this life or the next.

It is my anxious desire to found all my metaphysical opinions upon the Bible, because I think this book contains an explicit statement of God's mind as regards all that is essential for us to believe, in order to our everlasting prosperity, both as intellectual and moral beings. The sacred volume, indeed, is not constructed on philosophical principles, because it is God's word, and therefore there is no speculation in its announcements; for God does not propose to theorize on his own work, but yet whatever can be proved true in philosophy and science must be found in keeping with scriptural statements if these are true, since one truth can not contradict another. I believe in the truth of revelation because I have not been able to discover any thing of a demonstrable kind, either in the science of matter or of mind, at variance with it, and therefore if I now hear of a doctrine like that which asserts the non-existence of any thing but what may be seen, heard, or handled, and find that it does not agree with what we know of physical, mental, or divine teaching, it is no difficult task to determine to what class of productions the said doctrine belongs.

But what does revelation as well as common reason announce concerning the soul as a distinct spiritual existence?

There is much dispute about the words spirit and matter, but what we want is meaning. Probably all men understand by matter something capable of impressing the senses, something to be estimated on physical principles. Now that which thinks and wills can not be perceived by our senses, nor have its properties and forces tested by physical means. We can not see thought with the eye, like light; we can not cause it to travel by a wire, like electricity; it is something more subtile than either, but yet it operates on matter, and causes it to impress our senses; and thus you, my reader, have before you a visible expression of the ideas in my mind. But the ideas are not on the paper; you see the signs of them, and by the eye of the mind see them in your own soul, where they are formed as they are in mine, because we are both of us thinking beings. We can not now perceive each other by the bodily eye, nor could we if we met; we should only see the outward form of an inward power; because it is not the thinking being that is seen, but that which the thinking being acts upon. Yet a consciousness of our thoughts and desires is not a consciousness of any particular object as present to our senses, for we think of ideas, and ideas have no physical existence, and yet they are real and potential in their influence on our conduct and comfort. Now that which thinks and wills we may call spiritual and immaterial, since we find no analogy between its nature as experienced by ourselves, and any material object.

Those who deny the existence of immaterial or

spiritual being are obliged to conclude that the Deity Himself is material, and some have daringly asserted that they intend this. But we will suppose they are using terms in an unusual sense, and that they really mean that the matter of a spiritual existence is different from any of which we have any notion. If so, it is manifest that neither we nor they can comprehend what kind of matter they write about. If the matter they mean is incorruptible, and immortal, and thoughtful *per se*, then it is not matter in its common sense character, but something else, and this something may be called spirit, to distinguish it from things that are insensible, corruptible, and mortal, or liable to atomic change and integral destruction.

Unless moral law be the same as physical law, there must be moral existence as well as physical existence. Does not reason every where acknowledge that love to God and our neighbor is utterly different from elective affinities and the forces that bind materials together? Have we no conscience, no response within us to the rightfulness of doing unto others as we would that they should do to us under similar circumstances? Yes; we can will in keeping with an ordinance that is not a physical law; we can acknowledge the benevolence of our Maker, and consent to His demand upon us to act in keeping with His love.

Physical law is an ordinance that has nothing to do with obedience; it is irresistible, and yet capable of being altered by Divine determination, so that the visible universe might cease to be what it is; but moral law is unalterable, because it expresses the character of God himself, and therefore we may infer that the beings to whom it applies are also indestructible; but of course only because Divine will constitutes them responsive with respect to the Divine attributes—"That which is born of the Spirit is spirit." Spiritual laws are addressed to spiritual beings, and we can not be otherwise than of the nature of spirits if we are enabled so to think and will as to desire truly to adore the Deity, who is a Spirit; for surely intelligent worship is but as the conscious response of an understanding soul bowing through all its being in the felt glory of Jehovah's presence. It is mind apprehending the terrible beauty of holiness, and looking, in the consciousness of dependence, for Almighty sustentation, because it feels itself created on purpose to receive its own sufficiency only from the fullness of its God.

If we believe the Bible we believe that our Maker calls men spiritual beings. It is true that, in the sacred scriptures, from which alone we can learn anything concerning existence beyond sense, the word spirit (πνεῦμα) is used in several significations, but still it is certainly often employed to designate the power or attribute of a distinct conscious, active agent, and by implication, therefore, to designate that agent itself. God is a Spirit—not the energy of a being, but energetic being itself. The spirits of just men made perfect are perfect men, and so with regard to beings of every order to whom the word spirit is applied. It expresses both the mode or state of an existence, and the existence itself, because mode and state can not be predicated of that which does not exist.

A great degree of confusion exists with regard to the use of the terms *mind*, *soul*, and *spirit*, which probably might be obviated by considering the word *soul* as significant of the self hood, which is exhibited by will and understanding, these together being called mind, or the soul, in relation to emotion and perception; the term *spirit* being restricted to designate the attribute, character, or nature of the mind. Thus man is proved to be a psychical being, or soul, by his mental faculties; and these prove themselves, by the mode of their operation and their motives, to be essentually spiritual, in distinction from physical.

It is not for us to determine whether a created spirit is necessarily conjoined with some kind of body or not. Conjunction is not unity. We neither know what spirit nor what body is. The elements with which we are familiar are but different forms of force according to the fiat of Omnipotent will, and, for aught we can say, spirits may always embody their wills by expressing them in appropriate forces, so as to be sensibly seen, heard, and felt, by beings in a like order of existence. We need not, however, speculate curiously concerning this subject, since it is enough for us that, whether in the body or out of the body, it is the expressed purpose of our God to provide means for all the happiness which, as confiding creatures, we can require. There is a spiritual body, we are told, and the idea of a body is necessary, in order to convey to our conceptions the idea of action, because a bodily form is essential to all we know of outward operation; nor can we imagine mental influence but in relation to a body; but yet it is the influence or power of one thing upon another, agent and subject, and therefore they can not be the same things.

But the term *soul* (ψυχή), as employed in the New Testament, is most peculiarly significant of a conscious individuality. Though it is often translated *life*, *mind*, and *heart*, in accommodation to the English idiom, it has always a personal property and power, and it is evident that it was understood by the Apostolic writers to mean something besides bodily life, or any thing pertaining to existence limited to earth, since it is mentioned in reference to a continuance of being after the death of the body. Thus our Lord says, "Fear not them which kill the body, but are not able to kill the soul." (Matt. x. 28.) And his beloved disciple uses these emphatic words: "I saw under the altar the souls of them that were slain for the word of God." (Rev. vi. 9.) "I saw the souls of them that were beheaded," &c. (Rev. xx. 4.) Here we can not mistake the intention of the writer, since, whether the language be figurative or literal, it is clearly meant to state that those spoken of were veritable men, notwithstanding they had died.

The word *soul* may almost invariably be understood to signify a selfhood, and therefore we so often find that the personal pronoun may be substituted for it. We have a striking instance of this in relation to the resurrection of our Lord, as stated in Acts ii. 31.— "His *soul* was not left in hades, neither did his flesh see corruption." Here is a broad distinction between the actual personal being and the body: and as if the more powerfully to convey a sense of this distinction, we find the word signifying soul is not in the original of this verse, and the passage really stands thus:— "He (David) seeing this before, spake of the resurrection of Christ, that *He* was not left in hades." That *I* and *my soul* are equivalent terms, is seen in the Divine announcement,—"Behold my servant, whom *I* have chosen; my beloved, in whom *my soul* is well pleased." To deny oneself for the sake of following Christ is the same as to forego one's own soul in order to save it, as we find, on comparing Matt. xvi. 24, with Mark viii. 34, 35. In short, great part of the Bible might be quoted to show that the soul and the self are the same, according to inspired language, as when the Son of the Highest, groaning under *His* sense of man's iniquity, said, "*My soul* is exceeding sorrowful even unto death."

Can we suppose that Paul could employ the following phrases without believing in his own existence, independent of the, *corpus humilitatis* of which he complained: "I desire to depart, which is far better." "We are confident and willing rather to be absent from the body and to be present with the Lord." *Probamus magis peregrinari e corpore, et incolere a Domino.*

(Griesbach.) "Lord Jesus, receive my spirit," said the dying proto-martyr, when he committed himself to his Saviour for eternity, and the thought next before death was becoming a resister of sin and a follower of the crucified One—" Lord, lay not this sin to their charge. And when he had said this, he fell asleep." Fell asleep; is it not somewhat strange that this gentle and frequent phrase, which so sweetly expresses the peaceful departure of a believer, should have led to the conclusion that the Christian soul continues without wakefulness until the end of time? Strange, that because the man of faith closes his eyelids upon the light of earth and reposes as confidently in the arms of his God as a weary child upon the bosom of its mother, therefore the soul awakes not to the light of heaven, although the very scripture in which the phrase is placed also tells us that the Lord, to whom the martyr had committed his being, was seen by him in spirit at the right hand of God, and with God's glory, in that heaven to which he looked.

A name* famous in the subtleties of logic is associated with the defense of this notion, but it appears as if it had been with a total abandonment of his accustomed acumen, and in a desperate hope of modifying the objections of materialists to the broad and unaccommodating language of revelation. It is a grief of soul to see the benevolent efforts of a lordly spirit so completely defeated by the extravagance of his ready accommodation to those spiritual paupers who so sturdily ask charity because they have no faith. Not being able to discover the least glimmering of a reason to infer from the words of the Bible, or its spirit, that man dies with his body, the gifted writer referred to, met the smiling skeptic half way, with a surmise that as the body seemed so essential to action in this world, it might be the appointment of Omnipotent wisdom to keep the

* Archbishop Whately.

soul in a sound sleep, somewhere, until the resurrection, when it would find itself suitably provided with a machinery to work with. But this purposeless slumber of the soul served only to excite the greater ridicule of the unbelieving and profane while deepening the sorrow of the devout; for the notion seemed to imply that the Maker of all worlds being deficient in materials to employ human and departed spirits, laid them by in dormant idleness until a new organization could be conveniently arranged for their use, which might be after indefinite ages had rolled over their transmuted dust.

It is said, "Them also who sleep in Jesus will God bring with him." In keeping with this language is that most ancient and unfulfilled prophecy, "Behold, the Lord cometh with the myriads of his saints." "The Lord my God shall come, and all the saints with thee." (Zech. xiv. 5.) Now if they come, they must exist; but do they come as resuscitated frameworks and nerve systems? No, unless we are deluded with a nominal revelation, there is another mode of being besides the visible and material, and in that mode they come.

In insisting on the spiritual existence of man I would desire to guard against conveying the notion that material existence is contemptible. That God is the maker of both souls and bodies, is sufficient to give dignity to both, and that the fact that every being but the Infinite must be localized, is sufficient to prove that human beings must be corporeally accommodated with media of action and manifestation in whatever sphere they may dwell.

Those who doubt that the soul may perceive out of the body, should inform themselves how and why the soul perceives in the body. What relation has an object to the sensation which it produces? There is no sensation but in a mind: there is no other necessity for the connection between an image on the retina and the idea which we call sight, than that it is the ordinary law of our constitution while in the body. It is the soul that sees, according to this law, but it sometimes happens that the soul does not see according to this law, but to some other still more inscrutable. Thus in certain states of mind the soul does not perceive the idea of the object really before the eye, but some other idea suggested by that object. This often happens in delirium and mental derangement. Therefore it is manifest that the mind itself makes the idea in such cases. And, indeed, it always produces its own ideas, in so far as there is no idea but by an act of the mind. Thus to confine ourselves to sight, by way of illustration, images are constantly impinged on the retina, but we do not discriminate between them unless we attend to them. We must look at them with the mind's eye, or we discern nothing; as we find, if we are busy in thought instead of minding what is about us, we run against a post and beg its pardon. We might always live in such abstraction but for the demands of the body, and, in some diseases, this is a permanent state. Sensation is but one mode of the soul with regard to this objective world, and we know that there is at least one other mode of perceiving—namely, memory, which includes imagination, and by the exercise of which we realize our past experience and make it available knowledge.

We recall ideas in a great measure at will, and we reason on them, and strongly feel them too, without using our eyes, or ears, or tactual organs. Ideas are sometimes vivid enough in meditative minds to obscure all present objects by their brightness. We actually reproduce sensation by pure mental conception and association, and that so powerfully as that emotion also is excited even to a greater degree than when the sensation was first experienced. Thus I have often known a person so disgusted at the remembrance of a disagreeable medicine as not only to seem to taste it, but really to suffer a repetition of all its effects. We do, then, perceive objects again without their presence, and ideas are compounded and multiplied also in our minds, without the use of the senses, so that we may be capable of thinking out of the body, so far as the continuance of mere sensation is concerned. We may have thoughts even if we may not have sensations out of this body, and thought is quite enough to make us either happy or miserable, according to the habits and convictions of our souls. But as sensation is a mode of the soul, and is subject to variations according to the mental states, there appears to be no reason, in the philosophy of the subject, why sensations also may not be experienced in other modes than any with which we are familiar in this world, since those we experience are but mental states and adaptations of our minds in relation to our present life.

Brown, Butler, and other metaphysicians distinguish between outward and inward affections, as if sensation were not mental as well as memory, pain, and desire. In dreams, are our affections outward or inward? I dream, for instance, that I receive a letter, and actually seem to read it with deep interest; I feel the strongest emotion, and on waking I remember many of the sentences, just as I thought I saw them in my dream. Now these sentences were not produced by memory in the act of dreaming, for they had no evident connection with any thing previously in the mind; they were fabricated by the mind without the use of the senses, and without extraneous impression. Therefore the so-called external and internal affections have the same source.

Some persons always dream; others never. Are those that do not dream justified in denying that others do? No; the testimony is too strong to be resisted. But supposing there was but one man in the world who could affirm that he had dreams, ought we to deny the fact simply on the ground that we could not understand it, and it did not accord with our experience?

Exceptions are not contradictions, but they prove the existence of other laws than those in common operation. St. Paul informs us of facts in his experience, by which we learn that a man may enjoy a wondrously higher mode of perception than ordinary: whether he were in the body or out of it he indeed knew not; but yet he in rapture entered Paradise, and in unutterable words received a superabundance of revelations. This was at least an exalted and superior state of mind, something above ordinary sensation—a vast but sudden development of perceptive power, concerning the reality of which we ought no more to doubt, than when an honest person relates to us a dream. We can no more account for the dream than we can for the heavenly ecstasy, and, under certain circumstances, the one might be as common as the other. There are, then, various modes of mental sensation and perception, so unlike each other, that they can scarcely be compared, and therefore we have no reason to question the possibility of still other modes of mind in other conditions of that which is mind, since it is constituted to experience an incalculable variety in its emotions and its perceptions, under the government of the Power whose resources are infinite.

The doctrines of the Bible are in direct contradiction to much that goes under the name of philosophy. The former teaches us, that the universe is controlled by spiritual agencies or beings; the latter, that mental and moral existence is the result of physical arrangements, and consequently, that action, affection, feeling, faculty, reason, and religion, are properties of matter. On this system the cessation of cerebral function is the death of the thinking being. Death is the annihilation of the mind, says the materialist: it is departure to a life far better than this, says the Christian.

What is materiality, but the result of certain im material forces co-operating to produce resistance, form, and whatever property any thing may possess in relation to any other thing? As a natural body exists by the laws of matter, or on the principles of a material manifestation in obedience to the creative will, so a spiritual body exists on other principles, or in keeping with another system of laws or forces in obedience to the same will. Now we see and feel that there is a material body, but how do we know that there is a spiritual body? For the very same reason that we know the one, we know the other also. As we infer from their effects that there are physical forces, although not perceptible through our senses, so we infer that there are spiritual forces, because their effects are demonstrated to our reason. In short, the physical properties of things indicate the existence of forces which are immaterial; and the material world itself is a proof that there is a world of spirits, since matter can exist only as the result of will and purpose, in keeping with beings that think. Omnipotence constitutes every agency. A spiritual body or system is but another mode of accommodating the willing being. We know that our senses and our mental faculties are limited and restrained by the organization through which they now act. There are forces at work that are interferences with sensation, will, and thought. The mind may be withdrawn from these interferences, so as to act only in connection with agencies that may facilitate action. The medium required is always and every where present. The universe consists of forces mutually influencing each other, and all forces are subservient to spiritual influences.

The medium by which life and thought are brought into action is probably the same in all worlds. It is not air, nor heat, nor light, nor electricity, nor magnetism, but something by which these become what they are in relation to matter in general. There is something universal, the law of which is polarity. It pervades all other things, and produces a tendency to union among individuals similarly constituted or related to each other with regard to negative or positive state. It is not subject to gravitation and cohesion, but is fitted at once to the demands of the spirit; and in it the spirit that thinks and wills may perhaps be as really and substantially accommodated and evinced in selfhood and sociality as in the palpable materiality of this lowlier body; for the one mode of existence as well as the other results from spiritual forces put in operation by the will of God. Even now there is a spiritual body as well as a natural body belonging to each of us; and as the consciousness of our existence in human form depends not on our continued consciousness of this flesh and blood, so, if we were at once to depart from this frame of things, we doubtless should still feel a bodily existence, since our spirits would exist in a system of their own, by which we should be altogether human in form, affection, and faculty, and as capable as now, or more capable, of reciprocity and intercourse with other spiritual beings.

As far as reasoning by analogy can prove any thing, it has been proved by Butler and others, that death can have no influence upon any thing belonging to ourselves or our souls; it expends its power upon the body. But if *we* depart from this body and this world, we must pass into some other state, in which some other mode of soul equivalent, or even superior to sensation and perception may be developed. We go to some place, and place implies objects as well as souls; for objects and souls are created for each other. Some mansion is prepared for us. He who ordered our entrance and accommodation here, arranges for our entrance and accommodation elsewhere; and as it is by an operation of the Almighty that we perceive and understand now, so we believe that, hereafter, He will not leave us without means of discerning his wisdom and obeying his will. Before we conclude that the soul can be injured by being merely separated from the body, we must prove that the soul is not provided for by its Maker, but cast adrift upon eternity without a home, divested of all faculty of appropriation or of rest.

Millions have asked what is the nature of the soul, and have received no answer except from death. We know not what any thing is; but we become acquainted, through sensation, with certain properties of matter by their impressions upon ourselves, and thus distinguish one thing from another; and this is the extent of our demonstrated knowledge. But whoever attends to the operations of his own mind, and considers the marvels of his own consciousness in remembering past ideas, in comparing, in reasoning, in foresight, and in all that mind has done, and can do, is learning the nature of a soul. Had Adam lived till now, among his fallen progeny, his soul would have been still young and undeveloped. Earth and time are not large enough for the unfolding of a soul to the full. We look for the forest in the acorn; we look for the universe and its Maker in the soul. Eternity must manifest it, or rather that light, which is God, must so fill the profundity within us, to reveal eternity unto us before we can know the vastness of our own being. In the soul lie hidden powers which are like the living seeds that the Almighty cast with his own hand into the new-made earth, which have not yet produced all their fruits. The dew of ages beyond ages, the eternal sunshine, the tempering of seasons by the breath of Jehovah forever, are requisite for the germination and mature development of all those capabilities, for bliss or bane which reside within ourselves, and can not die.

The salvation of the soul, or the perfect health and safety of the man, is the object we are directed to seek in the revelation of God; and the redemption of the body, from the claim and rightful dominion of death and the grave, is insured in that of the soul,—the full price was paid for both by the Just for the unjust; therefore *God giveth it a body as it hath pleased Him, and to every seed his own body.*

The man who has passed into the life beyond decease or severance, will never be destitute of the means which may be necessary to complete the manifestation of his character, whether it be good or bad, malignant or benevolent. The glorified body of our risen Lord is the type and representative, before all heaven, of the body proper to all those who through faith in Him obtain the restoration of the Divine likeness in their moral nature. The sanctification of the man, or his separation in soul to the obedience of righteousness by love, includes the sanctification of all that may pertain to the body or medium of his spirit. But it is necessary for us always to remember, that we are not saved by any thing derived from earthly parentage—it is the birth by the Spirit of God that gives the title to the heavenly inheritance. Hence the difference between the first Adam, who was made a living soul, and the second Adam, who is the quickening spirit. The former had no spirit of life to communicate. The man of the soul (1 Cor. ii. 14) can not even perceive the things of the Spirit of God, but this power of discernment is imparted in the Divine regeneration effected by the second Adam, the Lord from heaven, who is the life-giving Spirit. In their resurrection-life, true believers are to possess bodies in keeping with this spirit, and thus to resemble the celestial source of their new existence. Blessed beyond utterance must they be who feel within them the germinating power of this God-life; but unless both the soul and the body are brought under the commenced dominion of this quickening spirit, even here, it is manifestly a woful delusion to call ourselves Christians; therefore, *let every one who nameth the name of Christ depart from iniquity.*

Every believer has his own reasons for his hopes. and of course those who receive the Scriptures as their creed have no doubt about the immortality of the soul. But no one fully appreciates the life that is brought to light in the Gospel, unless he desires to possess it as a state of being totally exempt from all liability to departure from the source of holiness and truth. Arguments why we should believe in the immortality of the soul are wasted on those who do not know why they should wish for it; nevertheless we will proceed in the next chapter to say a few words on the subject.

CHAPTER III.

IMMORTALITY.

DEATH is every where; but man can not die. He exists forever, and therefore he must think, and agonize to think; and it is because he is capable of an endless succession of ideas with an incessant consciousness of his own selfhood, that the desire for life becomes intensified into an instinct for immortality in man. Reason is born dogmatical, and she asserts her nobility by demanding a life suited to her nature; she discourses with intelligence, and draws an argument for her deathlessness from the fact that to love truth is to love existence for its highest purposes, since all the truth she learns so far reveals God, and therefore prompts the hope of enjoying a perpetuity of supply from the fountain of wisdom and goodness. But to suppose a desire for acquaintance with the wisdom of God, is to suppose a desire also for his goodness; and to feel this is to have in the heart that right love which believes itself incapable of death; to look for a continuance of life beyond the grave from any other motive, is to expect existence, only because we expect a retribution and an eternal vengeance suited to the rebellion of a fallen and malignant spirit. All our ideas concerning a futurity of living, thinking, and acting are mere phantoms seen in the dark, without revelation; and yet there is no reasonableness in reasoning, unless a man seek something more than daily amusement, occupation, and aliment; if he knows what he wants, he will seek for eternal life, and truth, and good, to live upon forever; since, whether we think of the right means or not, what we wish for is happiness without death. Would you tell a man he is to perish to-morrow, and forever, and then exhort him to thank God? He can not be truly grateful to his Maker without the hope of an imperishable existence as an irrevocable boon. But there is really no possibility of finding any distinct evidence in favor of such a hope, except in the Bible; for however ready men may be to promise themselves what they wish, they only deceive themselves with their desires, and rest only in the Rhadamanthine dreams of natural heathenism, if they found not their hopes upon what God offers.

It is of small importance to determine when creation began; but it is of vast importance that neither reason nor revelation will allow us to believe that what is can ever cease to be. Form may alter, and the elements may be newly arranged; but omnipotence would be opposed to omniscience, could there be annihilation. The material world has existed an indefinite period, but we, as individuals, are but just now created, and we are intent to know where and why we are; and, in endeavoring to learn, we find that nothing of the past is lost to us, since what has been still is, and eternity is before us, to throw all its light into our being. An immortality of mind can be conferred only for mental purposes,—to know and to love, to will and to act.

Not a particle of even the insensate world can be altered in its nature as a center of forces, but yet it continues not everlastingly without change; it must be relatively altered, although in its affinities the same, and so it must be with the soul. Every atom of every block of granite has been otherwise situated than it is, and it is in process of being put in new relations to the other elements, for nothing has yet reached the ultimatum of its existence. The progress must be onward, without limit, in subserviency to the Mind, from which all power, motive, and purpose originate. God is the eternal cause of eternal consequences. Each atom of each element must answer its end, and so must we, and that according to our nature. Atoms act according to physical laws; beings of thought and will, according to the state of thought and will, in relation to spiritual laws. The subtile and unsearchable mind of man, although, as mind, unalterable, must yet be exposed to mutations from without, and in the exercise of its affinities, according to orderly appointments yet to be evolved from the hand of the Almighty. But whatever results toward us in the eternity to come, must still be in keeping with the nature of our minds, as evinced in reason and affection; for the soul, like every thing else, is formed on fixed principles in relation to the rest of creation, and therefore subjected to laws which can not be abolished, because the unchangeable is their source, and His glory their fulfillment.

Morality and religion are based upon immortality; and not only so, but the emotions proper to moral and religious conduct necessarily indicate deathlessness. In short, we can not entertain a notion of right and wrong, without believing in a future state, or a life in which good or evil dispositions find their results. We are bound to right conduct, because the laws of heaven are the laws of eternity, and we can not escape the judgment *already* against us if we neglect our salvation. If nominal death, the death of the body, were the end of man's being, he might dismiss the claims of conscience from his soul; he would then have nothing to mind, nothing to concern himself about but to take his ease as long as it lasted, and to seize upon the accommodations of this world of promise and provision to the best of his ability. Might would then be right. No one could blame another for trying with all his heart to have his own way in spite of his neighbor's claim, since he would have no account to render to any one who did not demand it before his death, for in that event his Maker would forever absolve him from all his obligations. Those who do not look forward to a life beyond the grave really act on this unaccountable principle—"Let us eat and drink, for to-morrow we die." And they would be quite justified in so doing, if something did not say within them—you can not die—your God has to do with you forever.

Indifference to results is all the ethics of ignorance. The *profanum vulgus* of all conditions are those who, practically believing in death as their *finale*, endeavor to pass their lives in desperate disregard of the coming event; and lest it should abbreviate their guilty pleasure before its time, even by its shadow, they resolve to look another way. Thus desperado is the becoming name of every consummate criminal, and the dark souls that crowd our jails have usually advanced in vice without the visible fear of any judgment higher than that which here condemns them. They are adversaries to society, perhaps because society has been adverse to them, and has not convinced them that heaven reigns in righteousness forever. They have not been trained on principle to subdue impulse. No revealing light has entered the chambers of imagery to show them their own characters: they have not seen the hideousness of guilt, boldly raising an unblushing brow in the presence of the Holy One: they have not been taught, or in their habits they have been oblivious, that darkness holds no secrets from God. The doctrines of existence as to power, purpose, and eternity, they have not listened to: the light that awakens conscience has not fallen on their spirits. Eternal life, therefore, has not dwelt in their thoughts; and thus men have been prepared for murder as only a transitory matter, forgetting that the soul of the slain and of the wronged will call for vengeance from beneath the throne of God, and, in a world without mistakes, will meet the murderer and the oppressor face to face, and say, "Thou art the man."

Repentance is not demanded, but because immortality is revealed and a day of judgment appointed for the world, the certainty of which is known to all who have received the hostages of God and looked into the evidence—Christ is risen. If indeed there be any virtue, it can not be without results; it must be productive of present happiness, either in the enjoyment of what is passing or in the hope of what is to come; it must give a warrant of future bliss, not from a possibility of merit, but simply from the assurance which a mind rightly engaged can not but feel that it is walking in the way that wisdom appoints, and hence in a path that, though it may not be naturally pleasant in itself, is yet evidently conducive to a perpetuity of peace and joy, because God has ordained it as a way to an end. There is, however, no virtue in merely pleasing oneself—the word means nothing unless it signifies a state of mind with regard to Heaven, a state that is blessed, because it is an obedience to some law acknowledged by the mind as good in itself; for both the motive and the joy of virtue consist in conscious fulfillment of duty. But duty depends on relationship between the mind that yields obedience in love, and the mind that commands in love. Without love there is neither authority nor duty. Therefore there is always reason in moral law, and every man who can apprehend it is bound to submit to it, or to suffer in his conscience, because he sees it to be perfectly good; and he could not be required, as a rational being, to obey, except in the faith and affiance of a soul satisfied that righteousness in God is one with benevolence. But where is the reasonableness, where the righteousness, where the benevolence, in the Omnipotent, if He grant only a short lease of life and enjoyment to His reasoning and confiding creature that in love submits to His will? Does not the Almighty himself, in man's brief earthly life, inspire him with gratitude only because he is also inspired with a hope that his present happiness, in the emotions awakened by God, is but a foretaste and earnest of an unending abundance from the same source?

Surely there are contradictions and inconsistencies innumerable in the short-lease philosophy, without renewal, but none in the Christian Testament. Here Jehovah is seen as the constant rewarder of those that diligently seek Him, and those who thus seek, feel that, because they come to God as the Everlasting Father, in Him they possess not merely a quiet life for a few years, while obedience may be possible, and then death, but rather an eternal inheritance of active and happy service. Within them stirs a sublimer spirit, witnessing to their consciousness that, as they have a right to call God Father, because they love him for His love, they are not thus born as heirs of death and unquickened dust, but to an immortality of honor in the faithful exercise of those endowments bestowed by Him, and by Him sustained in motive and power for evermore, and by the possession of which they know themselves as sons of God. Any thing short of an eternal inheritance in God and His universe, reason itself, when roused up to its vocation convinces us must be thoroughly incompatible with the idea of Divine existence, as related to man, and manifested in man; and if the Deity were not thus related and thus manifested, man would have had no capacity to believe in the existence of God. But he does so believe as soon as he is capable of thinking religiously and consecutively, therefore he must act and expect accordingly, with the consciousness of being either at one with the Almighty, or else in will opposed to Him, and that forever. Now if a man feel assured that the Omnipotent owns and loves him eternally, he can not faint under

His hand. He must have seen the Saviour—God, and therefore be capable of incessantly acquiring strength, from the touch of the Divinity by which he lives, to bear all things well, because his heroism is religion. Hence he sees that trial is but the path of glory; he sees the end already. The spirit that moves him to obedience and to hope is the spirit that confers perfection and eternal freedom, and therefore he looks forward undauntedly, expecting, without doubt, to be mighty in thought and in action, but incapable of suffering when he shall enter into that world and state of life where there can be nothing to oppose a will submissive to Heaven.

The immortality of the soul was implied in all the commandments of God under the Mosaic economy, and in the history of the patriarchs, and in all the trials of men's spirits from the beginning, because there was no sufficient end to be answered by the Divine permission and providence as regarded man, unless in sustaining him in the hope of a future and enlarged existence. Hence the great cloud of witnesses adduced by Paul (Heb. xi.) as having acted under the power of faith with respect to the better resurrection, believing as they did in God as the rewarder of his worshipers. And the translation of Enoch and of Elijah was the visible regeneration of the body itself under the act of the Almighty's will, by which man was fitted in a moment to exchange earth for heaven, as a spiritual being accommodated to a physical universe by a mediate body, capable of change according to the demands of the inhabiting spirit and the place in which it was required to dwell. There was always sufficient evidence on earth to induce the hope of another life, and plain facts asserted, to all who could credit honest testimony, the reasonableness of looking beyond this world for the fruition of a soul set on finding its Maker.

The reasonableness of such a belief may be shown not only by reference to the evidences which revelation bears in itself, but also from the natural constitution of things, and from the unavoidable inferences of reason concerning the Creator's purpose, as evinced in the existence of mind and matter. But I will briefly sum up the arguments that prevail in my own mind.

1st. Human immortality may be inferred because a mind that is constituted to look forward to futurity with religious hope, and for the satisfaction of rational desire, can not have answered the purpose for which it was created without the fulfillment of that hope and that desire. He who satisfies the desire of every living thing, has not yet satisfied this desire. This argument, however, can have no weight but with those who experience the expressed state of mind. Those who are in the pitiable condition of being without this hope and this desire must be living without any consciousness of Divine existence, and they need to be roused into spiritual vitality and vigilance before they can listen to arguments for eternal life. This is the work of God, and He is engaged in it by constraining men to reason from their experience, and their hopes, and their fears; for even doubt is an argument for immortality, since it implies the question of a mind that can not rest in the expectation of nothingness, but believes only in an ever-coming to-morrow.

2d. If there be no future or continued existence, then the Maker of man has made him capable and desirous of learning more of His wisdom from His works, and yet has left him without any code of laws to govern his moral being, or any instruction sufficient to guide his inquiries concerning his future destiny; for moral laws are not binding on creatures destined to perish, and that doctrine is only deceptive which points to the light of Heaven, and then leaves the soul to be quenched in everlasting darkness.

3d. If God has not left man without revelation, then man is immortal, because the only intelligence which man has received with any indication of its being revealed from God, is that which informs him of eternal safety as a reward, and eternal damage as a punishment, as the necessary consequence, from the essential order of moral government.

4th. As what we learn concerning our Maker from his works and his word, begets in all devout minds a happy reliance upon him and an adoring love, because of the cumulative proofs thus afforded of his benevolence and wisdom; and as this reliance and this love are in relation to a being who can not cease to be adorable, there would be an incongruity of God's own making between the power to adore and the object of adoration, if man were not constituted, when actuated by indwelling truth, with a ceaseless capacity of worshiping and loving his Creator. But to suppose incongruity in God is to deny him.

5th. Without immortality, man would be a total contradiction to every idea of Deity; and all earthly mental existence would be useless, because, although it seems to serve the purpose of manifesting God, it only serves, in fact, to excite hopes, to end in disappointment, and to afford a taste of life which yet conveys to the spirit only death. The insect at the fountain may sip and sustain its powers, to fulfill the purposes of its little being; but man must drink destruction at the source and streams of life, since his eagerness for intelligence and enjoyment leads only to his being lost amid the flood that flows from beneath the throne of God, unless he be immortal.

These arguments are mutually resolvable, the one into the other—and, after all, merely express an intuitive conviction that, because we are what we are, we must be something greater hereafter, and that we must continue to exist, since we can not suppose our present state to be other than as a stage in our progress toward the full purpose of our existence.

If we do not believe in our future being, we must believe in something still more difficult to apprehend, for to expect continued life is according to our habit and our sense of probability; but not to believe this, we must believe in annihilation, but this we can not, because we find no ground on which to proceed to such a conclusion, since there is no instance of such an event in all our knowledge, and therefore there can be no possibility of our supposing the Omnipotent engaged in blotting out his own work. We will not, however, enter on the argument by analogy, since that is exhaustless, and has been abundantly expounded. The preceding are the reasons which determine my own convictions, and they appear to me most consonant with the doctrines of the Bible and with man's moral consciousness. In short, I believe the soul is immortal, merely because it is a soul; but without revelation there could not be a sufficient reason for a man's believing in immortality, since without that he would not have known enough of himself. What the heathen philosophers wanted in order to satisfy them, or at least to impart to them a hope full of immortality, was a true knowledge of God and of man. A mythology without an omnipotent Deity is a system without a sun—there is no cause of light or life in it—there is no being as the source and center of existence, no mind interested in all other minds, no unity in intelligence, no bond of reason, no parent of spirits to whom they might come to dissipate their doubts. What was needed was a *Logos* to demonstrate that the divinity was not a multitude of conflicting attributes, which men had imagined and adored as distinct deities, but that God was one, who, reconciling all things to himself, came forth to show himself as the Father of our spirits. When God was seen as love manifest in humanity, man was visibly immortal. It is in vain to reason of life everlasting without a demonstration of its cause, and that was never seen, except in as far as the Almighty made himself known as the immediate friend of man. In the book of God we thus behold him.

In the early ages of our race, the tradition of God's pledge to man as the conquerer of him who originated death was clearly taught. This we see in the religion of Egypt, and in all the old nations of the earth. Of this tradition, immortality was, of course, an essential part. The unity of the Divine nature, though so soon concealed in vulgar symbols, was a doctrine associated ever with the idea of immortality; and the deathlessness of the soul was never doubted until the unity of the divine nature was lost sight of. But wherever a glimmering of this one light was seen, there the notion of immortality began also to arise, and that not as a gross continuance of life through mysterious metempsychoses in earthly forms, but as the progress of a veritable spiritual being advancing in life on the principles of justice and of love; to be happy in the knowledge of God, or in the retribution that visited a rebellious soul, left with a disordered will to its own eternal misery.

There is much said by religious writers concerning the difference between a natural or necessary immortality and a derived immortality. Let us understand our own words. What God wills, that is nature—what he does, that is necessary; and he does what he wills. If, then, he wills that man should be immortal, man's immortality is natural and necessary. All that the creature possesses is, of course by gift. God has immortality, but he has it to bestow: "the gift of God is eternal life by Jesus Christ." Such is the scriptural view of the matter. Immortality is, then, conferred; but is it conferred on all men? We find that some persons who are ready implicitly to submit to the doctrines of that established authority, the Bible, nave, notwithstanding, come to the conclusion that the emphatic death so frequently mentioned in that book means annihilation, or return to nothingness, in contradistinction to the life obtained by the atonement. It is not the purpose of this volume to discuss the difficulties of theology or to expound the doctrines of the Gospel, but yet a few observations, on a question which is now disturbing not a few pious spirits, may here be not inaptly considered. For my own part, I see no more reason to believe in immortality for myself than for any other man. I have no reason to suppose the free gift of the Lord of life to be the monopoly of any class. Yet, as the authority of the Scriptures is incontestable, we are bound to forego our conclusions if therein we clearly find the doctrine we deny. But is the notion of annihilation derived from the Bible? We wot not. The word, as well as the thought, belongs to Epicurus, who invented it, in contradiction and despite of his own theory of the self-existent eternity of matter; and one who knew not the Scripture nor the power of God might easily so contradict himself.

The word *perish*, and other forms of expression of similar import, frequently occur in the New Testament; but if we look into their meaning as interpreted by usage and by the relation in which they stand, we shall find them in no respect favorable to the idea which some minds entertain of them. Without pretending to erudition any one may see the force of the few Greek words translated *perish* in the New Testament. First, there is *αποθνησκω*; this is usually applied to death, in the ordinary sense, as in that passage where it is said, "In due time Christ died"—he was not annihilated. Next there is *απολλυμι*, which means *to be lost. He came to save that which was lost;* the word is used also in the case of the woman whose piece of money was lost—this was not annihilated. The same word is employed by St. Peter, when he states that the world at the deluge, being overflowed with water, perished—it is not annihilated. But perhaps it would seem to signify more when hypothetically employed, as by St. Paul, when he says, "Then they also which are fallen asleep in Christ are perished;" but the verse before explains his idea of perished: "*If Christ be not raised your faith is vain; ye are yet in your sins.*" To be, and continue to be, with all the weight of unatoned sinfulness, is to be unjustified by a risen Saviour. There is a word, *καταφθειρω*, which, being in one place translated *perished utterly*, might seem to mean annihilation, if any did, but we find it signifies only, *shall become thoroughly corrupt;* and the same word is applied to men of abandoned disposition, as if to intimate their utter departure from all excellence. But to proceed further would be a needless waste of time and patience; it is enough to observe, that wherever the word *perish* occurs, it expresses a state of something that exists, and therefore can not mean annihilation. And so with regard to the word rendered destruction, perdition, and so forth—it indicates, in every instance, condemnation, as of something pernicious, perverse, or frustrating right purpose, as in waste or the misapplication of means; and when limited to the body, as it often is, it signifies dissolution, as opposed to its edification. We may then fairly conclude that there is no word in the New Testament which must mean annihilation in the strict sense—for in fact it implies a contradiction in terms—*a production of nothingness.*

Death is the negation of life, say you? True, but what is life in the scriptural sense? "*This is life eternal, to know thee, the only true God, and Jesus Christ, whom thou hast sent.*" Death, spiritually considered, is the opposite of this life; that is, to be ignorant of the true God is eternal death—a death, such as a man without faith must feel; a state, the reverse of that for which the breath of God first inspired the heart of Adam. Destruction is not the contrary to creation, but to the right use of existence; and damnation is not merely condemnation, but danger and damage, as opposed to salvation, or health and safety. Those who contend so literally for the true significance of death, ought to conclude that the grand serpent was no deceiver when he said, "You shall not surely die." The prohibition had been enforced with the penalty—"In the day that thou eatest thereof thou shalt surely die;" as if to show that disobedience is death, and that the proper life of a reasonable being is forfeited by the breach of Divine law; the moral vitality, the likeness of God is departed, and as a mirror without light is no longer a mirror, notwithstanding its substantial existence, so the human soul is dead to its purpose if it reflect not the glory of God. In this true and full sense, the busy people of this world are living in a deadly dormancy—"*Awake, thou that sleepest, and arise from the dead, and Christ shall give thee light.*" (Eph. v. 14.) Life and death, then, in Scripture language, are used not in respect to creation and its contrary, annihilation, but with regard to our happiness, as rational and voluntary agents. Life is a great fact, death is a great fact, but life from the dead is *the* great fact. If it be the purpose of the faithful and ever-living Creator ultimately to annihilate some portion of mankind, why is there a resurrection both of the just and of the unjust? "*By man came death, by man came also the resurrection from the dead. As in Adam all die, so in Christ shall all be made alive.*" We are not to limit these words to suit our whims of interpretation; the life is as extensive as the death, the quickening spirit is vaster than the living soul, and has abolished the last enemy. The price is paid for the ransom of all, and its value must be testified. "*We trust in the liv-*

ing God, who is the Saviour of all men, especially of those that believe." 1 Tim. iv. 10.

Of course, the declaration of our Lord, that *God is the God of the living, and not of the dead, and that* ALL *live unto Him*, will be a sufficient argument with those who believe the record. But is there not an indisputable reasonableness in regarding man as the property of God, and that man, as God's, can not cease to exist in relation to his Maker? The authoritative announcement and natural argument with which our Lord met those Jewish materialists, the Sadducees, is as plain a statement of man's necessary immortality as words can furnish. (Luke xx. 27–38.) The children of this world, that is, all men, are put in contrast with those of the *anastasis*, or future state, which therefore refers to all; and as it is in keeping with the condition of bodily mortality, that the race of man should be replenished and perpetuated in this world by marriage, so it is in keeping with the coming condition of life to be without the power of multiplication because without the capability of dying. *They can not die any more;* the body died, and that was all that could die. As it is consistent with Divine ordinance that human souls should enter on that state of existence, so it is but congruous that they should henceforth be "on a par with the angels" in regard to their immortality.

The idea expressed in the existence of a tree may, perhaps, be expressed by any tree of its kind; yet it can be expressed only to a mind, because it originates in a mind, it is the living manifestation of a design, from its embryo in the seed to its full expansion: but the idea of a mind, as a whole, can be expressed only to itself, and therefore only by its continued existence, as a being having memory and desire. Material or compound things exist for the sake of minds, but minds themselves exist with especial reference to the attributes of Deity, since minds alone are capable of good or evil. If a mind be not indestructible, it must be a compound of elements that may go to form some other thing, just as the carbon, hydrogen, and oxygen, which form the plant now before me, may be resolved, and become the aliment and ingredients of other living or dead beings. But one mind or soul can not be a part of another. Hydrogen, carbon, oxygen, answer a thousand purposes, and exist in a thousand combinations; but mind exists individually only, and with a simple unity of purpose. It is a mind, and can exist only as a mind, that is, to be conscious, or what is the same thing, to perceive and will. The existence of any thing is the expression of God's purpose in that thing: an element answers its end, as the element of some other thing, but a mind answers no purpose but as a conscious being—in perception and will it fulfills the purpose of its creation, and it is thus, and thus only, related to its Maker. Now the intention of the Omniscient with regard to any being is expressed in the nature of that being, but to intend annihilation is really to have no intention, since there can be no purpose in that which is not; God can have no relation to non-existence, and therefore the annihilation of a human soul is an unimaginable event. *He is not the God of the dead, but of the living; for all live unto Him.*

Is there to be an eternal tradition of the Divine glory, as manifested in the annihilation of beings brought into existence by Divine energy? Does reason teach us that it would be an appropriate demonstration of God's power, as the creator of light, to extinguish the sun, and blot it out forever? And is the soul of any man a lesser light, to be forgotten of its Maker, or to be spoken of in angelic story as a thing that was? That must be an insane charity that would distrust the judgment of God, and think it impossible for the Almighty to prove His benevolence, without annihilating those whom He created. Our experience does not speak of such a Father in heaven. Know, O man of tenderness and terror, that perfect love casts out fear, and that thy Maker has more charity than thy small heart can hold. All the love in the infinite universe is but as the breathing of its Maker over it. The full utterance of His heart you can not know, without inhabiting eternity in union with Himself. Not until you so dwell, and so live, shall you be able to fathom the abyss, and see how love is there. It is in vengeance, but still it is the vengeance of love—love that wills that all men should be saved, and that proves He will have mercy rather than any sacrifice but that of self-devotedness to the recovery of the lost. Yet let us not deceive ourselves by our habit of catching sounds instead of sense. The figures of speech employed in the Holy Volume are not like the poetic ornaments of Corinthian discourse, but veritable illustrations of truth, and therefore who can doubt that these words "the place where their worm dieth not, and their fire is not quenched,"—are meant to express a perpetuity of pain existing there? Is Divine justice revenge? We can answer this bold question without denying the eternal condemnation of the wicked and impenitent; but we must enter into the modes of the spiritual world, before we shall be able to apprehend either the darkness of hell or the light of heaven. This we plainly perceive—the seeking of glory and immortality in God insures eternal life in the fullest sense, because it is consistent with His will and nature that he should be the everlasting source of blessedness to all creatures in a state of soul to receive from His fullness with the acknowledgment of his favor.

I hope always to be able to join in the prayer of the Liturgy—"That it may please Thee to have mercy upon all men:" God willeth not the death of a sinner; but in order to the possibility of a remission of the Divine sentence, that banishes a soul from light, it is necessary that there should be a change of mind; for while malignity continues, hell endures. The soul that wills not to be holy denies that God is good, and can not have forgiveness, either in this world or in that to come, but is in the danger of eternal condemnation. But it is the business of theologians to propound and adjust whatever difficulties they may discover in the divine Scriptures; yet we dare not entertain any interpretations at variance with the character of Jesus. In him alone God is manifest. We know nothing of holiness, nothing of divine love, and nothing of justice, but as seen in Him. He came to show how God was just, and yet a Saviour. He told his most beloved disciple that he knew not what spirit prevailed in his heart, when he would have called down fire from Heaven to devour those who rejected Him; and he tells us all, that he came not to destroy men but to save: still it is nevertheless certain that to reject His salvation, as the cure for sin, is to continue under the dominion of evil, and that is itself *anathema maranatha.*

Ceasing to breathe this common air is not itself alone death. Men are accustomed to call it so because it is that part of mortality that most strikes the eye; but death itself is what sin gets as the wages for its every day's work—a deadliness of heart, a state of affection excluding God. Those who keep the saying of Christ, or obey His teaching, alone live truly and in a godly sense; for, as He says, they can not see death, because they are in spirit one with him who is the resurrection and the life. To feel under the eternal burthen of unforgiven sin, without a hope of deliverance, because without a disposition to receive regenerative life as from the blood of the Saviour's heart, is death, and all the proper purposes of being are then lost in the immortality of torment belonging to a mind distrustful of its God. Even now we feel that to reflect on the bare fact of immortal existence without a consciousness of God's love is intolerably awful; what, then, must it be to have all our faculties open to the everlasting reality of having voluntarily rejected mercy on the only terms on which it can be offered by the Holy and Omnipotent Author of our being?

CHAPTER IV.

MAN IN RELATION TO HIS MAKER.

Were not deathlessness a felt fact, there would be no motive for writing or reading a volume like this, which has been commenced, and it is hoped will be completed, with the conviction that both the writer and the reader have an everlasting futurity which must be influenced by present mental engagements and the nature of the will to which we yield obedience.

Qui obdormierunt non perierunt. Because man is immortal, and the awakening up from death will be with a restoration of the past to the spirit, in as far as all intelligence and the final destiny must grow out of remembrance, we have good reason for earnestness whether we set ourselves to meditate upon the means of self-improvement, or would rouse other minds to think of the purposes of life and thought.

Man is the only creature on earth that meditates. He alone treasures ideas, compares them with each other, and reasons concerning what he may expect from what he has experienced. Hope and fear look beyond the horizon of earth, and every exercise of intellect influences the tendency of our affections and our faith, either by extending our acquaintance with goodness, with freedom, and with truth; or by binding our souls more closely with the fetters of error and of falsehood. These, like siren sisters, meet us smilingly every day and unless we are fortified by the virtue of an indwelling and uncreated light, we must be deceived by their pleasant songs, and soothed into a slumber from which we shall awake only to find ourselves bound with grave-clothes, and buried deep in the marble dark ness of a tomb which can be penetrated only by that Divine voice which said, "Lazarus, come forth."

We must be taught. By whom? By our Maker. He alone is capable of instructing us in the truth, since He made it and possesses it, and He alone knows what we need, and how we can bear the impartation of knowledge. The Almighty must make enjoyment safe. All our business on earth is to be educated both feelingly and intellectually, and God has filled the earth with objects from which we are to learn the Divine will, and think of the eternal relation of that will to ourselves. His great facts are before us, but unhappily men are rather disposed to learn of one another than of the All-wise; consequently the world abounds with deception, and life is apt to become a lie, and history a romance. Thus education may be either good or bad, merely human and delusive, or divine and determinately excellent. What is education? It is every thing that influences the mind, and it includes the consideration of all circumstances and all affections. Its means are those of reason, the knowledge both of good and of evil, pain and pleasure, the sympathy of mind with mind, and any thing by which a soul may be induced to desire and to determine for itself as an associate spirit in God's company of intelligences. The end of education in its highest sense is to form habits of mental fellowship, and to beget love after the celestial mode of feeling and thinking. To ascertain how a human being should be trained, it is therefore necessary to inquire what are his capacities, and what are their objects—what are the soul's appetites, and what has God provided for them? We need not puzzle ourselves with refined disquisitions on the nature of the mind, since it is enough for us to know that every variety in moral character is simply a variety in the state of our will with regard to objects of sense, and that no improvement can be effected in the moral aspect of any being but by increasing love for what is absolutely good, while teaching it properly to appreciate what is good, relatively considered.

The will is the spring of action, but its character is determined by the nature of the affections, for what we desire is what we love—and, therefore, unless the affections be rectified, the understanding remains in darkness. We labor in vain to be learned, unless we also aim at being wise. But wisdom is not acquired by dint of study—it is the gift of God to a spirit, that kindles into earnestness by a desire duly to fulfill the sublime purposes of existence, humbly, yet boldly, comes before his God with all the burden of his being, and seeks to sustain himself upon the unupbraiding Giver of all good.

Here we pause as if in the twilight, on the edge of a precipice, from which a boundless ocean stretches before us. The infinite heavens reflected in the deep oppress us with their inscrutable vastness. We feel how vain is our desire to fathom the profundity which surrounds us, and we are glad, throughout our souls, when a star gleams forth amidst the purple gloom to assure us that the Maker of all worlds is our friend, and wishes us to behold the glory of his boundless dwelling-place, lit up by his own hand to accommodate his creatures. Here, with light upon our brow, we may stand and ask, What is good? And cheerfully, and without doubt we answer Light. Why? Because we can enjoy it without fear. There is liberty in light, and it seems to call on us to exercise our faculties to their fullest extent, with the understanding that wherever the Almighty throws a sunbeam or a ray of starlight, there the way is safe and holy, and open to us. We may travel as far as we can in any direction indicated by the luminous footsteps of the Creator, since he has illuminated all his works to attract our attention to the truths, which through them he would convey to us. Nature is the shadow of divinity, and both are manifested by the same light. Why do we enjoy light? Because it is opposed to doubt as well as to darkness, and it penetrates our being with a sense of beneficence, and the reality of our Creator's good-will toward us, appealing to our hearts from heaven to draw our desires thitherward. As long as we see light, or hear of it we do not feel forsaken. God is light! As surely as the universe exists in pervading glory, as if folded in the embrace of God, so surely does the power by which we gaze into heaven, with its countless realms of light beaming around us, speak to us of eternal love. O God, I believe in thy goodness, for it is over all thy works. Blot out the sin of my doubt, says the convinced soul; I had feared I was alone and forgotten, and doomed to tangible darkness for ever, because I had not seen and felt that the light which clasps this diurnal world so tenderly, was the revealer of thy love. But now I know the everlasting truth is to be ceaselessly opening before me, like worlds evolved from worlds at the touch of thy finger, and in the breath of thy mouth, which is life. It is good to live in light—*Deus lux est, et in eo tenebræ non sunt ullæ.*

But the enlightened mind is humbled, and would say—How dare I look up rejoicingly when the eye of the Holy Searcher of hearts is visibly upon me! He sees through the depth of darkness in my soul; but he sees also that it is to be enlightened that I dare look up. I open my eyes that light may enter—I come to be reproved—I come openly before the open heavens to call upon Omniscience to supply my exigencies, and save me; I come ashamed and silent, yet with words heard by the ear of God. He listens to my uttered soul—search, purify, lead me, O thou Way, Truth, Life. I dread the darkness in myself, and I would escape into light—and now I see life and immortality brought to light by the revealing Word. That removes all restraint, and bids me go on eternally in peace and hope and thankfulness, because gratitude and joy are the properties of those who believe in the faithfulness of the Creator, and desire heartily ever to obey the love that has revealed itself as always ready to bless the soul that trusts it. He will not forsake the work of his own hands.

Beautiful colors, forms and faces, speak to me responsively. My soul goes out to seek for objects on which to express my love, and I meet a face to smile on me with a happy recognition of my heart, and in confidence and joy our loving thoughts become prayers in the presence of the Majesty that filleth heaven and earth. And my little child knows that I love him, although never told the fact in words—deeds have revealed it. He intuitively perceives and understands love; for he is constituted to need, expect, and believe it, and therefore he takes my hand, and calls me Father, and trusts me to guide him home through the darkness. O my God! this is thy mode of teaching—may we never forget thy instruction, but praise thee in thought and in action; let our thoughts be actions and our actions thoughts, because thou hast manifested thy goodness in life, in light, and in love.

There is a disposition in every reasonable soul to inquire into causes and consequences. To be pleased, we know not why and care not wherefore, is animal enjoyment, mere instinct, the working of a consciousness that can not ask for a greater good, because it knows nothing of purpose—asking no questions, it can get no answers.

Whatever comports with the orderly advancement of our being as endowed with spiritual life, whatever tends to enlarge the sphere of our intelligence and fill it with divine light, whatever improves our affections and causes intellect to pursue the truth in love, is good, and all else is evil. Thus in a summary manner we arrive at our conclusion—whatever is fitted by our Maker to the improvement of our moral life, our understandings, and our feelings, is good, and that alone, because it is the will of God toward us as the lawgiver and rewarder.

Good education includes appropriate enjoyment, and whatever opposes this is in the nature of sin, and death, and condemnation; but obedience to the will of Heaven is safety, and health, and life, and bliss. The will of God is good for man, because it alone is truth, and truth alone is the end and satisfaction of reason. If a man, in his madness and wickedness, seem to enjoy evil deeds and erroneous thoughts, it is only because he is perversely ignorant of goodness and truth, and so in love with the false that his affections are awry and unreasonable. The perversion of his heart sets him altogether beside his proper place and purpose. It is of the very nature of his soul to be governed by the object of his love; but he is apt to embrace a demon in every creature of his desire, and to wander in a desert without rest, and without light, and without fellowship, startled and frenzied by the glaring hideousness of his own thoughts, unless some mind, having faith in the faithfulness of Jehovah, the Creator, the Saviour, meet him boldly in the spirit of that Lord, and take him by the hand, commanding him to repent, believe and obey, because God is the proprietor of souls. It is manifest that such a one must be convinced of his being thoroughly wrong, both as regards his will and his understanding, before he can be set right. There is no way of accomplishing this but by showing him he may trust you, and this he can not do without some proof of your love for him, and a better proof you can not give than by opening before him the books of God—creation and revelation; in other words, show him plainly, and to the best of your ability, what you know of the true nature of things in relation both to him and to yourself. Show him that God is his providence and yours forever. But you will only prove yourself a willful and conceited bungler, unless you really sympathize with sinners as a sinner with a new heart. Then do not be afraid—Faith will remove the mountain. Believe you work with the power of God, and you will find that power is nothing but intention, and intention is action in the Omnipotent, and he means what you desire—salvation, therefore be strong in Him who is unfailing.

Above all things, do not be afraid of finding the handiwork of the Almighty in nature at variance with the word of His covenant with man, as expressed in the Bible. But do not take a step without His book. He does not contradict Himself, and therefore creation is nothing but a consecutive indication of his wisdom, power, and love, to minds capable of appreciating the language in which He has thus written His attributes. *Because they regard not the works of the Lord, nor the operation of his hands, he shall destroy them and not build them up.*—Ps. xxviii. 5.

All nature, physical and spiritual, is a theology to enlightened reason; but yet, for a perverted soul, in the profundity of its ignorance, to look for the revelation of life and immortality in the elements of earth, is to look for the living among the dead. Earth would be but the grave of our hopes, but for Him who spake with Mary at the sepulcher concerning the ascension to his Father and our Father. The Lord *is* risen, and our life is hid with Him; and through Him alone shall we find it. Yet, "*without Him was not any thing made that was made*," consequently we may wisely worship and glorify Him while endeavoring to investigate and apply to our improvement some of the great facts of existence, and the interests of our natural relationships to each other as alike the creatures of His goodness.

Every mind has its select wonders, but existence itself is the grand mystery to all of us. It points from eternity to eternity, from the unbeginning to the unending. Man is the only being on earth that recognizes this mystery; none but he thinks, and therefore if there be any design in the creation of the human mind, the perception of this sublime subject must be intended for some end in relation to the well-being of that mind. As far as we can at present conceive, this end is only to direct us to a self-existent, all-productive Being, who intends to make Himself known to us, and therefore confers on us a disposition to inquire after Him, and in keeping with this disposition, and as necessary to its fulfillment, He imparts to us a desire for an existence never to terminate. Thus, in meditating on creation, thoughts will follow thoughts in higher and higher series, until man, from his intellectual elevation, gazing into the boundlessness that surrounds him, finds no rest for his spirit but upon the bosom of the Eternal.

The appreciation of our existence as intelligences related to the Everlasting is, then, the basis of all becoming effort to attain whatever belongs to the true dignity of man. If we know not our nobility, we shall not behave nobly. If we feel not our constituted capacity for greatness, we shall not desire to be great. If, in the strivings of our souls toward the light, we do not recognize our fitness for fellowship with heaven, we shall shrink back, and clothe ourselves fruitlessly in darkness, and, losing sight of the eternity in which we really live, shall in our misery find no time for mental improvement and moral progress. We may talk of life and enjoyment in our gloom, but it will be with a mortal taint upon our spirits, and our gayety will be like the delirium of persons smitten with the plague, turning the sounds of lamentation and the signs of death into laughter and madness. It is, indeed, but too prevalently true that we are so busy in watching the phantasmagoria of successive fancies, that we rather seem to dream than to realize the objects that surround us. Even while we gaze, delusion takes the place of sight, and when we would seize what appears so substantial and so pleasing, we destroy even the shadow at which we grasp.

It is not until some unselfish real love, like a spirit from heaven, takes possession of our hearts, that we obtain the full and inmost consciousness of our individuality. In the fixed attachment of our souls with the feeling of an everlasting affinity to some other being, we begin to doubt of death by recognizing the true purpose of life, and in the ceaseless nature of love, with its possibilities of agony and bliss, we experience the full weight and burden of the awful mystery comprehended in the fact that we are and must be. We may long for knowledge, we may long for power, but it is love alone that appropriates and employs intelligence and energy, and until this felt capacity of loving becomes as one with our life, we find all teachings but as the play of sunshine and shadow on a troubled stream.

When we acquire this new kind of consciousness, our existence is no longer instinctive, imitative, sympathetic, physiological, and reflex, but spiritual, and in felt relation with the Divinity who originates all things but for the purpose of expressing himself as love, that we may trust him as our sufficient good. Then we feel no longer little and limited, but capable of becoming expansive, vast, immovable, eternal, real as the heavens, and formed to regard the universe as a creation suited to ourselves, to elicit admiration, and satisfy our research, while awakening love within us as the response of our spirits to our God. Until this godlike animation enters into man, his morality, philosophy, and religion seem but as the speculations of vanity instead of the visions of truth, coming close in upon the soul like the revelation of Heaven, still obscure to us because of its intolerable glory. Incomprehensible, thou must sustain us; thou must satisfy us from thyself with thy knowledge and thy charity. O Light, thou must illumine us, though now we look and are blind; soften thy glory to our vision, that we may see and worship.

By our aspirations we are heirs of the Everlasting, for we feel, when brought to reflect on our capacities and requirements, and to set our hearts upon attaining truth, that our fellowship with creatures is not enough for us; since they can not comprehend us nor completely sympathize with us, being able neither to look back upon the strugglings of our secret past, nor forward to our coming necessities, they can neither rectify our wishes nor supply our wants. They can explain nothing of the mysteries we would solve, they can only respond to us by questions like our own—Whence are we and why? The Being who made us thus largely necessitous, dependent, and inquisitive, must have made us for himself; and he must reveal himself in all his fullness as personally bound to us forever, as our originator and our end, in order that reason, looking abroad on his illuminated worlds, should be able sufficiently to hope, sufficiently to believe, sufficiently to love. It is the Infinite in power, the Infinite in love, the Infinite in will, the Infinite in means, that can alone fill us with ideas large enough to satisfy the longings of our souls after the good, the beautiful, the true, the immortal; for it is not an indefinite notion, but a growing idea which possesses the soul that seeks satisfaction in seeking to understand the relation of the Self-existent to his creature, man.

Since He has given us the understanding and the will to look to Him, it must be his intention to supply us out of his exuberance; he can not have directed our desires by his promises, in order to disappoint us; but rather that he may bestow more and more abun dantly at each advance of our spirits toward Himself, in dependence upon his hand and thus on forever, world without end; for every good hope is a prophecy fulfilled already in the divine plan and purpose of our being. All things consist—nothing is but as a part of all—God's all. As we scarcely feel conscious of living in eternity until we look outwards and onwards, with the scrutiny of reason directing the eye into the blue ether, inquiring, Where does it terminate? and finding our only possible answer is, Nowhere; so, until we look into ourselves, we do not perceive what it is that discerns the everlasting, and *is* the everlasting. In the visible universe we see the works of Mind; these must be changed, in conformity to Divine thought—"As a vesture shalt thou fold them up, and they shall be changed;" but the constituting Mind itself is unalterable, and therefore essentially eternal; and the mind that apprehends must be akin to the mind that creates. We recognize in ourselves the reflection, at least, of the forming force of purpose and of understanding, and because of our inability to think in a godly manner, without desiring and expecting to think forever, we dare not, with respect to our own existence, say we see its termination. We can not determinately meditate on thoughts and say, for certainty, our end is in the grave. Reason boldly asserts that the possibility is otherwise; but our hearts go before our logic, and speak more positively still, for either our hopes or our fears take us beyond doubtfulness at once into the untried being of unavoidable futurity.

Why is this? Is it not because the life of man is the breath of God? When the Almighty had fashioned the dust into a form of beauty and majesty fit to be animated and actuated by a spirit that should assert its relationship to Himself, He imparted to the wondrous organism a principle of action and of thought, and man became a living soul. Thus life is not an inherent and detached principle, but the indwelling power of the present Deity. To enjoy divine life we must feel that it is imparted; as the light and warmth of the sun enter the substance of a flower, and fill its fibres and its fluids with expanding life, so the Divine power vivifies man by pervading all his existence, and thus the quickening Spirit of God himself is the immediate cause of a living, reasoning soul.

A living soul is a distinct but dependent being, susceptible of sympathy with every other being, capable of perception and emotion. Because the whole immediate creation was constituted in correspondence with the faculties of the new-made selfhood, man looked abroad upon all things, and saw the reason of existence by thus beholding the wisdom and benevolence of his Maker. This was the original prerogative of humanity, and if it has been forfeited, it has also been restored and increased, after the manner of an endless life, for eternity must still reveal the purpose of God in making man as his own image. Man alone, amidst all the creatures of earth, can recognize in nature the attributes of Jehovah, for no other creature on earth can know there is a God. He was from his origin inspired to respond to the Creative Spirit. His inmost being, his very self, became conscious of divine impressions, or was impelled intuitively to inquire, with the expectation of obtaining intelligence concerning God, because reason itself does not assert her power but in seeking to know the Divine will, and in doing it. This reason dwelt once unclouded in man's bosom, and therefore he at once apprehended, or inferred, or hoped aright, since all he saw, or heard, or handled, or in any way experienced, referred him directly to the Author of all and called him rather to worship than to wonder. He alone could believe, he alone could conceive of meanings, he alone could acknowledge the great first and final Cause, the Mind conforming the elements to His own purposes, and inducing existence every where to express His love and power.

Thus creation, however marvelous in itself, was but as the mirror of the Almighty to the eye of man, and therefore to perceive was to adore. He found in his Maker alone a perfect object of study, of faith, of hope, of love, and all sensible objects were but as *media* between the Ineffable and himself. He saw the All-sufficient, and was satisfied. In Him man felt himself possessed of an omnipotent friend, who as his originator, must especially and everlastingly love him, the highest earthly production of His energy. He who is the Creator of reason, must supply the ceaseless and ever-growing demands of His rational creature. Thus, as long as the human spirit walked in confidence and fellowship with the Holy One, man could feel no desire but as an intimation that it should be fulfilled in further evidence of the favor of his Patron and his God. Man's faith was then absorbed in his love, and he wondered not at the goodness and greatness of the Eternal, for then there was nothing in his own nature at variance with light and with love. There was then no occasion for patience, because there was no unholy disposition to be worn out, but heavenly affections grew strong on their own enjoyment. Such is our notion of the pristine or perfect state of man, because it is the state for which human nature, when rectified and regulated, seems to be designed. The test of creatureship, however, is law; and as man was to know himself safe only in union with God, the simplest temptation of his nature, as a creature of desires, was sufficient to prove his incapacity to obey and live through his own power. Without a better understanding of weakness and of strength—weakness his own, and strength to be perfectly manifested through it—he could but fall. The first man being left to do the best to fulfill God's law, with reason alone, fell; but may we not say he gained ultimate honor from his degradation, since the compassionate Creator took occasion thus to evince His infinite love, by giving man a divine hope with a divine power, by which to vanquish evil; for is not Omnipotence revealed in reconciling all things to Himself through human nature; and are not fallen beings thoroughly exalted, and yet the Holy One in wisdom vindicated, when the human will itself is so renewed in righteousness, through faith, that it becomes just in God not to impute sin?

We are fallen, and great is the depth of our fall. In our ignorance, our doubt, our distrust, we are overwhelmed in amazement the moment we truly think, for pure thought brings us as if into the presence of God, but does not reveal him to us. We are afraid to trust ourselves alone with the Almighty. When we think of Him, we try to turn away from the awfulness of his felt presence. We divert our souls with "the sweet music of speech," or by seeking the smiles of those who, like ourselves, are in love with the earth and its objects. We shun the thought of our only Benefactor, and thus we can not rest, because we can not rightly love; and we can not thus love because our thoughts are hard, and dark, and suspicious. We imagine the Almighty to be a revengeful being, a despot surrounding us with spies and accusers, instead of a parent beseeching us, by every means, to be reconciled, and to be blest in trusting to His heart and to His hand for constant protection and supply.

These ideas are not irrelevant to our purpose. Man is an awful fact to himself. In order to feel this fully, it is important that we should dwell upon the truth that our spiritual life is manifested by our consciousness of being more than we seem, and of having desires not to be satisfied on earth. We do not wonder so much at the existence of objects, and at their insufficiency, as that we are conscious of them and of ourselves, but as an intimation of something yet to be known, and of an existence beyond this. But all that philosophy might infer, or reason in her guessing might surmise, concerning the future, would be unavailing, futile, cold, dead, unless religion kindled and quickened our hopes with her own life. The creation of mind is indeed the only manifestation of God. He is known only in a soul made after his own image, an intelligent being, constituted immortal by the will of the Infinite, so that the perfection of Divine existence might be forever revealing itself to a reason preserved in correspondence with it, by the operation of the Spirit inhabiting humanity. Hence He who manifested God as love, and thus illustrated the law as the code of His own honor, is the brightness of the Father's glory, and we are to be like him, when we see him as he is, for we are to be thus created in righteousness and true holiness, after the image of the Creator. This resemblance to God, in the character of man, made perfect in spirit, is the sufficient end of our being, the reason why we exist. But this we should never have looked for, had not heaven informed us what to aim at and to hope. Everlasting progression and development are involved in our spiritual union by faith with Him, who is the Head over all. Had not reason been too busy with phantasms, she might have seen that truth. The objects of creation, spiritual or material, new or old, can not have been produced, but for the purpose of expressing to created intellect what exists entirely at once, now and ever, in the Self-existent. Mind answers to mind. Each of us must say there was a time when I was not; but no man can say the time will never come when I shall know all that has been. It may be, that as the believing man looks through the light of God into eternity, he shall be as if he had himself forever ex isted; for is not spiritual consciousness capable of rec ognizing all the past, as if now present? and shall we not, of course, feel, in every manifestation of Omnipotence, that He designs all things in relation to man? Are we not taught, concerning that wisdom which was from everlasting, that before the heavens were prepared, or the circling deep spread forth, Jehovah possessed the thought of this habitable earth, as his own delight with the sons of men, and that therefore He calls upon them to give heed to His instruction, that they may find life, and be blessed in following the footsteps of their God?

By thinking on existence we learn, first, physical order—the relation of matter to matter, world to world; then, moral order—the relation of mind to mind. The absence of physical order is chaos, the absence of moral order is misery. Order is law in operation. Thus nature is perpetuated. But moral law is distinct both from mental and physical law. Every element and material mass is governed by a constitution of its own, it operates always in the same manner in similar circumstances, and the mind has also fixed laws by which it also acts. Thus no man can avoid remembering from association, or prevent his will from being excited by pleasure or pain. But moral law is addressed to the will of man as a spirit capable of choosing between good and evil, because he is capable of thinking on the fitness of things as appointed by God. A consent to this is mental conformity to the law of God as good; willing opposition to this is sin, consistency of conduct in obedience to this is holiness. That is good which is congruous with the happiness both of the individual mind and the community of minds, and the reverse of this is evil. The law which requires this congruity is love or benevolence; and the mind that yields to love because it is love, is of similar disposition. The man who does good because God is good, partakes of God's spirit; his will coincides with God's—he obeys from the heart. This is the doctrine of Christianity. Therefore it is that love relates equally to God and man, and it is impossible for a man truly and religiously to venerate and adore the Creator for his goodness without manifesting kindness to his fellow creatures. "If ye love not your brother whom ye have seen, how can ye love God whom ye have not seen?" But oh, the jesuitry of the human soul! Men hunt each other to bloody and burning death in the name of Charity, while knowing nothing of him who died for all of them. If God were not good, it would be unreasonable to worship Him; and none can worship him without good-will to man, for benevolence is the glory in which God reveals himself.

Human knowledge is the progressive perception of Omniscience and Omnipotence, the reception indeed, so to say, of an atom at a time of the meaning of the Infinite Mind. Every production of that Mind bears in it the evidences of all its attributes, and successive revelation is but the development of a single truth. Thus, if we could detach a single point from the universe of matter, and look at it in the light of pure reason, we should see the force of the Almighty there, imbuing it with properties and affinities, fitting it for its place in the harmonious whole. The will of God gives it inherent faculty of existence, in relation to his own purpose. Infinite power and infinite wisdom are there, and if these exist to the apprehension of our minds, must not our minds exist in relation to that power and wisdom?

But if beings like ourselves are conscious of Infinite Wisdom and Power, how can this be but in connection with Infinite Love? What purpose can there be in the revelation of the Deity to His creatures but to express a reason why they should confide in Him?

Thus we are constantly obliged to revert to the

standing truth—"God is love." The doctrine of utility is the doctrine of love. Now there is a use in every thing, and in every atom of every thing. But what is a use? It is an order or purpose in the creation of whatever exists—an inherent quality or property in the constitution of a thing which renders it subservient to the benefit of some conscious agent. Thus all creation in its minutest parts becomes an evidence to thinking persons of the Divine intention toward themselves, as beings feeling and acknowledging the Divine goodness; for every act of Omnipotence is consistent with all other of His acts, and is directed to an end, which must be the eternal, infinite good of every mind that depends on the wisdom and benevolence of Almightiness.

The use of any thing is, then, resolved into the proper employment and enjoyment of the means which are provided for the formation of ideas and the rectification of desires. Right desires are all provided for. All that we can know concerning the use of any thing is therefore summed up in the word submission, for it teaches only this—Let your intellect and then your will, yield to the instruction and to the law of God, and you will find yourself satisfied at the source of love, power, beauty, and thought. In every instance that we discern the use of any object or any idea, we discern a benevolent adaptation, and it is an appeal to our understandings, an appeal of our Maker to our souls as an evidence of His interest in our own existence. He has made us capable of perceiving His perfection, as far as created things, thought, and inspiration reveal it, that we might love, and obey, and be blessed; for salvation is not an appendage to Jehovah's plan in creation, but an essential part to every being that needs it, and beholds God as love, and cleaves to Him for sustentation, for will, for ability, for intellect, for all. Thus the confiding spirit worships and glorifies The Father, and rejoices in His fullness for ever, and that not blindly, but from a sympathizing relationship, and therefore with the actual enjoyment of an everlasting heritage in His providence and graciousness.

CHAPTER V.

MENTAL MANIFESTATION.

THE living organism is the medium between objects and the soul. In this respect it is divisible into two principal parts—the sensitive and the active; the sensitive being subservient to sensation and perception—the active, enabling the soul to seek objects and to evince its feelings. We will to move the foot, for instance, and it obeys us in the 1,200,000,000th of a second, and impression from without becomes ours at the same rate. Such is the velocity and inscrutable nature of spiritual action, even through the medium of matter. The motive power of the soul in its action on the limbs, and also the sensitive faculty associated with this motive power, are demonstrated by the physiologist to reside in the brain and spinal cord, as the centers of the nervous system; and therefore the ability of the human spirit to perceive and to act through the body must mainly depend upon the integrity with which these nervous centers fulfill their office. It is manifest that disorder of sensation and of muscular action must result from disease in the nerves, because will and perception are never exercised in this world but in connection with nerves. The lesson we learn from this liability to morbid manifestation is mutual charity. We ought always to regard each other with every allowance for bodily constitution; as the state of the soul is mainly dependent on the accommodation thus afforded for the operation of the mind.

Disease, whether personal or relative, is the most prevalent test of our affections and our faith; and through it the spirit of man when rightly established in truth, grows mighty in endurance, and triumphant over fear and death. We are required to look compassionately upon the faults of others, considering that we also are in the body; and while throwing the light of a loving heart over peculiarities that may not please us, do our utmost to ameliorate the physical condition of those whose minds are diverted from their right objects by discomfort. Let us teach, at least by example, that it is only in the right use of the body that mental integrity is proved—and, although temptation and torment may assail us through the nerves, let us show that a soul fortified by faith in God finds the victory in the condition of its will, and comes forth more than heroic in the conquest of evil by the might of good.

The soul operates with nerve-matter; the will causing currents of energy to be excited in different portions of that matter, according to the purpose of the mind in attending and acting, so as to induce a state of muscle and nerve in keeping with the state of feeling; and of course, therefore, disorder in the materials of mental manifestation disorders the manifestation itself. We are indebted to physicians for this knowledge; but reason, without the help of physiology, teaches us with sufficient clearness that the personality of a human being does not consist of nerves and muscles subject to physical derangement, but that there is something superadded to this organism which through it perceives other things and expresses itself. This something is, as we have shown, the true man, the soul or self, and every influence, either from without the body or within it, affects him as a personal being related by creation to other beings; and, therefore, the most comprehensive method of studying the endowments and destiny of the soul is to investigate its personal relationships, and their influence upon individual character and experience.

As regards the doctrine of ideas, disputes are end ess. I am quite content, however, to believe that thought is the soul thinking, and ideas are but states of mind, or soul at work under the impression either of present or remembered objects. Emotions in man are connected with ideas, and, in proportion to the vividness of thought, will be the feeling associated with the thought, always, of course, according to the state of the body and the habit of our affections. We will not, however, involve ourselves in the mists of metaphysical disquisition concerning affections internal and external, and faculties definite and indefinite. With regard to the habit of viewing the mind as so many distinct faculties, we may say, with Locke, (Book ii. chap. xxi. sect. 6.) "This way of speaking has misled many into a confused notion of so many distinct agents in us, which had their several provinces and authorities, and did command, obey, and perform several actions as so many distinct beings; which has been no small occasion of wrangling, obscurity, and uncertainty, in questions relating to them." We would not cavil with those who, in studying mental manifestations, divide these manifestations, as if distinct from the mind itself; things must have names in order to be scientifically considered; but we may well object to a nomenclature that, instead of indicating the mere instrumentality of organization, represents the organs as one with the faculty evinced through them—and thus not only divides a man into thirty or forty imaginary cerebral sections, but makes him nothing more than a piece of mechanism, with about as much responsibility as a locomotive or a mill. In discoursing of faculties and susceptibilities, we only refer to objects of sense or of thought, and to their effects upon us; for all our experience, either intellectual or emotional, depends on the nature of the soul in relation to other beings. When, for instance, the benevolent man sees another injured, it is not a sentiment that is sympathetically pained, but the man himself, who, according to his character, exerts his faculties, and, like a good Samaritan, sets about relieving the sufferer, for whom he feels, because constituted with a nature in like manner susceptible of injury and suffering. It can only be a willing being that can respond to the will of another. If a man obey the known commands of God, it is not a faculty of conscientiousness and veneration, as powers operative of themselves, but a soul that is conscientious, and venerates and obeys.

A man acts either from instinct, which relates to some bodily necessity, or else from some purpose having respect only to the mind. The motive of organic sense is instinct, the motive of mind is reason. Man combines both in his present state; his organism supplies physical impulse, and his mind operates partly in obedience to bodily appetite, and partly for the attainment of some spiritual advantage, which he expects only because he has affections and faculties which can not be satisfied without the interchange of thoughts with other minds.

All that any man can really recognize as truth in the doctrines of metaphysics, he must know from the study of his own mind. "Know thyself" is, however, a maxim too deep for men in general, and we are all apt to wander in a barren waste of speculation, and rather bewilder ourselves with the mirages of a weary imagination than quietly draw water from the fountain of truth, or sit beneath the tree of life, and eat its fruit with a thankful heart.

A feeling of personal identity is, of course dependent on the will of the Almighty; but it must, in the nature of things, imply self-consciousness; for that which does not feel its own existence, can not be aware of the existence of other beings. It must also imply successive impressions, or successive states of consciousness, and the power of recognizing the difference between them; so that memory and comparison are essential to conscious selfhood. All our passions, emotions and reasonings arise from the consciousness of self, in relation to objects as remembered things. Hence knowledge, habit, and physical condition are the only causes which modify man's affections. On the affections is founded all we conceive of agreeable or disagreeable, and desire is but the state of the will with regard to what we know and feel, for we can not desire, for its own sake, what is merely painful, nor avoid, for its own sake, what is pleasant. If we look beyond immediate gratification, it must be from attachment to some other being, or for the sake of qualifying ourselves the better for companionship with what we love, or because we fear the consequences to ourselves in offending the Being who has the right to command and to punish us.

There is an inherent relation of our souls to certain objects, for without any previous knowledge we are at once affected, either painfully or pleasantly, by their presence. Our *natural* attachments are born with us. The visible and audible expression of strong emotion, in any creature, affects our nerves in such a manner as to convey its own meaning. This susceptibility to emotion, irrespective of intelligence, is properly denominated affection; and as no training can have produced this, so it is manifest it must be the especial ground of all the ideas which occupy a man's mind. Whether true or false, good or bad, a man's ideas will be grouped and associated according to the qualities of his affections, or the adaptation of his soul to objects as capable of awakening like or dislike, love or hatred. These feelings express the intrinsic quality or condition of the mind, and therefore, if we know a man who intellectually perceives the beauty of any truth, without being moved by the love of it, we at once see that the will of that man is engaged in a manner not approved by his reason; he is in a perverted and profane state of affection, and can not be brought into an appropriate disposition of mind for seeking eternal fellowship with the intelligence that is one with goodness, until he has undergone a process of rectification by teachings and trials, in connection with whatever affection may have predominated in his heart to the detriment of his conscience.

Man is so apt to overlook the unity of his being, that it is quite common for him to lose all feeling of responsibility, by supposing himself a compound of incongruous parts over which he has no control. Heathens, giving form to their fancies, and outward expression to the state of their minds, have, in all ages, carved their own characters in marble or in wood, and have deified their own affections, desires, and ideas, by making them visible in all imaginable combinations of beauty and hideousness. Having thus rendered poetry into sculpture, and made feeling a permanent presence they fall down to adore their own conceits. They divide their divinity, by personifying their own lusts and think they see a god when they behold an image of themselves; they people the empyrean with heroes that outrage humanity, and crowd their heaven with horrors that earth can scarcely tolerate.

Perhaps a disposition has always existed in human minds to represent their own feelings as different from themselves, and therefore it is no wonder that, in this respect, the philosopher but emulates the savage. A modeler of minds here and there demonstrates his rational status by presenting us with casts of his mental faculties and affections as distinct from himself, but resident in the numberless cells of his brain; while the savage, with equal ingenuity, evinces his mental condition, by attributing the powers of his own soul to insensate substances, which he calls gods, because he is natural philosopher enough to know that bodies do not act without spirits residing in them. Philosophers of the more material kind settle their incongruities by arranging them in opposite compartments, like prisoners in a penitentiary. There is, however, this difference in the cases: in the penitentiary one individual inspects many others, but the philosopher distributes himself in fragments through a multitude of darkened cells, and thus disposes of his faults and his faculties together, while the individual is lost and the mind is nowhere. Others would analyze intellect and volition, as they would the soil, and having separated its elements, and set them aside, they wonder what we mean when we ask them what they have done with the soul? The *ego* has been so complacently busy in research as to forget itself; and the man believing only as he works, through his eyes and his hands, observes that, having submitted humanity to a dry distillation, he finds no residuum, but a *caput mortuum* of dust.

We are strangely taught, by some of our best ethical writers, that desires and affections exist without volition, but unless they mean more than their words signify, we can not understand them; for where is the desire without will, and where the affection that is neither pleasing nor displeasing? Will must be excited in every manifestation of self, for all we feel is but the result of the correspondence between the sensitive soul and its objects; and if these be so indifferent to us as not to produce volition, we must soon lose sight of them, and, falling asleep, enter the world of dreams, for even dreams are more real than sights and sounds without effect upon us. We never attend without an exercise of will, and the qualities of things induce a state of mind in the individual regarding them according to his intuitive perception, habit, or association. By intimacy with the feelings of others, we are apt to feel like them. Their tastes become ours; we sympathize with them until we resemble them. Thus our affections are educated as well as our intellect, and we are always capable of departing as widely from good feeling as from sound thinking by fellowship with erroneous souls; for to depart from God is not only to forsake truth, but to pass into falsehood, which is never an abstract negation, but an active evil positively at work to corrupt the will. Thus minds always both stray and suffer when left untutored and unrestrained by those wise spirits that care for others. We can not separate the emotion from the affection, nor the desire from the will, except in speculative words. Will in action is desire, and a will inactive is no will. The mind, operating in relation to objects of sense, is mind under more or less of emotion—self more or less impressed by what is agreeable or otherwise; thus the soul evinces its will; and the mind, attending to ideas and comparing them, whether from direct impression or in memory, is a thinking mind or intellect. Now it is evident, that both will and the power of knowing or being impressed are essential to a conscious being. And man's superiority, as a mind, is shown in his capacity of abstracting his attention from objects to fix it upon ideas, so as to reason concerning them. His reason is his faith. So then man, fully manifested, wills, knows, believes, and loves. This is his nature. Therefore he must be provided with objects in keeping with his nature—things to desire, to understand, and to believe. And in as far as man is created with a capacity of thinking of the Creator as the originator of all things, he must be constituted to find in Him the supreme object of desire, of knowledge, and of faith. In other words, man's will and intellect must find their satisfaction in God, and in what He provides; for man can not rationally enjoy any thing in creation but as he finds in it the expressions of his Maker's mind toward himself; therefore an irreligious man is so far unreasonable—his reason is without its chief end, the efficient object of love, the only source of light and joy.

To know truly, to love truly, to believe truly, is to know, love, believe, what God has provided; and to be deprived of this, is to be ignorant and unhappy. But He has not left himself any where without witnesses of his tender care for human beings. He has given us all something for the exercise of whatever faculties we possess, leading us on in thought from the deficiencies of the past and the present to the fullness of the future, that we may be conscious that we hang upon His unfailing Providence for all we have and all we hope.

Let us not suffer ourselves to be beguiled out of our birthright as intelligent beings, by the vapory modes of speech invented by the misty order of metaphysicians, or the more mechanical surveyors of our brains, but let us remember, that whatever the peculiarities of our mental manifestation, we are still individuals, and not complicated thinking machines. *We* hear, feel, see, taste, smell; *we* desire, hope, fear, confide, venerate, determine; *we* compare, reflect, reason; *we* exercise intellect and feel emotion; *we* sin; *we* suffer; *we* live forever; and *we* need a Saviour, that knows our nature in all it is, and all it can be, and who is capable of providing for us according to the vastness of our necessities.

Superinduced upon the vitality of his physical framework, man, in his present state, has two modes of psychical manifestation, which distinguish him from animals. He is capable of living in an ideal world produced in his mind by the impression of exterior objects, and he is capable of enjoying thoughts which the material universe could not engender nor suggest, unless to a reason enlightened by underived Intelligence. Man is the prophet and the seer, the expositor of nature, the student of events, the only being on earth that concerns himself with the plans of Providence and the prospects of the future. And while he voluntarily dwells upon his own past for the renewal of its pleasures, or to indulge in the luxury of recollected sorrow, he feels called on to look further back, and forward, and around, not as if he were alone the subject of his own insight, but as if the inheritor in spirit of all that has been accomplished and all that is to come. It is true, that he alone beholds the autobiography of the heart, and sees written in his memory, as in a book, the indelible record of his life. But his individual experience is but a small part of his treasury of facts; he glances in the retrospect of thought, to witness, as in a moment of time, and as in a living panorama spread before the eye of his soul, the grand lessons of history, as the especial science of his race, in respect to the promises and providence of God; he mingles in imagination with the generations that are gone; his heart glows at the songs of bards two thousand years old; his nerves thrill at the eloquence of men that can never die; his spirit is kindled by thoughts that have passed from soul to soul since souls have been; he sympathizes in the struggles of human spirits erroneously laboring to be free, and, where truth brings the liberty of knowledge and of power, he seems to join the nations in their welcome to the light; he weeps at their griefs, and laughs when they are glad; every utterance of humanity affects his own heart, like a familiar interest, and he feels the touch of kindred and of love that vibrates through all time; he trembles in agony, to behold mighty souls losing their way and groping in the darkness of tradition, and feeling after God without finding him; and, if a Christian, he burns, perhaps, to speak of Jesus to Pythagoras, to Plato, and to Socrates; and, to satisfy his hopes, expects to find them learned in the Word of God and glorious in his kingdom. Thus the human spirit can take its part in all the progresses of its race; go back, as if with Milton, to the beginning, when "the heavens and the earth rose out of chaos;" associate in soul with the first Adam in his perishable Paradise, and then, deliberately looking through all the passages of a fallen and redeemed world, go forth in the strength of an unfailing faith to meet the second Adam, the Lord from heaven, returning to establish among men the immovable dominion of righteousness and love.

Man's character is formed by his ideas, and these are of three classes:—

1st. Those which he has in common with inferior creatures—the mere reflex of nervous impression.

2dly. Those that are purely human, rational, reflective, but limited to natural or physical objects.

3dly. Those that are revealed and divine, and tending to bear the soul onward to futurity, in consequence of what it perceives as the moral necessity of its own existence.

Perhaps there is not a being in human form so unhappily associated or so miserably uninstructed as to live entirely in the lowest or brutal state, unless from necessity, as is the case of certain idiots, who can obtain no associate ideas, in consequence of some defect in the organization of the brain through which the soul perceives. The relation between thoughts and things is lost in such cases, because the soul can not rest upon sensation so as to make comparison distinctly. Perfect idiots can attend to impressions only so far as to act instinctively; they are, therefore, removed beyond the pale of humanity, excepting as they serve to exercise our faith in Omnipotence, and lead us to look forward to the manifestation of His benevolence in the emancipation of souls from the imprisonment of incommodious and impeding bodies.

It is manifest that when the mind has not the power or opportunity of working, whatever of the inferior cast belongs to human nature will then operate unrestrained. The history of idiotism is a doleful illustration of this truth, but yet, like every evil, it points to good, and calls us to exercise faith in God, as the provider of means against misery. Idiotism proves the debasing influence of neglecting humanity. Even in its worst forms it is still somewhat amenable to kindness and to skill. Whenever a human soul can be reached by another, so as to feel a good intention, there is an improvable being. As long as the organization of the senses and their associate brain are not so imperfect as to prevent connected attention to objects, it is in the power of one man to elicit the light hidden in another; and many men, seeing this, and devoutly loving human souls for love's sake, have set themselves with patience to the task of redeeming idiots from the hideousness of confused instincts, undirected and without aim. By persevering efforts, in attracting and fixing their attention steadily and sympathetically to the actions of their teachers—teachers, so to say, by contact—multitudes of such forlorn beings have been brought into smiling association with humanity and reason; thus proving that those left to neglect and ill-treatment must be the pests and terrors of social and domestic life, until the unconquerable philanthropy of practical wisdom and charity is brought to bear upon them and bring them forth from degradation into rational relationship. If asylums for idiots had done nothing more than teach us that beautiful souls may lie completely concealed under disgusting coverings, they had done much; but they have also taught us that the might of patience, sympathy, and kindness, is greater far than the world yet knows. They have, moreover, indicated how much may, in general, be done to restore human nature to its right place, by true knowledge and love, duly exercising the authority which alone elongs to them, by showing how mental and physical evils may be prevented by moral restraints, and remedied, as far as man may remedy, by *insisting* on obedience to the laws of nature and of God.

If the brain be not so diseased or deficient as to preclude the soul from attention, through it moral education is probably always possible. A superior mind asserts its power, first by controlling its own impulses, and then by the orderly purpose of action in visible self-management, sympathetically governing the minds of others also. Thus, by persevering determination in regulating muscular movements, by bringing the senses steadily into use, and by exercising the will intelligently in every action, M. Sequin, and others on his plan, have succeeded in training the most unpromising idiots into conscientious agents. The philanthropy thus beautifully and wisely at work, opens to our view more of the practical science of education than all the discourses on mental discipline with which schoolmen have afflicted us: it has demonstrated that mind rules mind most effectually by *asserting its right* to be attended to, and that none can be lost to improvement who can be brought into willing obedience, and that this obedience, or yielding of self, is induced by the visible and constant interest of the governing in the governed. Mere coercion fails, even with an idiot: the mind is not brought out into intercourse, except by a strong will dominating over it by engaging it agreeably. The state of the body is a state of will, in as far as it tends either to pleasure or pain; and if the mind be perverted by an ill state of body, the only way to recover it from wrong desires is to command attention to other perceptions than those produced by the disorder or ill condition of the body or of any of its organs and functions; a new state of will must be induced. This is exemplified to the full by M. Sequin's treatment of the perverted and disordered idiot. He at first governs the idiot's mus cles for him, by putting himself completely in the idiot's way as, so to say, his only object. All the senses that poor imbecile may possess he confines to his own movements: he masters the forlorn being by infusing a new will into his limbs; he takes hold of them gently and firmly, and slowly moves them, as he wishes, consecutively, and for the attainment of certain ends. Thus the mindless, purposeless pupil moves with his master, until his muscles are educated into associate action. In short, the teacher adopts the only method open in such a case to obtain any degree of fellowship, and thus he draws out the idiot's mind into consistent action, as far as possible with so incommodious an organization of brain, nerve, and muscle, as an idiot existence implies. And all embodied minds must be reached and ruled on the same principles—the will of one must be brought into relation to the other by physical helps; there must be co-operation until there is established sympathy; and then, where sympathy is established, if mental development and manifestation be not a physical impossibility, an order of kindred thinkings may be conducted through one mind to the other, and that moral intercourse will result for which reason exists and language is given.

The exercise of memory is generally the chief part of education, as usually conducted, but this is really the least important in itself; for if memory alone be cultivated, a man may learn to have no thoughts of his own, although as full of words and facts as an encyclopedia. The intellect may be quickened into such intense activity, *memoriter*, as to be ever busy with associations and comparisons, and even to be poetically and even mathematically insane, but yet make no progress in practical truth. The man of large remembrance may be not a whit the more moral, or the more religious, or the more useful to society and home, for all his knowledge. He may be only a man of ideas, after all,—a mere psychological curiosity,—unless he learn to regulate his body as the outward and visible part of the formal social system. Religion and morality are not ideal things. We recognize, indeed, most fully the fact that man is a psychical being, a soul: for physical senses and frameworks would be useless if an operative and percipient agent were not engaged, through them in forming ideas. Objects and sensations can never become thoughts but to a thinking being. But a man must perceive and understand his relation to objects before he can justly reflect or properly feel. Thought is altogether wide of its purpose, but as from an intuitive sense of the fitness of other created things to the individual mind. Without this the symbols of thought are never interpreted, and the senses serve only to awaken impulses that have no meanings beyond those of the idiot and the brute. The human being must be taught to perceive and feel his relation to other intelligences before his moral nature can be developed. He must be drilled as well as disciplined. His will must be brought into coincidence with others; he must move with them as well as reciprocate their affections, before there can arise a sense of duty or a disposition to act with respect to another's claim upon his conduct. Free will does not begin to be evinced until the mind perceives this duty, and until then moral consciousness is not awakened. The distinctive attribute of man slumbers until the mind is conscientiously cultivated by practical lessons, or by the embodiment of good thoughts in good actions. If a man have never seen any but malignant or evil passions at work, how can he have a good thought? Human minds must not be judged by the heavenly standard until they have been brought under Divine doctrines, and that not in abstract terms, not in words alone, but in words interpreted by the language of life, by example, by excellence made visible in deed, just as the Son of God taught the bewildered sons of men. Thus Christians stir the world, agitate spirits, rouse wills, grapple other minds, and shake them with the truths that shake you; propagate the energy that is to regenerate mankind, because it is the will of God that is in you.

There are many among men so satisfied with the brutal kind of accommodation, that they forget that blood, nerve, and muscle were placed in relation to the human soul only to subserve it with means of learning truth and of exercising will, so as to prove that mind is eternal and irresistible when in the possession of ability from God to believe in Divine goodness, and thus to conquer evil. These men, having their souls biased by depraved habit, prefer what they call sense, and so modify their reason with the constancy of their search for pleasures of sight, sound, taste, and touch, as not to allow ideas of a higher order to remain before the eye of the mind, or even to enter on the field of their perceptions. Their Paradise is not merely one of fools, but of idiots, since to be quite fit for it men must content themselves with the grossest bodily sensations.

A third class are on earth—but are they not few?—whose ideas are not all convertible into dreams and phantasms. There is a reality of life about these men as regards the purposes of their minds, which will not suffer them to limit their attention to images of objects merely; they have moral notions, and believe in God, and in a grand arrangement to take place in a world to come, on decisively righteous principles, so that each soul shall stand eternally in relation to happiness precisely according to the state of its will and affection toward the Holy One. Men with these convictions and expectancies are, of course, disposed to use this world without abusing it, and always aim at the subjection of the animal nature, both in sensation and idea, that their conduct may tend to demonstrate the excellence of reason, by proving its power to rule on principles derived from Heaven, and from motives, that, as they arise from love to the Lord of life, must defy death, and regulate the springs of thought and action forever.

This is the really reasonable class, for in its full exercise reason is always religious, since veneration to the Supreme is the only truly exalting tendency of the soul; and it elevates the whole man, as if by the Divine attractiveness of light and love, into fellowship with the Maker of heaven. If we are not capable of recognizing the power and wisdom of God in the objects of creation and in its ordinances of harmonious co-operation, we are not, indeed, rational, and can not discern right from wrong. The law of heaven is then hid from our eyes, because we have not entered on the proper exercise of our higher faculties, since for these there can be no occasion, except in the investigation of truth, as revealed to our understandings in the workings of the Almighty in matter and on minds. If men discover nothing of God in nature, or in the spiritual revelations of thought, they must be dark at heart and unreasonable in conduct; for this is that form of ignorance that makes deities of lusts, and fate of lawless will, because men living under its influence, being filled with falsehood and delusion, can believe only either sensually or superstitiously. Being tyrannized over, in one case by their sensations, and in the other by their fears, their ideas have nothing to do with logic, nor their morality with love. They tolerate each other only from convenience, just as a frightened herd crowd their heads together for mutual defense; they begin to butt at each other as soon as the motive for such association is past, and obedient only to selfish impulses, they separate, to roam or to ruminate, as the bodily state of each may suggest

The reason why many really live a brutal kind of existence arises, as we have seen, from the circumstance that human beings are constituted in a great measure with relation to mere animal life. They possess bodies formed on natural or physical principles, and confining their attention, either from ignorance or from indolence, too much to this body and its conveniences, they lose sight of the supernatural or spiritual relations of their minds, and satisfy themselvesas, well as they can, with brutal comforts and bodily enjoyments.

In these days when so much ingenuity is evinced in endeavoring to reduce man to the elements of nature, it is important clearly to see wherein the human mind, when permitted to be manifested, differs from that of mere animals. If a dog had a brain like a man's, say some physiologists, he would be reasonable and religious. This is the same as saying, if a dog were human he would not be a dog. All such *ifs* are simple impossibilities, because what is one thing can not be another. A human brain belongs to a human being, and no other being ever had such a brain ; and yet the brain no more makes the man, or the dog, than the man or the dog make the brain. God constitutes his creatures, and he has determined that no creature on earth but man should voluntarily control his impulses for moral purposes. Man can train himself by the apprehension of a will wiser than his own, but animals can not will otherwise than as their senses may impress them and excite desires. Man can believe in God as a Lawgiver, and he can *wish* to love his neighbor as himself, because he can perceive that it is essential to the well being of all intelligences endowed with active powers, that they should mutually regard each other's interests, or they would be mutually injurious. Where are the morals of beasts—and what are their charities ? Can a brute reflect on the probable effect of his conduct on the feelings of another ? Can it perceive any evil in its will? Is it capable of acting conscientiously? Can it put itself in relation to history? Can it arrange past facts into new pictures? Can it obey God, from love and gratitude? Can it trust to His hand? It can do nothing of the sort—and, therefore, until those expounders of natural history, who include Omnipotence only as a part of the theory of development, have brought forth for us some specimen of a quadrumanous or other mammal, not born of woman, but yet devout toward God, and consequently conscientious toward man, we must take the liberty of doubting their admission to the councils of the Almighty. But, alas! it is easy to find men so far resembling brutes, that they neither venerate the Author of their being nor justly regard the claims of their fellow creatures. But they are not forced to remain in such a state. If they are not idiotic, they may so attend to the doctrines of nature and revelation, as to see that the Maker of beauty is a proper object of love, and that He who harmonizes the universe by light must be the source of blessedness to all who obey His laws.

Whatever similarity may exist between the mental manifestation of brutes and the actions of some men, there is still an immeasurable and impassable gulf between the human mind and the brutal, which can be accounted for only from the supposition that God has imparted to the soul of man a power of desiring and of acquiring ideas in infinite succession, through which it may learn and love for eternity. The human soul can be educated on moral and religious, that is to say, on rational principles, because it is constituted to reflect the mind of its Maker, as evinced in beauty and order, or law and government. In short, man alone can acknowledge a Creator, or be instructed from his works and his word, to trust him and to honor him. Reason is the mirror of God, and reflects his image —and the soul of man, perceiving in itself this reflex of perfection, is able in some measure to appreciate the love and understand the power, which belong to Him—who, as the one origin and end of being is the only object demanding his devotion and worthy of his worship. Until we find animals equally endowed, we shall have no reason to compare man with them. When they begin to exercise free will and conscience, we may talk of their morality, and then consider their expectations of immortality. They can not desire a spiritual life, or a conformity with the Divine will, by its embodiment in person or in action. They see neither life nor death, and truly, as before said, the man who lives not in truth, and loves not God, is so far like them. The lower order of mind from physical defect, or groveling mismanagement and ignorance, is humanly brutal: the next order is rationally intelligent, so far as the use of this world's elements of knowledge and advantage may serve the purposes of thought and action. The third order of minds is devoutly spiritual, from some degree of Divine illumination in the understanding, by the entrance of truths addressed directly to the heart and intellect of man, as being conscious of entire dependence on the All-wise for every endowment that shall qualify him for association with the intelligences that bow adoringly and hearken to the words of God. In this order of minds the thoughts are apt habitually to take the form of prayer. They trust actively, they praise actively, they pray actively, they live silently, unostentatiously, divinely, efficiently, because they live feelingly upon the beneficence of the Might that thus always operates both on earth and in heaven.

Without spiritual knowledge, or the consciousness of good and evil, man has no free will, and can only choose evilly, selfishly, or simply to answer the sensual purposes of this bodily life; and thus it must be, until he so understands the character of his Maker as to love it, and to hate whatever is opposed to it. This perception and apprehension of Divine perfection can be conferred only by God himself; for how can man willingly conform to the law of God, without being instructed by His Spirit? Thus men do the will, and learn the wisdom of God, by the operation and impartation of a creative power, which induces a change of mental direction, equivalent to a new nature in the thoughts and purposes of man, so that he becomes holy in body, soul, and spirit, by acting in faithful obedience to the demands of his Maker. Instead of seeking for a self-satisfaction for to-day, the really religious man should live, every conscious moment, with his mind set upon conformity to a higher, holier will, and thus seeking an unfading glory, and looking to God, find in Him the happiness, the end, the sufficiency of his being. He who is thus spiritually alive can not but believe in eternal life, because he has already begun to enjoy it in earnest; and he can not but believe in everlasting love, because he knows that if we, being evil, give good gifts to our children, our Father in heaven will much rather give His Holy Spirit to them that ask Him; and thus religion proves itself divine—the end and purpose of reason to the man who receives the revelation of Heaven.

CHAPTER VI.

SELF-MANAGEMENT.

WITH an endeavor to simplify the science of mind, it has been my aim, I hope not presumptuously, always to keep in view the unity and individuality of the being which feels, thinks, and acts. It is a self, or a soul that is conscious of sensation, thought, and will. Whatever be the experience of the mind, it is a condition of the *ego*, with relation either to objects or the ideas of objects. It is a personal being, existing experimentally, and in the actual perception of realities, or in the remembrance of them, and weal or woe is the state of the individual in his inward life and self-consciousness. But the soul of man has relation to a three-fold order of consciousness—of thought or intellect; of feeling, or some degree of emotion; of desire, or some exercise of will. These correspond with the three-fold division of the nervous system, the cerebral, the cerebro-spinal, and the ganglionic. But it is important to observe that this division destroys not the unity of the soul, since in thought, feeling and desire are involved, and in every degree of emotion, thought and desire are included, and in desire, emotion is blended with thought. Willing and feeling are essential to intellect; and either the one or the other predominates, according as the soul manifests itself in its different bodily relations. This division of manifestation is a practical truth, that demands to be borne in mind in our endeavors at self-cultivation; for all defects in education are traceable to mismanagement, both of the body and the mind, in one or all of these divisions; and it is in the relation which these divisions bear to each other that we find the limit to the power of mental training. We have to preserve a just balance between intellect, emotion, and will, or the mind becomes more or less deranged in operation. The person whose thinking faculties are cultivated at the expense of his affections and natural desires, lives in a world of abstractions, as if amid ideas that find no representatives in the universe of God. One whose thoughts are left to wander at random in the region of romance, becomes a being full of sentimentalism, and is lost in inordinate affection, either in idea or reality; while he whose natural desires are neither restrained by natural affection nor regulated by thought, descends to the baser madness of the habitual sensualist.

Thus we see that mental and moral fortitude, or virtue, consists in maintaining that adjustment of our nature which includes the management of bodily impulses, under the feeling of those superior motives that spring only from the understanding of our duty to God and our neighbor, and a firm resolution, under the encouragement of Divine and ever ready help, to do it. It is in this way that man walks with God in health, and enters heaven as his natural home.

I would thus define the three-fold division of mental operation :—

Intellect is the self, or soul, perceiving physical and logical relations, and acting on them.

Moral feeling is the self, perceiving the relation of conscious beings to itself, and acting accordingly.

Emotion is the effect of ideal or present objects upon one's sense of self, as regards pain or pleasure.

Each of these conditions of mind is modified by bodily state and the employment of the senses. Healthy organization of nerve and brain is essential to the exercise of that attention on which clear ideas depend while using the body; and, therefore, in as far as attention modifies emotion, our feelings must be influenced by the body.

Moral perception will of necessity be obscure, where reason itself is darkened; but its defects ap pertain rather to the will than to the understanding, though will itself is limited, in certain respects, by physical necessity.

Emotion, as far as the mind can act voluntarily in controlling its own feelings, will be evinced according to the state of the intellect and the acuteness of moral perception; but in as far as the susceptibility to impression from objects depends on nervous sensibility, it is manifest that whatever modifies this sensibility will also modify emotion. Hence it is, that sex and temperament exercise so large an influence over the formation of character, and in the conduct of individuals, under the same rational and moral convictions.

In considering the connection between the mind and the body, it is of the highest importance always to remember that the mind, or rather the being that thinks and wills, is the active agent. The body, with all its beautiful and wondrous adaptations, only supplies the means of perception and of acting. Nerve-matter is the evident medium and instrument of the being that perceives and acts through it. Physiologists appear to have demonstrated that an imponderable principle, akin to electricity, is evolved in the nervous system, and that currents of this fluid are constantly traversing the different sets of nerves, according to their office and function, either as the media of sensation, volition, or of vegetative life. There is, in short, an action going forward in all the nerves and their centers, similar to the electro-magnetic, and consequently every nerve is polarized. The soul appears to operate upon these electro-magnetic currents, and to be impressed by them. The imponderable *energia* passing in these currents is apparently the medium between the soul and the more palpable materials forming the body. This may be inferred from the fact, that whatever alters the force of these currents alters the condition of the mind in relation to the body. Thus the arrest of the current in a nerve subservient to voluntary muscular action, whether by chemical or mechanical means, prevents the mind from exercising will in the use of the muscle with which the nerve experimented on is connected. The same occurs, also, in the like case with any nerve through which we obtain sensation of the presence of any body which, in a natural state, would so affect the nerve as to produce feeling. Another evidence that the soul acts through this fluid is afforded in the circumstance that, by strongly directing attention to any part, as, for instance, the eye, a new sensation is perceived in the organ; and if this kind of attention be persisted in, or frequently repeated, the eye becomes inflamed and painful. It is also evident, that those nerves that belong to parts, the natural functions of which are carried on without our consciousness—such as the stomach—may be rendered sensitive by a strong action of the will; and the operation of all the reflex, or ordinarily involuntary system, is modified by mental emotion. In fact, every thought changes the nerve-current. Moreover, the brain itself, and all the nerves connected with it, are so far influenced by the will of the individual as to be not only directed into new modes, so as to effect an entire alteration in the habit of mental and muscular action, but also to such a degree, that "the completely organized brain is partly a creation of self-directing and self-repeating mental activity," (Feuchtersleben, p. 123.) It is, so to say, developed by the habits of the soul.

The rapidity of the mental processes seems to require an electric or some similar medium, by which they may be effected in connection with the body, since they result so instantaneously that the will to move for instance, and the motion, are simultaneous. Professor Wheatstone has proved that electricity, like light, travels at the rate of 192,000 miles in a second: and this appears to be an agency sufficiently subtile to answer all the purposes of the soul as an active being. Probably electricity and light are but one agent, acting under different relations. It is interesting to consider ourselves as operating, by each act of our will, upon embodied light; but whatever be the immediate agency between mind and muscle, it is vastly more interesting to know, that the willing being is something as really and distinctly existing as the light itself, but in its nature infinitely more subtilely and exquisitely constituted, since it is indivisibly and inscrutably associated with the Being who said, "Let light be, and light was."

If we advance further in contemplating our mental existence in connection with the body, we shall more clearly perceive, that the body itself is not the cause but the instrument of mind. In order that it should be a ready instrument, it is, as we see, constructed on electro-magnetic principles, so that it serves the purposes of the mind in many spontaneous actions, without even awakening consciousness. Whatever is essential to the processes of life is carried on in the economy, without our consent; and until some demand is made by the body, requiring our voluntary interference for the removal of inconvenience or for the supply of aliment, our attention is not so far attracted to the body as that our desires are distinctly perceived to arise from its state. Thus we feel hunger or thirst, and use means for their removal. But our emotions and affections are at all times influenced by bodily condition, and in many respects, may be traced to a physical origin. They are so far involuntary, that their causes are in operation before we are aware, and they are apt to evince their power against our wills; yet reason is tested by their presence, and she prevails over them in proportion to the clear perception and experience of spiritual motives, or those moral convictions which arise from religious enlightenment. Were it not that our connection with the body subjects us to feelings against which we are conscientiously and reasonably required to contend, we should be incapable of that self-consciousness by which we distinguish ourselves from our bodies In fact, those who find no other inducement to thought and action than the body affords, are really incapable of apprehending any other than bodily existence, and they live not according to spiritual but sensual motive

The passions being heightened impulses, consented to by the mind, are evidently connected with the emotions. They are strong expressions of pleasure or displeasure, according to the state of the will or the mental intention at the time of the impulse. We desire whatever promises us pleasure, but this desire may be removed from the mind by the previous consideration of the nature and consequence of such a pleasure in a moral view. The enjoyments of sense may give place to those of thought. The inclination of reason will be directed by the knowledge of results and by its disposition to yield to what it recognizes as Divine law. The object pursued by rational choice will be according to our apprehension of the nature of that which is presented, with respect to good and evil morally considered. But, of course, without the reception of the Divine moral law as a standard of conduct, there can be no other sense of good and evil but that which many infidels have advocated—namely whatever the individual may find agreeable or otherwise, with no other modification than that of selfish convenience.

Those who deny that our Maker has revealed His will as the rule of life, are perfectly consistent in representing every heart as being rightfully a law to itself—not from conscience but for pleasure, not for eternity but for time, not for life everlasting but for speedy death.

The emotions and passions, as regards man, are in deed but different conditions of the sense of self; but then they receive modification, according to the degree of mental culture and the purity of moral motive and purpose, as well as from the state of the body. Let us consider that state of mind known as cheerfulness. What is this but an undefined pleasure in the consciousness of life, with that degree of satisfaction which is felt during the absence of any thing annoying, and without the presence of any object that excites passion? Yet it can never exist without a quiet hopefulness, and hence the man who busily sets about doing his duty is most disposed cheerily to whistle at his work. A certain forgetfulness of consequences, whether from a careless disposition or from the influence of a stimulus, often induces this state of mind, but a wise man is not likely to rejoice without a good reason.

Some metaphysicians include certain emotions in their catalogue of passions, and others classify certain passions among the emotions. This discrepancy probably arises from a disregard of the fact that both our passions and our emotions, with reference to objects of sense, are but states of self, in relation to impression, and the energy with which they may be manifested depends on the state of the body and its organs at the time that any impulse acts upon us. To illustrate my meaning more fully, I will examine anger—the most violent of our emotions, and emphatically designated passion. However sudden the seizure of this *furor brevis*, it springs directly from a feeling of interference with the accomplishment of some desire; it is the energetic expression of offense at the resistance of our wills. It therefore operates throughout the muscular system, and makes a strong demand upon our hearts for a rapid supply of blood, and summons the brain to put forth all its energy. The degree to which the brain and heart may be excited will depend upon their state. We well know that the nervous system and the blood may be in a condition to favor irascible feeling, and render even a wise man in danger of appearing both foolish and ill-tempered. Who has not seen or heard enough of the mysteries of madness, to be aware that ungovernable rage is one of its most terrible modes, in consequence of the feeling of offense coinciding with a state of body so predisposed to promote its expression, that total exhaustion of energy can alone terminate the paroxysm? That the cause of the emotion may sometimes be purely mental, and sometimes physical is, in this case, very evident. The state of the body suggests the angry ideas, and any slight cause of mental disturbance at once rouses the brain and circulation to the rage point. All our passions are more or less subject to the same reciprocal influence, and hence, in the New Testament, self-government is enforced by commands that require us to keep the body in subjection while seeking a conformity of will to Divine example. To be angry without sin, is the standard of perfection; since such a state of feeling is but holy zeal in the vindication of God's character, as the faithful Creator, and a resistance to whatever would tempt us to doubt or disobey Him.

There are a thousand degrees and kinds of indignation: the moral condition, together with the intellectual cultivation determining the kind; for an exhibition of conduct that would only excite an offensive sense of meanness in one man, will produce in another the most earnest expressions of compassionate concern. A feeling of anger exists in both; in the former it is pride and wrath, constituting contempt, but in the latter it is a sense both of the impropriety and the danger of the individual offending. In short, every emotion acts as a stimulus to the brain, only to elicit an expression of the general character and habit of the mind; since whatever impulse a man may feel, he will act under it, according to his moral and religious convictions. Thus the temptations of one man drive him to the secret place of the Almighty, while another is led captive at the will of the tempter; one seeking comfort in prayer, and another in potations.

We shall do well to reflect still further on anger, as the type of passion. In the human mind, without religious motives, anger is essentially hatred; but a well constituted man can allow it no rest in his bosom, except in the form of that constant odium with which he regards any thing positively unjust and injurious, as opposed to the universal law of love, to which he himself wishes ever to be obedient. Love is the proper antagonist both of anger and of hatred; and as he who hates his brother is a murderer, devoid of all idea concerning eternal life, so he that truly loves the human brotherhood has passed from death to life, and feels the value of the price paid for man's redemption. The method by which God reconciles men to himself is the only method by which men can be perfectly reconciled to each other. There is no other cause of peace in the world. Men may, indeed, be too busy in their pursuits to quarrel; but the very eagerness of their engagements produces war whenever they come into collision without love, because the natural will can not then be excited to anger without also awakening hatred, and that is a desire which knows no rest but in the extermination of whatever opposes it.

There is an instructive distinction between animals and man, with regard to the irrascible disposition. As animals are not capable of moral emotions, they are incapable of malice; for this requires intellect and reason to engender and to foster it. This fact is illustrated by reference to the tempers of lower animals.

It may, I think, be questioned whether they can experience anger in any respect similar to what man feels. They resist any opposition to their natural desires or convenience, but they do not *resent* it, because, in fact, they have no real sense of wrong. Infants and idiots, in whose minds moral motives are not in operation, are so far instinctive in their consciousness of resistance to the fulfillment of their wills: however they may struggle to overcome and even destroy what may stand in the way of their wishes, we hold them irresponsible, because they can not compare another's claim with their own, nor apprehend the law of right. Hence a sense of vengeance, or revenge, properly speaking, no more mixes with their emotion than does a sense of justice. As they are actuated by instinct to resist opposition, so the instant the obstacle is removed, or a new object attracts their attention, they are appeased. They harbor no ill will. Revenge is not a motive in their anger. The lioness robbed of her whelps will fight for their recovery, but their restoration obliterates her wrath in natural pleasure, provided the despoiler disappears. Man's anger is not of this simply protective nature; there is vengeance in it. He reasons wrathfully, he nurses his indignation, he maliciously exaggerates the injury, he reflects his own spirit upon it, he pursues the offender, not only as a foe, but as a culprit, whose crime can not be expiated but by a consummate punishment—he seeks his revenge. This is the natural course of man's anger, until religion changes the style of his affections, and directs his thoughts to God. He then foregoes all thoughts of revenge, because he feels that he could have no hope of salvation were not righteousness necessarily love.

There is some sense of justice in man, however wild, and this appears to be engrafted upon mere animal resentment, or that result of constitutional antipathy by which the different tribes are kept apart, for their better enjoyment of the means of life. But the spirit of revelation, of reason, and of religion, masters the animal in man, and causes him to feel an interest in his fellow man, commensurate with his own consciousness of eternity and God. All we know of man's nature from physiology, from the Bible, and from self-consciousness, shows us, that in proportion as the will is regulated by religion, will our emotions be kept in orderly submission, and our conduct be directed to right ends. There is no security against the tyranny of our passions but from that dominion of the spirit, which consists in the formation of correct mental habits, under the influence of Divine truths and proper objects of affection. These must take possession of our hearts and nerves, in order to our safety; for if they do not, ideas from evil sources will prevail over us, and that in such a manner as neither to be cast out by agony, nor controlled by terror. The enemies of God are the enemies of man, and the sensuality of our fallen nature is so far coincident with evil, that if we refuse to obey the exhortation that addresses us as the children of a Heavenly parentage, we must be ruled by the hand that can not suffer an enemy to prosper, because the Omnipotence of Love is pledged to promote only the devout and the benevolent.

The mightiness of those motives which Providence has appointed for our government, is strikingly exemplified in that most awful state of human degradation, insanity. We will refer to this subject merely to illustrate the influence of hope and fear under the most unfavorable circumstances. M. Esquirol employed the actual cautery, a red hot iron, in rousing the dormant will of insane patients, and thus succeeded, in some cases, in establishing the rational dominion of the mind over the confused emotions induced by disease of the brain. Pinel employed a plan, more humane but perhaps equally efficient. He directed the cold douche, not only as a means of changing the nervous action, but also as a punishment, where the mind was still amenable to the persuasions of fear, and he has recorded that he thus occasionally cured an obstinate insanity. But the more philanthropic method is now recommended to the world by the gentle firmness with which Dr. Conolly manages to engage the minds and interest the hearts of the numerous inmates of Hanwell Asylum, with employments, and with hopes suited to the different states of their affections and intellect.

But it is evident that many of the various diseases of the nervous system are of a kind that limits this power of appealing to the mind for motives to control itself. When disease so interferes with the action of the senses and of judgment, as to hinder the right perception of time and space by too rapid an excitement, then a whirling and confused sense of present objects begins, and is speedily superseded by imagined or remembered impressions. Responsibility is at an end—the man is no longer capable of comparing one thing with another—he employs not his senses under the guidance of knowledge—he is no longer capable of acting toward others with consciousness of moral relationship—he is mad as a drunkard.

But it may be said of any man, that unless he habitually employ his faculties and affections on their appropriate objects, his experience, however craftily acquired, is still but a self-controlled insanity, for to live without an intelligent and amiable purpose, is really to serve an inferior nature, and to aggravate the degradation of the selfhood by the indulgence of its depraved desires.

If self-control, and the subjection of bodily impulses be not founded on love to others as well as to ourselves, moral derangement is already commenced there is an established aptitude for *monomania*. This state of mind is usually no other than a perversion of intellect, in consequence of moral obliquity, or the habit of acting with a view to selfish gratification, irrespective of all that conscience may dictate or relative affection may demand. Hence, it is no uncommon thing for monomaniacs to charge their crimes upon the defects of their education or the mismanagement of their childhood. A youth, who, after a course of outrages against morality, murdered his father, thus addressed the dead body—"Ah, my father, where are you now? You and my mother have caused this misfortune. If you had brought me up better, it would not have happened."* Let parents so pray, and so act, that such a charge may not be valid against them before the throne of God.

Every remarkable instance of deficiency in self-management we regard as an evidence either of defect in mental culture, or of some disproportion and disorder in the organization by which the mind operates and is impressed. Mental derangement is complete whenever any disease of the nervous system in any of its divisions has so far advanced that the power of the will is insufficient to control physical impulse, or the impressions of the mind so rapid, that to compare ideas, and to determine with consistency, is impossible. Habitual misuse of the mind produces mental derangement as surely as disease in the organs of perception, volition, and emotion. The evil influence of bad example, of ignorance, or the immoral training of the intellect, encouraging malignant motives of conduct while restraining all the higher exercises of reason—these, and whatever else pertains to an abandoned soul, contribute largely to populate our mad-houses with patients of the least curable kind. And we might reasonably suppose it would be so, since such states of

* Georget, Discussion Medico-Legale sur la Folie, p. 144.

mind imply the habitual and voluntary abuse of those organizations which are the instruments of thought, will, and feeling. Yet every one of these wretched beings who has so much of sense remaining as to allow him to attend to his keeper, is controlled by moral motive. See the happy hundreds, in their festival at Hanwell. Having a purpose to fulfill, for their own pleasure, they hold themselves in order, and co-operate with their fellows in promoting harmony and happiness ; but the moment any one of them loses sight of the motive for self-control, some disturb ance of his passions commences—the demon again takes possession of the man, and he must be hurried off to his cell until the evil influence works itself out by temporary exhaustion of the body.

Our moral emotions are excited both by physical and moral causes, and if our desires be not habitually restrained by reason, and the love of truth and of God, our moral nature is necessarily deranged. As the Apostle exhorts us, so in fact we find it necessary to abstain even from the appearance of evil. The lion's cub is harmless till it has tasted blood, but then he becomes outrageous; and the evil in our heart may be dormant till excited by its appropriate aliment and indulgence, when it becomes uncontrollable. I refer to insanity, as the strongest exemplification of the influence of disorderly passions. Even in the York Retreat, 112 cases in 135 arise from that kind of disappointment which might have been prevented by the right employment of the senses, and by proper objects of thought. By reference to the records of insanity, we see, indeed, as by the united testimony of many thousands gathered together before us, as from all the Asylums of the world, in all the frightful forms of humanity deranged and demonized, that knowledge, faith, and love, alone furnish the soul with competent motives for self-management, amidst the many maddening influences of this world of trial. With our best appliances, we still rest in the hand of Mercy for protection from the evils around us and within us, through the disobedience of man.

Power is proved by resistance. There is always something to be overcome in exercising will while we are in the body. If it were not so, will would either act as a creative power, or otherwise it must be always so anticipated by the provision made by the Creator for its indulgence, as that moral cultivation would be impossible, which of course can only be the case where moral training is unheeded—that is to say, among perfect beings, whose wills can never contravene the holiness of God's behests, and with whom not a desire can be felt at variance with Divine wisdom and benevolence.

It is well for us that our physical constitution, with all its wonderful conveniences, offers, nevertheless, so frequent an impediment to the fulfillment of mental purpose, as to force us to reflect on our dependence on higher power; for otherwise malevolence might work its way without interruption from the necessities of the body, and instead of being sometimes obliged to limit its activity to dreams, it would always be vigilantly mischievous with the plottings and the powers of a Satanic malice and ambition.

As the existence of the soul as a distinct being is proved by its thoughts and by its power over the body, so its spiritual standing as a moral agent is proved by its self-control, and its resistance to the undue demands of those appetites and passions which appertain to its bodily habitation in this earthly state.

The mind must act with whatever motives it possesses. Its tendency is to act incessantly, but there are restraints upon us. We feel that there is nothing in the mind itself to hinder our willing and doing according to our own pleasure, forever. The impediment is not in that which wills and acts, but in the body by which it acts, or in the restraints of circumstances and connection to which Providence binds every spirit he has formed.

There being, then, no check upon soul-power in thinking and willing but in the motive which determines the choice of subjects on which to think, and of objects on which to fix our affections, let us exercise the reason God has given us, in soberly considering what He renders imperative upon us, in order to our reception of the happiness which, on fixed principles, He has appointed as the portion of every spirit that takes its right position in the universe.

If an insane waywardness may be arrested, and the charmed mind be led back to the path of sobriety and reason, by the gentle hand of wise, firm, indomitable kindness, how mighty and commanding must be that charity which is the spirit of Christianity, when made to influence as it ought all the relations of life. This alone has a touch of efficacy sufficient to dispossess wickedness of its willfulness, to attract the urgent soul from its chosen misery, and to conduct it to peaceful activity. If we possess not this spirit we are not philanthropists, but madmen, and have no more right to our own way than the inmates of Bedlam, since without it we can not rightly co-operate with others for mutual good.

We are strikingly taught the importance attached to our habits of action by observing that our mental constitutions are confirmed into evil, by our bodies themselves taking on a corresponding condition. Even the mimicry of a passion produces a state of nerve which excites the very emotion imitated. Garrick always, after acting Lear or Othello, suffered convulsions for some hours, from the struggling of his mind to resist the excitement of his nerves, produced by acting, in keeping with the supposed character of his heroes. Hence we learn how desirable it is that persons suffering from any strong emotion, or mental disorder, should refrain from those bodily motions which express it, and endeavor rather to divert themselves by adopting some action of an opposing kind; since otherwise they may yield to the indulgence of embodying their feelings in action, until the feelings themselves are prolonged into physical habits, and, by mismanagement, actually become confirmed into mad ness.

CHAPTER VII.

ASSOCIATION.

We draw rational motives of thought and action from experience through our senses. We become conscious of our own existence, and the existence and character of other beings, by their impression upon ourselves. Sensation is the exciting cause of ideas and of sentiments. We, however, interpret impressions according to a law implanted in our souls. Thus, if a child see an angry face, it need not be told what it means; and one who looks on an infant lovingly is intuitively met with a responsive smile.

Man, without possessing senses superior to the brute, is endowed with a far nobler faculty of perception, by which he associates thoughts with objects, and thus nature is representative to him of something higher than itself. We *con*ceive from what we *per*ceive, and that is far more than we can see, hear, or handle.

The human mind is so constituted, that every present object that awakens interest also suggests others, and by the law of association excites the remembrance of the past or the hope of the future; and, as both memory and anticipation are brought into exercise by our intellect, in relation to our own experience, we necessarily compare idea with idea with regard to probabilities for or against ourselves, and those in whom we are concerned. It is, indeed, the business of reason to consider causes and effects in their bearing upon minds, and therefore all rational research is but an inquiry into the design of things, with reference to conscious beings, and hence our feelings, in connection with objects, will be generally influenced by our sense of the importance of those objects in the economy of existence. In short, the full revelation of Deity is in humanity.

All truth is really experimental to us; and before we can fully believe any thing, we must perceive its relation not only to the senses but to our souls. Our faculties are all associated with reason, and therefore we infer from things perceived to things possible, and that because we can compare and combine ideas ana logically; hence, from space we infer infinitude—from time, eternity—from ceaseless effects, the unbeginning Cause. Wherever we turn the eye, there infinitude begins. We look into the limitless heavens, and feel that time is but eternity, measured to our conceptions by the everlasting revolutions of suns and planets; and perceive that the wonderful beauty and beneficence seen in the adjustments of the celestial mechanism are not due to extraneous influences, but to a Power that operates also in our own being, since we find that our intercourse with each other is governed by the visible laws of Heaven, and our daily experience springs from the correspondence of our frame-work with that of the boundless skies.

The very power which excites our imaginations, and conveys to our minds a sense of loveliness or majesty, suggests also some moral truth, because every thought has some personal relationship, and induces a desire to reciprocate the emotion we experience with some other being. We scarcely behold an object in nature, or receive an impression which interests our hearts, without thinking of some one who might enjoy it with us, or the expression of whose feeling and knowledge might not enlarge our own conceptions or increase our confidence, and thus tend to fill us with still happier emotion. This social tendency, in all the operations of our minds, indicates that physical existence, in all its parts, was designed for moral ends, in keeping with those laws of our minds by which we are drawn into fellowships with each other, while we feel ourselves to be equally the dependents of that Providence, to which we ought to look in adoration and in gratitude, as the source of good, and as our only guardianship from evil. In short, we shall discover, if we seek the truth, that morality and religion are essential to the right use of our faculties, even in relation to things that perish, and much more so in regard to those thoughts which are awakened in our minds by the constitution of our senses, in correspondence with the outward world, and which abide with our perceiving, reasoning, believing spirits, forever. There arises not in our intellect a single conception of beauty or sublimity, or an idea of good or evil, but from the adaptation of the wonders of this universe to the soul, as a being capable of loving truth, because it is the manifestation of the All-wise, who confers on us tastes and sensibilities correspondent with the properties of nature, and renders them all, when rightly exercised, subservient to our advancement in social happiness and the bliss of worship.

The laws of association are those of our bodies as well as our minds. Our nervous systems, and indeed our whole natures, are constituted in a two-fold relation to all objects: the one, as they influence our understandings; and the other, as they move our wills. Our emotions act on our intellects, and our intellects re-act on our emotions; and our habit of mind and nerve is determined by the manner in which our desires are engaged, for if we do not perceive the beauty of moral truths, and are not governed by the love of them, we must be actuated altogether by instinct and sensation. Whether the impression received by the mind be purely mental in its origin, as in a conviction from rational induction, or whether it be the mere idea of an outward object, it equally operates on the soul, and, so far as it continues to possess the attention, promotes the formation of our mental character. Whatever affects the organs of sense, affects the thinking being, and every thought that passes through the mind modifies the nervous system, and tends to render habit unalterable. Sensation and thought alike influence habit, and as the soul is engaged either in pleasing itself with the passing impressions of sense, or reflecting on ideas, so we are becoming either more sensual or more rational. The only method of preventing our entire subjection to sensual influences is to imbue the mind with moral principles, and to fix attention upon those facts which reveal to us the moral government of the Creator in relation to the consciences of men. If we yield not to truth, we shall to delusion. All appearances deceive us, except as they are interpreted by reason in reference to the designs of God. The pillar of cloud and of light which led the Israelites to safety, drew the Egyptians to destruction. The former recognized the Divine hand; the latter saw only a natural phenomenon.

If we would arrive at ends worthy of immortal beings, the daily course of our conduct requires to be regulated on spiritual principles; for if our common sympathies be not pre-engaged and governed by right reason, we shall be the slaves of a thousand successive masters. If we decide not for ourselves, by choosing our associations, on the dictates of a wise and informed will, our circumstantial associations will altogether determine our lot for us. To be free, we must judge whether we will obey the right or the wrong; and in order to this freedom, good and evil must be clearly presented to our consciences. But how can we know the nature of things, without instruction? If good and truth are not communicated, evil and error will be. But there is nothing in sights and sounds of themselves to show us spiritual relationships—Heaven must teach us to teach one another.

The seeds of a rank and dangerous fruition are scattered over us by every wind; the soil is prepared to nourish them; and unless pre-occupied by the good seed of the kingdom of God, the luxuriance of evil will cover the soul.

Bishop Butler but expressed the experience of every spiritual man, when he said that "he was all his life struggling against the devilish suggestions of his senses, which would have maddened him, if he had relaxed the stern watchfulness of his reason for a single moment." This exercise of his reason required that strong stimulus or motive which religion alone supplies. But what shall those souls, destitute of such motives, be able to accomplish toward the suppression of "the offending Adam?" How shall they bring the curb of reason to bear upon the mad impetuosity by which they are hurried on to death? O God, be merciful! Thou hast committed the lamp of life to the custody of men; but instead of diffusing that eternal flame, having in itself the seed of an endless increase, from house to house and from hand to hand, like familiar light, they have endeavored to hide it in the sepulchers of the dead, or confine its illumination to the temples they have built.

Religious conviction imparts the character to nations; and every individual mind is mainly determined by an apprehension of the Divine Being and His requirements, since every new conception of God modifies the spirit of man, and gives a new aspect to all the facts of his existence. But religion is nothing to a man, unless it palpably engage his body as well as his mind, his conduct as well as his thoughts; but when it is thus practically demonstrated, it takes possession of all his life and energy, because he then really feels it to contain within itself whatever is most interesting to our relationships, and most sublime in the hopes of a deathless spirit. It is by the associations of mind produced by religious ideas and actions that society is governed, and it is the reception of revealed truth alone that elevates either masses or individuals from degradation and degeneracy. Do we wonder at the wretchedness obtruding itself amidst the bustling magnificence of our great towns? A slight insight into the mental and moral destitution of the neglected classes would remove our surprise at their defects, and lead us to wonder rather that, with such associations, so much of a fine humanity yet remains among them.

I see now a squalid mother with four children by her side, whom she loves like a savage. She wears the rags of a widow's weeds; she lives by the compassion of passers-by, who fling her pence to avoid the pain of her presence; she can not smile, and never had any reason to do so; her heart is strong in the feeling of fatality; she doubts not that her wretchedness is the inevitable appointment of a Power whose name she has never heard but in blasphemy, and with which the idea of love would be the most unlikely association. Her husband died in an hospital, where a medical student gave him a tract which he could not read, and whispered at last, in his dying ear, of Jesus and the resurrection; and in death that man wept and wondered that such words had never reached his ear before. His parents and his wife's parents were vagabonds and outcasts, and it was never known that any of their generation could read. The creed of the Egyptians under the Pharaohs was a creed of light, compared to the palpable darkness of their minds. That haggard widow can only be a whispering beggar in the metropolis of calculation and commerce. What wonder! Two little girls creep feebly by her side; their faces are livid, and withered, and sad; they will soon die The baby on her bosom is also wasting away. But the diminutive boy, about nine years old, standing at the corner, begging of those speechless ladies with feathered bonnets, has some vigor in him; he was born when his mother's heart was warmer, and his father was drudging on with some hope in his ignorance. That boy will, if left alone, probably be a thief, and come to the gallows, or be sent to Norfolk Island. He is shrewd, quick, sensitive, and already heroic in his efforts to cheat mankind, whom he supposes to be all against him. How shall that child be improved? He dwells in the midst of uncleanness and cruelty, catching the contagion of sin from the expression of almost every face, and he is in sympathy with polluted humanity in every form. How shall that susceptible young being be transformed in the spirit of his mind, so as to grow godlike, while all the influences about him tend to make and keep him hideous within? Educate—educate; stamp burning truth upon his soul, show him that you are in sympathy with Heaven; impress the character of Jesus on his mind; let him feel the Saviour's love in yours; let him see how you adore actively, because the Maker of worlds and of souls and of bodies is pledged to redeem us from all evil. Teach him the Lord's Prayer; bid him look abroad upon the universe of light, and give him the key to its glories; give him knowledge, and you will then furnish him with motive for behaving as if he might hope to become an heir of God. That boy may be either a Barabbas or a Barnabas. Under the guardian influence of Christian associations, and the spirit that unites souls in the love of a glorified Master, who was once crucified for them, the incarnated inheritance of evil would be exchanged by that boy for a godly heritage; and instead of growing up as an Arab among men, he would be able to smile like an angel, even if they should stone him, for he would still look into heaven and pray for them.

Moral law is founded on our sense of ourselves, for it requires us to consider ourselves in another's situation, and then imagine what would be our feelings, and what the consideration that would be due to us from others in such circumstances. Because we can sympathize, we can act conscientiously. We feel for those who exhibit painful emotion, and we smile responsive to the joy expressed in another's countenance. We detect what is good or evil in another's behavior by its effects upon our own consciousness, and our wills are excited to detest or to admire, to approve or to condemn, according as the action would be personally agreeable or otherwise, in relation to ourselves. Hence our minds are exalted with the tale of generous deeds, as in the noble philanthropy of a Howard, or horrified at the recital of murderous outrage and revenge. But unless we exercise our fine feelings amidst the realities of life, and by reciprocal offices of social relationships, our sympathy degenerates into morbid sensibility, that finds its indulgence in religious reports as well as in romance and the sentimentalism of trashy novels.

Our sympathies are intended to be practical, and to bind us with the ties of kindred and common humanity ; but if our fellowships and fellow-feelings are not governed by some true, steady, elevating love, we are but the subjects of instinctive impulse and of passion. In short, if our affections are not held in obedience to the directing will, and the authority of God, as the supreme object of love, we can not rise above mere accidental and circumstantial motives, and shall be incapable of attaining the high standing of beings amenable to the undeviating principles of rectitude and truth. We need an unerring standard, and the knowledge of a will altogether wise and good, in order to give a right direction to our desires or stability to our conduct. And where is this? It is nigh thee, and within thee. In fact, unless we purposely submit our minds to the guidance of a holy law and a holy spirit, we act without intending to be good, and therefore without the possibility of moral excellence, or resemblance to our Maker. We can not properly obey the precept to love our neighbor as ourselves, until we feel that He who thus commands us has a right in His nature to our hearts, and minds, and soul, and powers, and that because of his inexhaustible good-will and charity in personal relation to ourselves. Hence, thus to reverence God, to believe and obey Him is the whole duty of man. But how are we to distinguish good from evil? By conscience—by that power belonging to our reason, which acknowledges the righteousness of the law which is love. We can not mistake—it is impossible for us to believe that the two tables, fulfilled in the word *love*, can have originated but from the mind and will of Him who created the universe, because it is impossible for the intelligent beings formed by Him to live harmoniously together, and work out His plans for their mutual happiness, without obedience to that law, for that is the only principle that reduces a moral chaos, from darkness, deformity, and confusion, into light, order, and beauty.

To dwell together in peace, we must know why we are to esteem each other. In the first place, we should feel that we are not called on to judge any but ourselves, because we can not. Each one has an experience peculiarly his own, and therefore not to be judged according to that of another. There can be no hope of our agreeing with others, if we dispute about our differences, for every one has good reason for his own opinion; but that is the very thing to be given up, in order to live faithfully. Others can never have seen exactly as we have, and we shall never be able to see the same things precisely in the same light until "we see as we are seen, and know as we are known." Each man has a world of his own, by which all his mental associations have been formed, and to which they belong; and therefore it would be foolish, as well as unfeeling, to insist on his conformity to another's rule, except so far as there may be a wise and proper agreement among persons equally ignorant, that they may use the best means in their power to help each other forward in seeking after truth. To be faithful is to be full of love for truth, and valiant in defense of it; but the more we see of truth, the less critical and the more charitable we shall be, because the more we discern of the truth and rejoice in the love of it, the more we perceive of the Divine character and feel its charity. The highest angels are the most courteous; they love most. A man would never enter heaven, if he were not received there in kindness. The most gentle in dealing with ignorance and prejudice is God himself; and the Son of God would never have been the personal and familiar friend of Martha, Mary, and Lazarus, and of every confiding soul, if He had not been like the Father in heaven. If, then, the undefiled Immanuel endeavored to win the esteem of guilty beings, because He loved them, surely we may well bear with each other patiently, and believe, and hope, and act for each other, as with the certainty of being required to live together in love forever.

Our intercourse with each other is regulated by our notions of time and space. There could have been no order or harmony in our associations, had not the Creator, with his own hand, measured our movements, both of thought and action, on some common principle. We are all alike subject to the pulses of time, and one mind communicates its impressions to another by expressing itself, more or less, in keeping with that mind, as regards its sense of time; for every feeling is as if set to appropriate music, and the manner of its utterance is more or less either *adagio* or *allegro*, according to its nature. Individuals do not well agree together if their nervous systems are very differently strung, or if the expression of their feelings and affections do not keep time with each other. If the mode of one is quick, and that of the other slow, their states of mind scarcely ever correspond ; and if bound to act together, they become wonders and trials to each other, and perhaps perfectly intolerable : for if they do not deem each other somewhat deranged, they at least think one another excessively perverse, if not very wicked. Alas! there are few souls brought together so attuned to the music of the spheres as to move together in unerring harmony and fellowship. But the temper of heaven is true love, and that exhibits itself on earth in patience and forbearance, rather than in the radiance of smiles blending with smiles, and the happy response of heart to heart, conscious of nothing to suffer or desire. And the worth of love is demonstrated by its power to hold dominion over all the other passions, like a spirit so actuated by an intuitive excellence, that it can not believe any evil to be indomitable. It meets with opposition always and every where ; but, knowing that no one can be blessed without its presence, it ever addresses each heart according to the state of feeling that there is manifested ; for, without sin, it is in the nature of love to sympathize with humanity in all its tribulations, and so to adapt its utterance and expression to the agitations of the soul as to seem moved by the same impulse, until, gradually prevailing by an insinuated might, it brings the wayward spirit unconsciously into obedience to a better will. Like a master of harmony, it knows how so to mingle its voice with discordant sounds as to reduce them to the right key, and to lead the listening soul to join, as if from a spontaneous movement of its own, in a new and heavenly melody. Thus love never rebukes, but in order to subdue ; for

it acts in the consciousness that there can be no repentance unless the heart feel that it has sinned against a spirit which always seeks to harmonize and bless it.

Persistence in the habit of self-love must terminate in malignity and the positive and active manifestation of hatred, for it is in the nature of a mind always bent upon its own selfish gratification to become more and more dissociated, and therefore desirous of destroying whatever opposes it, since every passion grows in proportion to its indulgence. And selfish desire can know no corrective restraint but in the impossibility of its fulfillment, which is torment and despair, or else in regard to other beings, which is, in fact, the commencement of its destruction.

The habit of co-operating with others, even in drudgery, brings into action the social principle, so that a man's impulses are no longer altogether selfish. This is exemplified in the case of S. Jackson, who lately died at St. Thomas's Hospital. He was employed, with several others, in sinking a shaft for a railway tunnel at Blackheath. He was at the top of the shaft, which was forty-five feet in depth, and had drawn up by a windlass a pail filled with water, when, while in the act of tipping it over, he fell back. He immediately called out, "Below!" and thus warned those in the shaft, who saved themselves by moving on one side as he fell in the midst of them. Thus the safety of others was a consideration with this poor man, in the very moment of his deadly peril. And it is true that the habit of mutual help is the only efficient check upon the natural waywardness of the human will, and therefore our Maker requires us always to regard our neighbor as ourselves. Those who voluntarily isolate themselves from socialities and relationships are living on principles unfit for earth, and unless their affections are so set upon things heavenly as to absorb their whole souls in a continual ecstacy of worship, some less holy power holds them in thrall. In either case they are dead to duty, and becoming disqualified for all the happy activities of the near next world, while rendering themselves disagreeable impediments to the business of the present.

Religion is founded on mental association, and man's belief in the Self-existent arises from his capacity of reflecting on his own consciousness. This feeling of being refers him from objects to their origin, and by intuition rather than inference, assures the reasonable soul of the necessity of an unbeginning, never-ending Mind, which perceives and wills through eternity; as one infinite presence. The soul sinks beneath the weight of that thought into an abyss of interminable darkness, until God himself speaks, and calls the spirit back into light among the associations of creaturely convenience, by which He demonstrates His accommodating kindness. He comes to man in human sympathy, and demands his heart. He bids him not be afraid of the vastness of unsearchable power, since the Almighty effectuates nothing but good in gentle manifestations to the trustful soul, and shows it incessant reason why it should incessantly confide. And thus Jehovah hides the majesty of His might in the homely and hourly charities in which he trains his children by little and little, as they can bear the revelation of their own existence as belonging to the Eternal Source of all ability and blessing. Through kindred He teaches us kindness; and through humanity, obedient to law as love, He illustrates the Divine nature as supremely worthy to be loved. A God not humanly revealed is no God to man. We may, indeed, obtain, poetical, sentimental, and even philosphical notions of a Deity, but his moral perfections are lost in his natural attributes, and his love in his power, unless he be known to us as the giver and expounder of laws for the regulation of our intercourse with each other, in the acknowledgment of his goodness, and in acting upon the feeling of that goodness, as a sufficient motive to obedience and worship. Without this moral revelation, in personal appeal to our own spirits, the Godhead becomes an unapprehended and diffused energy, apt to be reduced to a mere word—and that word, Nature.

In this world, however, our faculties and affections operate, as we have said, in a bodily manner. As our senses are constructed on temporal principles, so also our memories furnish their stores of ideas to the demands of life, and reason with relation to time and the action of our muscles; thus we move in keeping with the movements of objects around us, and thus our intercourse with those we love is modified by motion, for motion is the only means of expressing feeling and power. From this universal fact we learn the importance of wisely controlling our visible actions, as they may influence the feelings of others, or embody to their view the state of our own souls; not that we should study to be hypocrites, but that we should be careful to attain such a condition of thought and affection that its natural manifestation in our movements should bring others into better sympathy, or at least demonstrate to the apprehension of the depraved that there is a nobler mode of energy and action than usually prevails among themselves. But this nobler mode consists only with true humility, which is the firmness of a mind well grounded, that stoops not to earth, but stands erectly upon it, conscious of God's power and presence and favor. Abandoned characters can appreciate this standing, and honor it; but they are very apt to imagine the existence of pride as the moving power of those who come to teach them bare lessons of morality, and therefore they often repel the approach of such persons, and scoff at and scorn them most madly; but when, by a man's style of action and address, they are convinced that he is governed by a simple, true, and obedient spirit, they bow like children in a superior presence, and listen but to learn. The success of Mrs. E. Fry and Sarah Martin, in teaching the most forlorn of beings, exemplifies these observations.

Unnaturalness, or that artificial mannerism in speech or action, which is acquired by minds aiming to imitate some real or ideal master, is of the nature of this repellent pride. No one is fit to be a Christian minister who does not honestly descend from all pretensions, and exercise the simple life-gifts with which his Maker has authorized him to act upon others for their benefit. How often have we seen a spare and chilly congregation of barren formalists under the unctionless preachings of men who could not forget themselves, while pretending to feel awfully alarmed lest sinners should fall headlong into perdition. Those that such men thus seem to tremble to think of, are, however, not such as they usually see before them, for men are not snatched from the hand of the mighty slave-driver, and gathered into the fold of the Bishop of souls by polished and polite rhapsodists, but by men in the rough, like John the Baptist, stirred up by the spirit of great truths, which have entered into them while reading the Bible. Such men have their senses all alive to the great facts of nature and of books, for free minds are always great in their grasp, and use all their knowledge so feelingly as to make all they know tell within them upon the formation of their own characters, and thus increase their power of influencing, by utterance and action, the characters of others. Such men are ministers of the Spirit, and they would be more numerous were it not for the pride of affectation and the disposition to substitute intellect for heart-work.

Unnaturalness in utterance and the distribution of ideas into sentences without euphony, hinder usefulness. Men, from an affected mannerism, or from aiming at peculiarity, or from too artificial a training, disjoint their language in a great variety of ways. Some, in pursuing thoughts, forget harmony—while others seem to set their ideas so completely to music, that their hearers or readers are apt to lose sight of the subject, in listening to the sweetness of the melody. Occasionally we find a man who speaks and writes as if his soul stuttered, so as to form a hundred periods in a page. The jet from the fountain comes in fits, so many times a minute. The conjunctions are all disjunctive. It is as if a long piece of music with all its variations should be staccatoed throughout, with a rest at every bar: however emphatic, it is apt neither to be understood nor remembered. Others take no breath, and rush on like a cataract, confounding the waters of life into foam. Sober reason instinctively adopts the medium, and measures her eloquence by the nature of the subject and the state of feeling proper to the occasion. The cause of so much ineffective utterance is found in the fact, that the thoughts and the feelings do not flow together. They are sought apart, and keep apart in spirit and in power, although seemingly wedded together by sound—*vox et preterea nihil.* This would be avoided if each man expressed his own thoughts in his own way, instead of seizing ideas from all sources and trying to fit them with those which he happens already to have trimmed in his own staid style. A natural ear can always detect an unnatural eloquence, and none but the habituated lovers of listening can feel the truth inviting them except from lips touched with its living fire.

There is an art in love. The only way of rightly influencing other minds is to put ourselves in sympathy with them. We must use means for this; we must in some degree feel *with* them as well as *for* them. Their perceived or imagined state must act on our own emotions, so as to excite an appropriate expression in our features, our action, our utterance. To withdraw them from unholy passion or disastrous pursuit, we must enter into their feelings so far as to show that we can sympathize with them in intensity of purpose, while superior to them in the direction of our wishes and the disposal of our means. We must fall into the same key, but only to utter emotion and intelligence of a higher order, guided by a will under spiritual control; thus counteracting the evil influence, not by vehement resistance, but as sunshine quenches fire, by the gentle force of a purer warmth, and a light unextinguishable, because it flows from heaven. Every feeling tends to action, and we must be conscious of the expression in our own persons, and be roused to a perception of the thoughts and affections in keeping with the excited state of our nerves, before we can set our minds to the counteraction of this state. In short, we must not only suppose ourselves in the situation of those whom we would persuade, but we must so far feel like them as to find it necessary to persuade ourselves. We must control the very emotions in ourselves which we wish to control in others. Not till we are brought to this state shall we fully be able to influence other minds with our reasonings, for not till then are those ideas suggested which are natural to the occasion. The associations of our minds will then become the associations of those we address, and their bodies, as well as ours, will be imbued with the same excitement. Thus the eloquent man utters the reflex of his own feelings in the contemplation of evils that he deprecates. Thus Hall, when he had busied and burthened his soul with the arguments of infidels, until he almost felt what it was to be destitute of faith, exclaimed, "Eternal God! on what are thine enemies intent? What are those enterprises of guilt and horror, that for the safety of their performers, require to be enveloped in a darkness which the eye of Heaven must not pierce. Miserable men! Proud of being the offspring of chance—in love with universal disorder; whose happiness is involved in the belief of there being no witness to their designs, and who are at ease only because they suppose themselves inhabitants of a forsaken and fatherless world!"

The orator felt that apostrophe, and all who heard it felt it too. But the plain words of Sarah Martin, in the prison at Yarmouth, told as well upon her audience, because she visibly felt for them, and could not be discouraged, because her faith was in God. It is the productive, creative, or poetic mind, that possesses power to excite other minds to the degree requisite to facilitate the vivid reproduction of ideas in the memory, so as to repeat the emotion first induced by them. This it accomplishes with great natural ease, from its own feeling of analogy, contrast, and comparison. Thus one idea is illustrated by another in such a manner, that the recurrence of one causes the re-appearance of the other, and renders both more distinct and more apt to be re-felt as well as remembered. The ideas of the persuasive man are not abstractions, but objects, that really influence himself, and which he desires others to perceive as he perceives them, with all the feeling of a spiritual correspondency. Our Saviour's teaching was the essence of eloquence and poetry, because it was truth spoken naturally, and with a feeling reference to the familiar incidents of humanity, thus ever leading the mind on to sublimer apprehensions of Divine power, and insuring the recollection of the ideas presented by placing them, so to say, upon the heart with its daily interests. If we do not regard nature as God's storehouse of truths, to be employed spiritually, we shall be but low disciples of the Great Teacher. Speech is thought and feeling, uttered to be heard, and letters, like musical notations, are the symbols by which language and sounds become visible; but the universe is God's uttered thought, to be perceived spiritually, both by men and angels. But there is a sublimer Word—the *Logos*—that created the heavens and the earth, and keeps them in harmony, as the vehicle of spirits related to Himself. *The Word was made flesh*, to speak as man to man. It should be our business to know the meaning of that Word, for it must be a personal revelation to ourselves, since it is in person and in presence alone that God addresses us. Intelligent beings are conscious for the purpose of understanding each other; and our Maker imparts rational consciousness to us, that we may understand his intentions toward us individually.

Every living creature is governed by language—either in visible or audible signs; for language is meaning, feeling, thought, intelligence, actively signified. Animals have a language of emotion, but not of thought; man's language expresses both. Hence, there are so many voices in the world, and none without significance; and an uncertain sound is itself the utterance and the occasion of doubt. If a man set not his heart determinately to obtain God's truth, and utter it, he is already in a state of mind and nerve indicative of a lying spirit—there is nothing decided about him but what is false; he is deluded by appearances, and therefore the expression of his mind is but the utterance of deception; his will itself actively lies, and his tongue is set on fire of hell; he contradicts heaven, and helps to disorder earth, by propagating falsehood; he is an antagonist of God, and must so continue, unless the omnipotent Spirit of Truth speak, through the voice of man, in such a manner as to strike the sinner dead with terror, and raise him again, with a new and living hope, in righteousness, after the likeness of the true man—God manifest.

If a man bridle not his tongue, whatever be his

religious opinions, they are all in vain. Why is this? Simply because there can not be a right converse without a right spirit. Every man is an oracle, either of truth or of falsehood; he must speak either life or death—for God, or against him. The man who feels his position will be well assured that indifferentism consists not with the order of the world. To be negative in one respect is to be positive in another. To be in keeping with the Divine mind is the purpose of the human mind; but to be thus harmonious with Deity, is to will like Him; and in order to this, we must attend to God, listen to His language, and learn His love; for not till we are thus imbued with His own Spirit, can we be free in will to serve Him as his sons. From the nature of things, and the Maker of all, neither the thought nor the tongue of the spiritually disobedient man can be at liberty; there is nothing in the universe in keeping with him but evil spirits. But love has no limits to its range or its language; it is always seasonable; it may at all times utter all it feels, for kindness must belong to its feeling; and it may be ever busy, and travel as far as the light. All it utters is truth, all it does is beauty, and all it aims at is harmony and happiness. This love is the response of the soul to the Creator, as when He first saw in his works the reflection of his own goodness, and the sons of God shouted for joy.

Emotions in man are ideas formed by his mind, and are only suggested by objects. The feeling of fear, joy, love, hope, is as strongly excited by an imagined object as by a reality; but the imagined object is formed by the mind, according to its habit of association with real things, or according to a man's faith. Thus one man dreads what another desires, because he thinks of it with different connections. A Christian, believing death to be only a passport to glory, may well long for it as a rapture from this wearisome, because wicked world; and being confident that the Father loves all that man ought to love, far better than man can do, a believer leaves wife, children, friends, to the gracious conduct of His careful hand, expecting to meet them purified hereafter. But what can make death beauti ful and blessed to an unbeliever? How wide the difference in the emotion produced by the same object, simply because the mind of one clothes it with light, and that of the other with darkness! It is the same in regard to all objects. If we would enjoy happy emotions, we must have a happy creed. We must believe in something besides earthly objects, to receive heavenly ideas from them. We must hold Divine truths before we can be moved by Divine affections. We must trust in the will of God as love itself, before we can be so governed by this love as to fear no evil; for as we think, so we shall feel, as long as thought and feeling together constitute human experience. Why, then, do we complain of our tyrant passions? Our ideas are wrong. We see not as we ought; we deceive ourselves; we receive not God's testimony; we believe falsehood; the truth is not in us, or we should be free; in the truth of real love, in the truth of real hope, in the truth of real joy, in the truth of a real Saviour and his peace, we should be free.

CHAPTER VIII.

LIKING AND DISLIKING.

MIND is the cause of all action and re-action. It originates polarity, or the existence of opposites. All matter is both negative and positive, because the will of Omnipotence is expressed in it. Each atom is related to other atoms, so as to be attracted or repelled according to their mutual states. It is thus with all things, because they are created—with souls as well as with bodies. But the human mind is endowed with the power of will, so far beyond that of any other creature, that it is capable of altering its own state in relation to other beings. Thus we use our senses, not merely according to the direct and immediate action of objects upon them, but in a pre-determined manner. We render the passive senses active by thought, and change the direction of the vital forces in the brain in such a manner, that through it we attend to ideas as well as realities, and reverse, so to say, the poles of those nerves by which we receive impressions from without, so that they seem to convey them back from within. According to the state of our wills is our attention. Our material as well as our spiritual relation to objects is affected by our capacity to will, and by the manner in which we will. Thus the state of our desires modifies our power to attend, for desire implies the engagement of the mind about some particular object. Inattention is either the result of bodily unfitness or of intense mental occupation—either excess of feeling or deficiency. In either case, there is something to be overcome before the mind so affected can be duly educated.

We have seen how the obstacle to attention is attempted to be removed in case of bodily unfitness. Excessive mental occupation is self-absorption, and to be remedied only by drawing the soul away from its inward objects, by presenting such external ones as must be attended to. The most direct way to divert inordinate feeling is to put one's self in personal contact with the patient—seize his hand, for instance, and at once address him with some intelligence concerning facts, some piece of news from heaven or earth. Common sense teaches us how to obtain the attention of healthy children; we must pleasantly take them in hand, and whisper to them face to face; we must be engaged with them alone, and soul to soul, in order to disengage them. Men are but children of a larger growth, and must be managed pretty much in the same manner, with all due allowance for their greater obstinacy in evil habit. Still let them have something real to look at, and with it some evidence of the sympathy of another spirit.

We must control ourselves and others on the same principles. We must polarize the sense-powers by an act of will; we must determine to set our attention upon what we know to be proper objects. If we are indisposed, we must do as Johnson did with his writings, we must go doggedly to work, and before we have done our best we shall be well pleased with our efforts. The reason of our pleasure is in the fact, that we have put our brains voluntarily into a condition to impress our nervous systems throughout with our new ideas—our thoughts become connected with emotions, we feel them in our bodies. We are constituted to enjoy novelties, especially of our own creating. They act upon us somewhat after the manner of outward objects that are agreeable to us; they are in keeping with our bodies as well as minds, in consequence of our thorough attention to them, and therefore their light, their sound, their motion, is ideally and essentially communicated to us so as to actuate our nerves.

We willingly polarize ourselves with regard to objects, so as to become passive to their action, until we are positively affected by them, and are in a state positively to influence the minds of others by our own force and energy. This is the way that men master each other mentally. They attend to things until the accumulated impressions overpower them, and to relieve themselves they must show others what they see, and express themselves in words and actions.

But, alas! those whose heads and hearts are full to overflowing of the great things of outward existence, can scarcely speak, but they seem like enthusiasts and madmen. It is, therefore, essential to the success of strong and sensitive souls, that they study all the arts of prudence and wisdom, in order to win their way, and persuade men to be happier. But with the best oratory, and the ablest argument, it is still almost impossible for even a wise man to speak from his heart the truth as he feels it, without presenting it in so individual a manner as to offend. It is, to a certain extent, his duty to do so; the scandal is not in the honest speaker, but in the uncharitable hearer. Minds that are equally positive are of necessity repulsive to each other, unless they are equally attracted to the same point. The truth, as it is personally felt by another, is, however, the very thing that a party man needs to tolerate with cheerfulness; for unless he can so bear it, and even enjoy it, he can never be converted from the popery of self-opinion and partisanship to the catholicity of Christdom.

Truth is intended to neutralize opposition, and to be the bond of union between all rational minds; but every attachment to mistake induces dislike and antagonism, because error is of the nature of evil or disorder, and therefore always tending to maintain disunion. Where charity is the only cloak a man wears, he is ready to fling it over the faults of any person, and press him to his bosom, if he have proved that he loves truth, by an uncompromising submission of all his faculties to its influence, as far as he sees it. Truths adapted to the prevailing fashion, and taken up and cast off according to convenience, do no more to enlighten and improve the world than the fireworks at Vauxhall. It may be true fire, but it is manufactured of evil materials, like the pyrotechnics of Milton's Pandemonium, to amuse miserable beings. Truths, to prevail upon many minds, must be constantly about a man, so as to seem embodied in him, like the glory about the sun.

Provided a speaker be understood, he usually excites just that degree of emotion proper to his words, and which he feels in connection with them at the time of speaking. But although the amount of feeling, between the orator and those who are attentive among his audience, be similar, yet in kind it is very different, for this depends on the previous state of will in each individual. Let us imagine, what is real enough, that a number of persons, in several mental conditions, go to hear the same sermon, and we shall see how liking and disliking depend on the state of the mind, with regard to love of truth. The preacher is ready to open the large Bible, and all eyes are up to catch the preparatory language of his looks, and all ears eager to receive the first sound from his lips. There is an Arminian Methodist, near the clerk's desk: he may be recognized by his light smooth hair, sprightly, sanguine face, and white cravat without a visible tie. There is a swarthy Calvinist, as unkempt as a Scotch presbyter, just at his elbow. There is a very gentlemanly Socinian, thoughtfully in ambush at the corner of the next pew, almost behind the pillar. Verily, there is a Friend in the organ gallery. In the pew with the Alderman, there is a Free-thinker, of a very German and billious aspect: he is foreign correspondent to a religious society and a great smoker. And what is oddest, there is an Infidel by his side, very much like him; and in that curtained pew sits an avowed Atheist, with a prayer-book still in his hand. The preacher solemnly, slowly, strongly utters his text. "The Word was God." He fully feels the force of these words, as the language of the Logos, and cleaves to the truth with all his might. He eloquently sets forth the idea—Omnipotence in union with human nature—God manifested in the flesh. He is apt to teach, and all who understand his plain words feel with him, just in proportion to their power of attending. But we may well imagine how the kind of feeling is modified by the previous convictions or notions of the hearers. Thus the Methodist is moved by a sense of duty, as if to co-operate with God, who is the minister of man. The Calvinist, believing in the majesty of Divine action, feels only the passive impotence of the creature, forgetful that to be moved by God is to move with God's might. The Quaker seems to hear the Logos as a voice in his soul, with a resolution that his life should speak of it. The Socinian mentally suggests a correction of the text, supposing the original might just as easily be read, "The Word was *of* God;" the Rationalist deems the phrase a figure of speech, and enjoys it figuratively speaking; the Infidel almost laughs as he listens; and the Atheist pants with hatred at what he hears, and curses cant, metaphysics, and priestcraft.

The points on which those who were real Christians differed were lost sight of by each of them as they thought of Christ; and no doubt, if they generally thought more of Him than of their private interpre tations, they would realize more of what is essential to Christian fellowship than can be found in the watchwords by which parties are kept in their places, as in centers of mutual repulsion. If we would in charity, or even from the hope of informing ourselves, give heed to the truth as it actuates any one, we should find more of a common attraction; for he who attends to man for the truth's sake that is in him, attends to God Himself, for all truth is His, and this it is that draws honest hearts together, because it attracts them all to the same center.

None can attend to truth felt, and therefore spoken, without a lasting influence. The speaker and the listener are put in bodily and spiritual relation to each other, as by the word that said, "Let there be light." The thought and feeling of the mind in active utter ance brings the attentive mind into sympathetic action with it; and the effect of that action continues forever in the soul of the man with relation to God, whose providence brought him into the position that tested the state of his will, and presented motive for the higher direction of desire. Hence the momentous consideration, how and what we hear. Truth is either the savor of life unto life, or of death unto death. It always meets us, according to our state of mind, to actuate hope or to deepen our condemnation, and yet it can never say, Despair—that is the teaching of truth's strong opponent, that incessantly flings darkness in the face of light.

We never yield attention to words without gaining good or evil, because it is the design of Providence that they should both be communicable by language. Hence we see the wisdom and the mercy of the evangelical institutions of preaching and teaching by words, uttered audibly or in print. By this means the treasury of Heaven's own truth is thrown open to the world of spirits; and thus the sustenance of souls, the bread of life, is distributed to dying men. Without the propagation of the Word, yea, the Word that was with God, and was God, human minds would become like a putrid sea, unmoved but by the corrupt and incongruous monstrosities bred within its bosom. The breath of heaven must ruffle the great deep, and the life of light enter into it. The Spirit must move upon the face of the waters, that a world for God to dwell in may arise out of them. But it is in tongues of fire that the Spirit comes as advocate, as comforter, and as witness to the truth, and to the triumph and glory of our risen Lord; and it is by the living voice that He is exalted in spirit to draw all men unto Him.

There is no tendency to improve the moral or spiritual condition of men except from the diffusion of revealed doctrines, because the genius that is not animated with their living power is really actuated only by pride and love of position. Society is constantly changing its character, according to the style of those ambitious minds that guide its opinions and fill its fancy. Some wizard is always scattering his enchantments, like the Sybilline leaves, before all winds, till the nations admire, and are mad. At one time the mighty influence comes in the form and with the native gloom of a demon, and at others in the glittering array of light. Now converting the horrors of history into amusement by the colorings of romance, and then bidding all classic remembrances speak the language of the misanthrope, genius flings its own colors over the multitudinous minds that, like the waves of a restless ocean, arise for a moment to reflect any light that falls upon them, and then sink again into a dark eternity. Whatever the direction of the prominent intellects of the day—whether merely imaginative, or also scientific and philosophical—still the tendency is never heavenward, except so far as the truths of revelation are standing too mightily in the way to be thrust aside without at least some reverence to their greatness. The reason why genius without grace only tends to refine evil is evident—the man of genius perceives the spirit of the times, and garnishes his soul, and makes it ready, that he may be thoroughly possessed by that spirit. Then the fire of infernal enthusiasm is kindled within him; he seizes the ideas prevailing around him, subdues them to his own purposes, infuses into them his own energy, polarizes them into new combinations, sees himself in every crystallized thought, and then sends back upon society a moral idol formed to express its own character, and which, therefore, for a time delights it, just as a flattering likeness wins the smiles of a vain beauty. The spirit of this world never rises above the clouds, except volcanically, to fall back again in dust and ashes, death and ruin. But that which is above brings with it an organizing and beautifying and animating light which attracts to its source all those into whom it enters.

It is necessary for us to be careful, above all things, lest the sensual causes of liking and disliking should influence our relative and social feelings to such a degree as to banish morality. We see that this is the case with the baser order of minds—their partialities and prejudices being founded on appearances, sympathies, and antipathies of sensual origin. The only means of counteracting this liability is to become imbued with principles of spiritual truth, not notionally, but practically, so as to be habitually acting and hoping in reference rather to what we know of Divine charity than with a view to the gratification of our natural tastes of any kind. Thus delight of a heavenly order will supplant earthly pleasure, and our desires, expectations, and faith, will grow in keeping with our apprehension of the beneficence of God, and we shall love souls for what they may be, rather than what they now appear. If we are earnest in our efforts to obtain a fitness for the inheritance of light, it must be by a transformation of character. The beauty of holiness must be on us as the beauty of God, and this is the beauty we then shall desire alone to see in all around us.

If we feel any thing of true loveliness, we shall, above all things, promote love. But alas! men dislike deformity, and hate evil in every one but themselves, because they find no mirror to reflect their own moral image, and will not look into the law of God. Hence they can worship exterior beauty while unconscious of intrinsic hideousness. So deeply deluding is our outward life, that unless we are honest at heart, the more that is said and thought of the moral and personal excellence of others, the more apt are we to question the motives that influence them. Those who are hateful are always ready to become calumnious, and those are already outrageous who seek for pictured and extraneous beauty rather than to be beauteous in their souls. The most horrible deeds of darkness and cruelty have been perpetrated by the worshipers of a pictorial religion, and the fiercest defense of nominal public virtue has been the fruit of intensest private vice.

The worship of a beauty, exalted and apart from any relation to a man's own soul, is consistent with a zeal that leads to massacre and murder. The fifty thousand victims of St. Bartholomew were sacrificed to the power that presided over imposing forms in the name of God. The men who would have bowed to a picture of the Blessed Virgin, as divine, could stab a living mother with a babe upon her bosom. Because they had no beauty in their souls, they pierced again the heart of Jesus while they seemed to kneel at his cross, and they thought to serve the Son of the Highest by execrating those for whom he died. Light had lost its meaning to their eyes. As sight is a spiritual sense, and we do not behold the objects as material things, but only perceive the different degrees of antagonism between light and darkness, which we call colors, so these zealots of beauty made their own colors out of the darkness that was in them when the true light shone upon it.

The love of beauty is one with the love of goodness, in a mind purified by holy truth. But a nice taste for the fine arts, as means of pleasure, may prevail in a breast without humanity. The mob of murderers, with guns and bayonets, in the French Revolution of 1792, pursued the fugitives from the Palace of the Tuileries into the gardens; but they refrained from firing on those who, in vain efforts to escape their assassins, climbed up the marble monuments abounding there; and, lest the statues should be injured, they pricked down their victims, murdering them at their feet, with steel dripping with gore warm from the heart. Thus the divine beauty of the human form was mangled by lovers of beauty in stone. As usual, men, women, and children were butchered at the feet of idols; for devotion to Apollo and to Venus is but the madness of pride and lust. The true perception of beauty was of course impossible in such savages. Men can not see beauty while they merely look at appearances, because the spiritual relation of things is not discerned by the bodily vision. It demands a spitirual eyesight and apprehension. Beauty in the abstract is truth—the embodiment of moral law: it is an attribute of God. But in our relative view of the Divine love and power as exhibited in the uses of created forms, beauty is, in fact, that order of things which tends to preserve the complacency of man; and, while pleasingly exciting his attention, encourages the social affections. It is, in short, the visible expression of God's purpose in nature, the end of which is to promote harmony between thought, feeling, and action.

Ideas of beauty must be as diversified as minds; for every kind of love meets with its corresponding object, and every taste finds something to please it. There must be an inward, as well as an outward sunshine to illuminate the true beauty; for it is formed of a light that is not visible but in union with pleasant thoughts; and hence it constitutes the poetry of existence, because it never appears but in association with love and hope: if it speak not peace, it is at once trans formed. Wherever there are smiles, there is beauty; and there are smiles all over the dimpled earth and the great deep. All nature is beautiful, when seen without an idea of danger; and the vast globe is a mass of beauty, when we contemplate it as floating along in light, with all heaven about us.

There is beauty in motion, while it means gladness—in rest, when it signifies content, yea, even in agony, when it expresses faith; for then we think rather of the coming cure than the present malady—of the salvation, more than of the suffering—the eternal weight of glory, rather than the momentary pang.

Beauty is never seen by the eye of fear, since the most fascinating being on earth turns hideous and hateful the moment it ceases to suggest ideas of heart-rest and confidence. Venus becomes like Hecate, when we see through her exterior, and in her heart behold the image of Mars. The more lovely the outward appearance, the more loathsome the felt reality, when the smile is known to be a mask. The angel hypocrite is seen only as the more infernal fiend, when detected through the disguise of light. The only unchangeable beauty is sincere love. Something of this love appears in all plain, manifest good meaning, such as Gods puts into innocent beings, and in all things in heaven and earth by which he would teach us to trust Himself. Not to know his love is to find his name our terror; therefore he every where gives evidence of infinite benevolence.

Beauty, in dead matter, is order, or many parts in unity of design, with becoming color. The true beauty in human faces and forms is the soul expressing itself as God's likeness, ready to bless any mind that can acknowledge Divine love.

There is always a sentiment of charity in whatever is pleasing, and a mind satisfied with its position is always generous. In order to enjoy beauty, we must feel ourselves safe; the instant we cease to trust, we cease to admire. The gentle hand of the young child was attracted to the burnished crest of the serpent that fed with it from the same cup; but when, in the dismay of its mother's face, it was taught that there was danger, the idea of a serpent, instead of pleasure, inspired terror. The tiger, with its gracefulness and waved dark stripes, upon a smooth, bright ground, charms us while we see her encaged, asleep, or playing with her cubs. Her maternal instincts enhance her beauty while we think of her as harmless; but should we meet her in the jungle, then she is a demon.

Where we can not trust, we can not love; for amiable thoughts can not be associated with treachery. We may, indeed, be conscious of an interest in the lineaments of one whose every movement and expression speaks of evil, but it is the interest induced by a fiend. We might say the form was lovely, if we could withdraw the spirit, but that is a power that forbids thoughts of peace in its presence. The value of beauty is estimated by every heart, according to its aptness to suggest ideas of happiness. The beauty that suffers us not to feel at home with it, soon becomes a hateful distraction; and that is beautiful in the highest sense, which elevates our minds with heavenly hopes, and seems, by the love that belongs to it, to assure us of a perpetual reserve of blessings, to be in due time enjoyed.

Whether we know it or not, we love beauty only because we love joy: and it is in vain for the most fascinating person on earth to expect to maintain any but an infernal influence who does not persistingly endeavor to promote happiness. Children, before they reason, and idiots and creatures without rational intention, may be loved after an instinctive manner, whatever their temper may be; but voluntary agents can not be loved without being amiable, or in the hope that the capacity of becoming so will at last be established.

The love of variety is essential to inquiring minds, because we know only by comparison; and our inner life is supplied with objects of thought by the scenes and sounds which memory furnishes for the employment of imagination. This disposition of mind is beautifully in harmony with the constitution of the world. The word of God in creation was the utterance of his will toward man. The wondrous exhibitions of Divine wisdom are seen but as beneficence. The arrangements of nature are most marvelous, in the means provided for the entrance of an endless diversity of enjoyments through the eye and the ear. Analogy and resemblance characterize all the kingdoms of nature; but uniformity and monotony, like discords, are only admitted as incongruous exceptions, as if more plainly to express the benevolence of God in harmonizing the elements.

The more extensive the scope of the mind, the vaster is the variety brought within the field of its perceptions; and the more minutely we examine the economies of existence, the more unsearchable they appear. The study of nature is, indeed, the study of the Divinity in action; hence, no mind can be freely and devoutly given to the contemplation of realities, without obtaining a sublime elevation and an enlargement of spirit, with a feeling of life, as if it were one with that of the Eternal. But the addiction of the soul to any artificial employment reduces and darkens it. Circumstances may constrain men into apparent meanness, but they become little, only from the littleness of their chosen pursuits. Like the Dutch, we may all cultivate for ourselves, so to say, an artificial nature, so that the world of God's making may not appear before our eyes. But, as Coleridge, I think, says of the Dutch—What is the consequence? They are artificially comfortable—in vain do you look for the sweet breath of hope and advancement among them.

Natural objects, whether beautiful or marvelous, produce ideas rather according to the state of the mind than according to their intrinsic qualities; for creation, in all its forms of loveliness or magnificence, is intended to impress the soul as a voluntary and reasoning being, and therefore it is that nature has ever a moral aspect toward man. If he have but one religious truth, or a single idea in relation to the claims of God upon him, he can not behold beauty nor look into sublimity, without some thought or feeling being awakened which shall cause him to become more conscious of his worth as a creature through whom and to whom the Eternal manifests Himself. The very joy that expands his bosom, as he gazes upon a wide-spread prospect, glowing in the life and light of the embracing heavens, fills him with a sense of unutterable hope, in the felt power and beneficence of the Creator of all things. That hope is a Divine promise to him, and while it burns at his heart, he prophesies to himself of the glories of a world to come, and confirms his confidence in immortality as if by visions of a deathless Paradise.

Thus the training of his conscience in holy sensibility will proceed with the cultivation of his taste for natural beauty; and the enjoyment of God's works will aid his reason in drawing those inferences which form his religious character, and establish his faith as a happy feeling, as well as an intellectual conviction.

Every object which affects our minds affects them

according to our moral state, or according to the manner in which our intellect has been cultivated, in relation to sociality and religion. Our sense of beauty or of sublimity is emotional. It is the awakening of association. Some objects, however, are intrinsically adapted to excite pleasing, and others, painful feelings Certain expressions of feature and gestures of the body induce agreeable sympathies, while their opposites produce corresponding emotions. They naturally express states of mind with which we are constituted to sympathize, when our own minds are attentive to them. They are the motives by which our Maker designs to influence our social behavior, and by these we are preserved in relation to our fellow beings. But if those truths which teach us our relation to our Maker are not fixed upon our minds, the expressions of life and feeling in our actions will always be perverted, so as to render our whole existence evidently sensual · for every pleasure apart from its moral and religious purpose, is merely a temptation and a snare, detaining the soul from the enjoyment and the end for which it was created.

There are other objects—those inanimate, for instance—to which ideas of beauty may be attached conventionally. The whole series of things, all the universe within our vision, may be regarded as the means by which our understandings are aroused, through emotions more or less associated with our desires.

In short, we are drawn toward hope or fear by every thing we contemplate—we are either disposed to entertain a hopeful complacency, or we become more susceptible to apprehension. Thus the verdure and the bloom, the songs of birds, the living streams, the blending of sparkling light with the billows of a summer sea, and the varied features of a picturesque and rural prospect, encourage sentiments of kindliness; and the heart, if not possessed by some painful bosom-interest, is ready at once to respond to any face that beams pleasantly upon it, and cordially to reply like a friend, to any one that greets it with a word of the bright weather. But when clouds gather, winds howl, waves roll, or if we find ourselves in a position otherwise sublime, if we speak to each other, it is with more or less of consternation and of gloom.

Unless we have an inner motive to abstract our minds, our thoughts are always in keeping with the scene around us; and hence we perceive the reason why men erect temples of stately or solemn architecture, with a view to encourage religious emotion, and that the place may accord with the intention of assemblage. A want of keeping between the object of a building and its ornaments and proportions is, therefore, a want of taste in the builder, and it requires a spirit devoutly engaged at heart to be superior to the influence of such incongruity. The fact that souls are so strongly influenced by appearances, is a sufficient motive for the study of those arts by which the properties of nature are made to bear upon the feelings of society. God himself has sanctioned such studies, and inspired men with skill to construct edifices, in detail and in general, suited to promote those solemn ideas which accompany devotion. To neglect these considerations is, therefore, to neglect Divine teaching. Our Lord Himself suited his discourse to the position of his disciples, and followed the intimations of nature in the sublime doctrines which He taught in the temple, by the sea, or on the mountain side, with the Divine magnificence of heaven and earth around Him; and the successful propagation of truth has always been influenced by these adventitious or rather Divine aids, and the direction of the mind impressed by objects in nature, and in those suggestions of nature which are supplied by art.

Our attention is first arrested by that which appeals to our emotions, before we regard arguments; and our affections must be aroused before we can perceive the validity of reasoning. We must feel that we are naturally God's creatures before we can apprehend our spiritual relationship; but if we are spiritually minded, the humblest hut, equally with the noblest fane, becomes an appropriate place of worship; and yet not a temple on earth has ever been erected that could reach to the idea of Christian worship in its august simplicity, holiness, and love. There is not majesty enough even in the starry dome of heaven; the rosy light of morning upon the mountains, and the sunshine reposing upon fields of ripening plenty, are not sufficiently suggestive of the peacefulness, benevolence, and hope of Christianity. There is nothing visible vast enough to indicate its dominion, nor a flower fair or frail enough to show forth the fostering gentleness of its Omnipotent Spirit. The Virgin Mother, clothed in light, with the Son of God upon her bosom, is its tenderest embodiment; but we can not obtain a sufficient glory in the pictured charity, the colors of light can not form faces so radiant as to image in our eyes even our faint ideas of Divine love made human. It is better seen in death than in life; for the love that is Divine must teach us to believe that God will raise the dead, even as at first he breathed life into the dust in His hand. It brings us with Mary to gaze into the tomb where Jesus was laid, and where the angel stood in light to say that He was risen. Hence the mature Christian feels that his heart is but mocked by attempts to excite its devotion by earthly objects. He can look at beauty and magnificence, in their symbols, and be thankful; but he realizes far more than these, because his spirit is truly worshiping in that heaven where no temple is seen, for the Lord God Almighty and the Lamb are the sanctuary there.

In proportion as men have been influenced by that pure spirit which freely breathes in Christianity, have they exhibited in their writings an admiration of nature as the work of God, and, while honoring the power, adored the love that constitutes the universe as the abode of various intelligences. Whenever asceticism has taken the place of active Christianity, the poetry as well as the science of existence has alike been darkened with artificial gloom, and the cloudiness of fanaticism has usurped the splendor which God designed to occupy the visions of the soul; for the soul was made expressly to be informed and delighted by Divine truth, as seen both in His handiwork of creation and the wisdom of His written word. Artificial and fictitious religion fastens fetters of iron on all the faculties of man, but that of truth calls the spirit forth to the fresh air, and to breathe vitality in open, happy light, and bids it contemplate what Benevolence has done to secure the joy and gratitude and praise of all reasonable creatures. If, therefore, we meet any ordinance against the intercourse of souls with souls, or the slightest interdict opposed to the spirit of inquiry after either natural or revealed truth, we may be as fully assured as if God himself had instructed us, that such ordinance and such interdict is not of Divine but of human, if not demoniac origin; for the doctrine of Christianity denies that man can attain his true nobility without research, and without seeing and feeling the difference between God's teaching and all erroneous and imaginary devices.

We are called to the light; let us walk, then, as children of the light. It requires only the courage of trusting God to act worthy of our vocation. Wherever we may dwell—in the luxuriance of the south or the chill of the north—we shall see enough in living tribes, in the forms and colors of vegetation, in the flowing waters, in the verdant plains, in the proud hills, in the sublime mountains, in "those eternal flowers of the skies"—the stars, in the endless heavens, and in the great deep, to lift our spirits from the visible to the invisible, and raise our thoughts above this grave of things—from moving time to steadfast eternity, from ourselves to God—in whom our hopes may rest for fruition, far beyond what the brightest and highest faith can promise. Thus we receive from the Parent of our spirits, if we trust Him, a sustaining consolation proportioned to the need we may experience in our pilgrimage. The beauties of nature are subject to decay; darkness may obliterate the skies, and a dart from the clouds may quench our sight, but there is no interruption to the benevolence of God, or to the peace of those that trust Him.

CHAPTER IX.

TEACHINGS OF LIGHT.

As, in treating of sensation in this place, it is not the object to teach its physiology, but merely to point out the influence of moral motive upon the formation of ideas, it will suffice to direct our thoughts more particularly to sight, since this is the most intellectual of our senses, and the medium through which we ordinarily become conscious of our moral relation to existence. Without light—poetry, philosophy, literature, and religion must have remained unknown to man. But we are not appointed like our kindred worms to house ourselves in darkness. Our souls, familiar with the light, expatiate in immensity, and converse with beauty.

The direction of the eye expresses the state of man's mind, but it turns not to Heaven except when we are excited by strong emotion, or by the urgent longing for comfort, light, and truth. Every feeling has its appropriate action. Adoration and pathos naturally express themselves in much the same manner, by raising our eyes upward, because these states of soul call those muscles into action which are peculiar to the eye of man. No other creature is formed voluntarily to look upward; but devotion and agony equally constrain us to turn from the troubled earth toward the calm of eternity and heaven, as if in our necessities to demand the help of the Highest.

Light was made for us, and therefore the soul looks for it in all directions. It comes to us in its sevenfold harmony from above, and the sublimest vision of our spirits is heaven itself. Whether we contemplate the abyss of stars, the serene moon walking in her brightness, or the sun enthroned in his glory, we are almost ready, in the bare sensation of unsearchable magnificence, to bow in worship to the visible majesty above us. Thus the earliest idolatry began when men looked up to heaven, and forgot their origin. But we have been spiritually instructed, and in spirit would adore the uncreated Light that in the beginning called all things into being. Thus the eye becomes the instrument of intelligence, and by its aid we perceive that the moral law is founded in the nature of physical, in relation to rational existence. The Commandments, written by the finger of God on the top of Sinai in the tablets of granite, and also in the heart of man, are but a condensed transcript of the law of the universe, brought into direct accommodation to the human socialities of earth. The grand code of God, as the moral Governor of all worlds, is inscribed by his own hand upon the starry firmament of his power, and all existence is the development of law. If we ascend into the heavens, He is there. In the Father's house are many mansions; the glories of the revealing night speak of the household of our God. Suns and systems indicate in light the overflowing beneficence of their present Maker, and it is not in the power of our reason to believe that the associated spheres revolving together in their varied radiance, and modifying seasons to each other, as they roll on in eternity, are without the doctrines of love among them. We can not believe that the ten thousand beauties unknown to earth, with influences innumerable, effectuating accommodations intricate and excellent beyond conception, belong to dead and spiritless worlds. No: a plenitude of goodness is for beings who can enjoy gifts, and praise the Giver. Those arrangements, so vast, various, and sublime, for the unceasing manifestation of benevolence and power, must be intended to meet the demands of moral and intellectual existence. The myriads on myriads of worlds must teem with appropriate inhabitants, who learn from the reciprocal ministrations of Heaven that the Creator is among them. We can not look up, and think otherwise than morally, for the socialities of heaven are visibly expressed in the very light that enters into our souls; and as surely as light is every where, and every where brings visions of Divine beauty to minds formed to receive them, so surely must we conclude that the worlds above and on every side of us are the abodes of beings having some discernment of their relation to each other and to their Maker.

There must be ideas among them, and ideas are but the responses of reason to the intentions of the Creator, in the existence of objects. Ideas, therefore, must be attended by corresponding emotions and affections; and wonderful beyond our thoughts must be the pleasures of beings who reciprocate sentiments of joy and of knowledge, in their contemplation of the magnificence, wisdom, loveliness, and love, revealed every where in the scenery and arrangements of the heavens.

All objects and all elements are but adaptations to the social necessities of mind. We may not be able clearly to infer the moral and physical constitutions of the dwellers in those far-off worlds, but we are certain that all their experience in the marvels of creative skill, so richly at work for their bliss, must largely teach the universal lesson—"God is love." All who can receive this word so far apprehend the Divine nature, and must feel that law which says, He alone is worthy of supreme affection who bids us love one another. This, at least, is the law propounded to man; and turning from the heavens to our homes, we feel that beings incapable of love are incapable of reason and of happiness. Moral beauty is the image of God, and we minister His spirit only when we enjoy and diffuse His charity. The world that is not constituted on this plan must be a world of darkness and disorder —a place of minds that would hide themselves from God, because they wil. not trust Him. Would they but think of Him as love, they would ask and feel forgiveness, and then walk on rejoicing in light.

Thus, whether we look to the associations of heaven or those of earth, we return, at last, to our moral consciousness, and therein seem to stand as upon the interminable firmament, from whence we every where perceive the operation of the same law wrought into the very materials of existence, as well as into the very being of our souls—love—the bond between the Creator and the creature, without the felt indwelling of which it is the manifest will of God that none shall be blessed. The absence of this principle is that outer darkness, in the unsearchable depth of which every spirit wanders who in selfish loneliness seeks a path to which wisdom has not pointed. There is no curse but in the essential malediction which the perverse heart utters on itself, and on all that oppose it; for the mind that is willfully set upon merely obtaining its own way, finds the happiness of others is apt to be an impediment to its selfish aims, since the law of righteousness is the law of charity, embracing all alike: hence disobedience is always associated with wrath, and its anger is so mad that it always acts as if it thought the law was hate; for to be at variance with heaven is to depart alike from love and from truth.

All power is God's; we see it in creation, we feel it in our minds, and our very eyesight informs us that love and power are infinite, and therefore impartial. We turn toward the heavens, and the boundary is not there, but in ourselves: we find no limit but in our capacity to expatiate, and if in thought we would follow our vision into space, and pass on, we become conscious that we have entered into eternity, for there is no chronology among the stars, and time as well as space is lost to our perception, ere we can take the first step along the pathway of unutterable glory that opens before us. Thus is it also in every attempt to contemplate the Divine attributes—" The center is every where, the circumference nowhere."

Begin where we may, there the eternal is before us. Wisdom, and power, and love, are visibly infinite and equal; though we could calculate with an angel's skill, we should find the hosts of heaven beyond our arithmetic. But yet, wherever we might fix our observation, we should perceive each system moving in all its intricate circuits with an equilibrium so adjusted as to prove that the touch of Omnipotence is there; for no other hand is gentle enough to hang worlds upon nothing, and roll them on in their inconceivable vastness and multitude, upon lines finer than an atom of light, through billions of billions of miles, undeviating and unbroken, both in their progress and their revolutions. And this governance would not be that of power and wisdom if it were not also that of love, for, as before observed, all the adjustments of matter must have been induced for the sake of minds. We can not imagine that the distant glories that gleam in faint starlight on our homes are wasted. There are intelligences every where to kindle into ecstacies of thought, amidst the sublimities and beauties that crowd around them, and bring into their existence the consciousness of the universal life. There must be reason where there is divinity, and there, too, must be worship, morality, and religion—for the mind that owns not God, both in thought and in deed, is not intelligent, but unenlightened, and either brutal or insane.

Whether with the telescope we search into the endless magnificence of heaven, or with the microscope we peep into worlds of infinite minuteness, all we see is that the Almighty is there, and therefore we infer that created minds are every where cognizant of the movements of His might, for His handiwork is the revelation of Himself to beings that can discern His power and learn somewhat of His wisdom. The glimmering intuitions of our reason thus assure us, with a faith immovable, that Omnipotence can only evince himself as love, and that He produces intelligent creatures only to supply them with the means and the motives of happiness, by expressing His will in His works.

The glory of God is a visible thing. When Moses said, "I beseech thee, show me thy glory;" Jehovah answered, "I will cause all my goodness to pass before thee."

There is much indefinite use of this word, *glory;* but as it is applied to the ineffable Author of all things, it can mean only what he has done, and the only way in which we can glorify him is to learn his character as expressed in his acts, and so to regard his character as to become transformed into its resemblance. To reflect God's light is, in short, to be glorified ourselves, and this is the manner in which the fountain of excellence is revealed in us. Whoever receives his supplies from this source becomes at once an overflowing spring of joy to other beings, for the glory of God is love and light, and their nature is everlasting diffusiveness without diminution.

I reiterate my thoughts, because I feel them. Creation is a fact full of this meaning—power, wisdom, and benevolence are one; and they equally announce to us also, though we seldom regard the truth, that happiness can be found only by acting and thinking in consistency with the working of this wisdom, power, and love, as expressed in the natural ordinances of earth or of heaven. The law of blessedness, thus fixed in the very nature of things, is the law of moral being, and declares itself unalterable; and therefore, if a will be found in any world at variance with that law, it can find no refuge from its doom of disappointment and perdition, but in a change of purpose, or by seeking to have desires consistent with its creaturely position and a life of faith upon the loving hand that can restore it to its proper place. The Almighty, because He is Love, must of necessity oppose the disobedient, and can only overcome the perverse will—perverse either from ignorance or design—by removing the means of its perversity, or by controlling its movements by still persisting evidences of loving-kindness and tender mercy, in always presenting impediments to its progress in misery. Thus we find, from our experience, that the physical government of God is never separated from his moral government, except in the abstract speculations of our bewildered minds. All we see assures us that we are in soul naked, and open to the scrutiny of God.—He who formed the eye, shall not He see? He who created light, shall not he perceive?

We might profitably follow out this stupendous subject into its details in relation to human duties, but every reader will find arguments ready in his own thoughts. This much may here be affirmed—there are no safe data for metaphysical investigations but in revealed truth; and therefore we shall save ourselves from a world of trouble, by grounding our reasoning upon revelation, and conforming our conduct to its light. It is true, that what we find received under this name is a humanized inspiration; and it would be useless if it were not so, since man can learn only in a human manner. God's truth speaks to common sense; we are required to believe only what is demonstrated—not, indeed, always to our eyes, but to our souls. By all we know of history, and by all that the highest class of minds have been able to discover in nature or in themselves, by prophecy and by fulfillment, by necessity and by supply, by all we are and all we would be, we are bound to the Bible as the book of God. Its doctrines are in keeping with all the intelligences and teachings of the universe; but without its culminating truths, all the light in all the worlds would leave such beings as we are as spiritually blind as ever, and utterly unsound, unsafe, unsatisfied. The religious men of old may have known but little of astronomy, but yet they knew the meaning of the heavens. To what degree Job, Moses, David, and the Prophets were informed of the physical laws which regulated the movements of the glorious hosts, we can not learn, but they saw and understood that the heavens and the earth formed but one universe in the hand of the Almighty. They could not weigh the masses of rolling orbs, with Newton, but they believed in Him who held them in the balance, appointed their places, and directed their influences. They felt His power was infinite, and therefore conceived no limit to His dominion, and named eternity as His abode.

Though the Cosmos has been reduced to mathematical admeasurements for us, and the ideal statistics of the skies are familiar in our schools, yet it would indeed be a feeble sentimentality to talk of mental cultivation taking the magic charm from the mysteries of nature; but alas! men are too apt to enjoy a sublime idea of the universe, while forgetful of Him who "telleth the number of the stars, and calleth them all by their names." This, however, is not the fault of knowledge, but of ignorance; for in contemplating the manifestation of creative power, the demands of creative love are overlooked, unless the spirit that perceives the order of the visible heavens also perceives that natural systems are but the outward symbols of inward and spiritual relationships. But the knowledge of the one conducts to the other; and as surely as the knowledge of natural phenomena is increased, may we be assured that moral truths are also to appear; since general mental development is no accident, but an accordancy with the Divine intention, that determined that all human history should subserve to the explanation of prophecy, and all science tend to demonstrate that the plan of nature is that of Providence, to prove that man was placed upon earth, and scattered over its face in families and nations, with reference, from first to last, to some grand consummation, which shall reveal the character of God as especially concerned with all humanity.

Thus informed, a youth stood on a hill at Bethlehem, waiting for the stars, and it was in his soul to sing, with a burst of adoration, "When I consider *thy* heavens, what is man, that Thou art mindful of him;" and that youth was fit to be a king of God's anointing. Though he seemed among men but as an amiable lad, his mind in worship had been conversant with the wondrous works of creation; and therefore, though still a rustic and a shepherd, something divine was manifestly in him. He could touch the chords of human sympathy, and utter melodious notes in praise of God, so as to stir the souls of others, as if with involuntary responses to his own spirit; and when the defense of the feeble demanded prowess, his knowledge of the ways of Deity filled him with a fearless virtue. The Lord of Heaven corresponded with his heart, and called him the Beloved; and his heart replied, "I will love thee, O Lord, my strength." The heavens declared the glory of God to him, not only as the Creator, but also as the Lawgiver. (Ps. xix.) He heard within him the intelligence uttered by the day and by the night; and it prompted him to meditate acceptably on the enlightening ordinances of Jehovah, as if the voice of the Omnipotent were addressed to his conscience, and caused him to pray that sin, presumptuous sin, might not hold dominion over him. Thus viewing the Almighty at work among His worlds, he at once associated the idea of the Power every where present with the Love that demanded obedience in the daily duties of his life. This idea was doubtless the source of that dignity which visibly ennobled his youthful manhood, and made him notable in Israel, as one honored of Jehovah. He wished his thoughts and the language of his life to be in harmony with the mind of his Maker, as the source of power and salvation; and therefore, though beguiled by the treachery of his own heart, he nevertheless heard the reproving voice, felt at once his contrariety to the holy law, abased himself, bewailed in secret his guiltiness of soul, and sought prevailingly the renewal of a rightful spirit. Hence he was qualified to speak the words of inspiration, and to pour the overflowings of his heart into the ear of Heaven, in songs of praises and pleadings of necessity, which mingled so eloquently with the music of his harp, that adoring angels might linger to listen, while demons were dispelled, and all things in nature seemed to feel him call upon them loudly to laud the righteous Ruler of all intelligence and of all elements.

In the Bible we are not directed to mental imaginings, but to *see* the glory of God in what He has outwardly and openly done. David thought and sung in the spirit of the universe; hence he says of Jehovah, "The heavens declare his righteousness, and all the people see his glory." (Ps. xcvii. 8.) And therefore those who trust in idols are called on to turn to Him. "The heavens declare the glory of God, and the firmament showeth His handiwork," is but the commencement of his song of praise. "Day unto day uttereth speech, and night unto night showeth knowledge." And then, as if the universality of the Divine beneficence were shadowed in the sun, he appeals in rapturous words to the world-wide diffusion of its light and warmth. He saw therein the type of truth; and, with seeming abruptness, he turns from the tabernacle that God had set for the sun, to show forth the glory of the perfect law. The exordium of inspiration concerning the visible majesty of heaven was a fit introduction to the spirit and meaning of all the Creator's manifestations—the enlightenment of man and the removal of moral darkness.—"Great and marvelous are thy works, Lord God Almighty," is but one part of the vast anthem of immortals; Just and true are thy ways, thou King of saints," completes the parallelism of praise; for in the greatness of Jehovah's works is seen the righteousness of His ways.

What made the difference between David and Laplace? Motive. Laplace scrutinized the universe with only himself before his eyes; David looked up only to adore God. Laplace never mentions the Might that made the heavens; he concerned himself only with their mechanism, and, though with an angel's ken he gazed into the temple of Omnipotence, it was not to worship, while David felt the sublimity of the boundless glory but as the shekinah of his Maker.

Now, as in nature, so in the book of God, there are no sentimentalisms and no mistakes. These are man's, but both nature and the Bible tell the truth, and tell it to *us*, if we would listen. The one shows us our littleness, the other our need. They both say that science is not salvation, and that truth is a practical and personal matter. The Creator thus addresses us by all visible things, to awaken moral motives into activity, and leads the mind at every glimpse to further light, until we see that the universal light, is the emblem of God, and that as there is but one source of vision to all eyes, so there is but one source of righteousness for all intelligences.

We can not imagine the power that set the universe in action, but we feel that it could neither have begun nor been *exerted*. Motion, space, duration, as manifested to us in what we behold of God's plan of action, are yet all inconceivable. We may multiply moments on paper, and calculate the rapidity of light as it travels from world to world, but the numbers employed appear only as figures; their sum is not apprehended as an idea by the mind. Light flew from the stars, as they were produced by Omnipotence, in all directions, at the rate of 200,000 miles in a second, and with this speed the light of those stars next and nearest to our system would probably require thirty millions of years to reach our eyes. Such is speed, such is space. What do we learn from these physical facts? Only this—the Almighty has to do with us, and has created light that we may look to Him.

We perceive that time and space, past and to come, are identical with regard to Omniscience and Omnipotence, since reason, in thinking of Deity, can not limit Him to possibilities, as we are limited by our creaturely organization. The Eternal sees not His universe on mechanical and material principles, as it presents itself to our senses. He sees things as they are, but it is in the nature of the senses to modify things according to their mechanism; thus the world wears quite a different aspect to two persons, the convexity of whose eyes in the slightest degree differs. What is real and true must be so to thought, and we—with awe may we say it—must perceive as God perceives, to distinguish the possible from the impossible, the true from the false. As we are situated with regard to the external world, we can not think, and at the same time use our senses, without being subject to organic laws or to the movements of things which of course can take place only in time and space. Even when we withdraw our minds from sensation, we still attend only to one idea at a time. We therefore can not perceive things as they are—God alone can do that, because He alone perceives without succession or interruption, and therefore without period, pause, or place. He who knows all things at once, alone knows them as they are, because in fact there is no break in the universe; and no mind can be taught the truth but by Him who addresses spiritual arguments to our reason.

To be every where equally, and to see every thing equally, and that forever, can not but be possible to Him by whom all things consist; and whatever is possible with God is not only practicable, but a fact. In short, whatever men call impossible, is that which Deity has done and is doing. He sees, at this very moment, every movement in every star that existed millions of ages before Adam's creation; and the state, place, and thoughts, of each of us, as they will be, myriads of ages hence, are now evident to Him. Reason must allow that there is no real past, except to finite perception, since all that is called past, not only remains present in the sight of God, but is also written in light upon the materials of the universe. Reason, however, can bring no evidence to prove the visibility of all the future as well as all the past; but yet we must believe it, because we must believe in the Infinite mind, in whom past, present, and future can not exist; because they are, so to say, but as organizations belonging to the creature. Omnipotence, Omniscience, Omnipresence, Eternity, are one in God; and by our abode with him, and by our capacity of annihilating time and space by thoughts of His deeds, we are involved in these attributes, and must forever be learning what they signify.

Motion results from mind, and it began in the will of God. None but a being whose intellect is biased by desires incompatible with the plan of creation, can fail to perceive that the Divine will and power are goodness in design and deed. If men look abroad over the works of the Almighty, and yet deny his existence, or fail to adore, it is because they prefer wor shiping something more like themselves. They can clearly see that all things must have been made, and therefore they can not doubt the eternal power and Godhead; and on that very account it is impossible for them to escape condemnation, since their inference concerning the righteousness of God must be as distinct as their inference concerning his power, for reason tells us that Omnipotence can not be unjust. "Behold the heavens," says Cicero; "must we not acknowledge that there is a perfect being?" By the *Logos*, the divine Wisdom, were all things made; but the darkness does not comprehend the light, and the evil in us still excludes it, or we should discover a world within in correspondence with Jehovah. We turn away from the glorious revelation, although it is but a personal expression of the fact, that, as a Creator, God is faithful and fatherly and loving. He calls on us to repent of our miserable contempt of true existence, and to submit to be informed and to be happy.

We have seen that the meaning of existence, as far as we can discern it, is love, boundless love. This is our idea of God in creation, and it implies created intelligence to recognize and enjoy it as a manifestation of God, for a latent Deity is a deity unknown; the natural light agrees with the light of revelation. The attributes of the Almighty exist only in creation, since, without action, Omnipotence is but a word. Almightiness is infinite, and acts in infinitude; and, like Omniscience must have infinite objects on which to evince itself. Immensity of means is the expression of immensity of power, and the scene of love must ever be as boundless as the Divine beneficence; and, therefore, to assert that there ever was a time when God was without intelligent creatures, is to assert there was a time when Deity was dormant. There is succession to the creature, but none to Him. Existence is His one act, His everlasting object; hence every thing which we can conceive is connected with all other things, boundlessly as to space, and endlessly as to duration, because all begin and end in the Infinite. There is no dissociation, because every thing is part and parcel of God's one eternal act of manifestation to created beings, by referring reason to Himself. We perceive successively; but to perceive truly, is to see as God sees—all things at once—and as they are, *in seculo seculorum*, with all their variety, a harmonious whole.

The eternal character and consistency of Jehovah's works have been used as an argument against the reception of any other revelation than that of science. What science will answer all the purposes of the Bible, we are not informed. Astronomy and geology show us no Saviour; and the heroics of infidelity have not been those of heaven. Its exploits, either at home or abroad, notwithstanding its pride in sciential appliances, have never evinced any tendency to promote the glory of God or good-will among men. To convince men of sin, of righteousness, and of judgment to come, has neither been the end of their doctrines nor the motive of their revelations. In fact, this kind of conviction is just that which infidels desire very scientifically to dispense with, and the fruits of their doctrines have fully demonstrated the bitterness of their nature. Yet let us not blame science, since this could never impede religion but in minds determined to find their own way, without the help of that light which the God of mercy pitifully offers them. That there is nothing in real science opposed to the Scriptures, has only been the more clearly manifested, by the astonishing trouble which infidels have taken in endeavoring to draw evidence from nature, against revelation. They have been digging into the earth, as if to hide themselves from the sun, and to bury themselves beyond the reach of the only source of life and joy. Geology will not help them, the mountains will not fall on them, the caves will not hide them, they are driven out as if by a centrifugal force to meet their antagonists in the light, if not to be convinced, yet to be silenced there. A fact will show how the motive with which a man looks will pervert his judgment. "Oh," says one, "it was found, that in sinking a pit at Jaci, near Mount Etna, seven distinct layers of lava, with *a thick bed of earth* covering each, were pierced through." This, observes the infidel, could not have occurred in less than fourteen thousand years. But true and eminent geologists, who looked with the fear of God before their eyes, found that there was no earth between the layers. The narrator who so confidently announced these ideal beds, immediately afterward states that "the country about Hybla being overwhelmed by the lava of Etna, became totally barren, but in a second eruption, by a shower of ashes from the mountain, it soon re-assumed its ancient beauty and fertility," Thus we see, that when he had forgotten his doubts of the Mosaic record, he found no need for the two thousand years in order to convert the lava into luxuriant fields. Real science tells nothing but the truth.

It is remarkable, that the facts of geology and other sciences have led to the denial of Christianity on the Continent, where the spirit of inquiry is trammeled by usurped authority, and Christian doctrines have been cast into fixed and unalterable forms; but in England, where the mind is left comparatively free to ask for itself, investigation has only tended to confirm the faith.

We must allow that time is not a consideration in the business of the Eternal; and we can well suppose that the ages which geologists believe to have passed over this earth previous to the formation of man, were preparative of conveniences for human population, and anticipative of human exigencies. Moses does not inform us how long the earth had existed, but only gives us the earliest chronology of events in relation to man.

The indefinite periods of geology may be the days of successive creation mentioned in Genesis, since it is certain that the orders of creation, as shown in the stratifications of the earth's crust, are exactly such as follow the order of creation as described by the first historian—a fact sufficient in itself to puzzle infidels to account for the information possessed by the Jewish legislator.

The use of the eye is to see what God has done. Can "God work miracles?" says the sentimental Rousseau; "can He derogate from the laws which He has established? The question, treated seriously, would be impious if it were not absurd." Yes, it would indeed be impious to suppose the Almighty at variance with Himself. But the impiety and the absurdity belong to the mind that conceives a God limited by His own laws, not as they relate to moral existence, but to natural phenomena. Surely Omnipotence may alter His own works, in evidence of His power, and for the instruction of intelligent agents, without contradicting Himself. But the infidel does not see God as the author of righteousness, or as a lawgiver to understanding spirits, but only as the power at work, originating and maintaining material operations. The scoffer looks up into the heavens through his telescope, and catches a few glimmerings of glory through his tube; he calculates orbits, and watches planets undeviating in their courses, and utters that very thought which Peter, the Apostle of Jesus, 1800 years ago, said he would utter—"There shall come in the last days scoffers, walking after their own lusts, and saying, Where is the promise of his coming? for since the fathers fell asleep, *all things continue as they were from the beginning of the creation.*" A power superior to nature is not acknowledged, and to imagine it is irrational. "The probability of the continuance of the laws of nature," says Laplace, "is superior in our estimation to every other evidence. What has a Christian to state, by way of argument, against this probability? Facts, facts—natural facts; nothing but fact is an argument. The testimony is experience, and there is no other evidence. We appeal to what God has manifestly done, in order to give a reason for our belief in His promises. He Himself always directs us to His deeds; He did so from the first—He does so now. The faith of Christians stands in the power of God. Let us not, like the unbeliever, be *willfully ignorant;* we do well to take heed to the sure word of prophecy: it is full of facts; it points us incessantly to visible things, accomplished, and now doing and about to be done. It told us that scoffers would plead the continuance of nature, *in statu quo,* from the beginning, as a reason for not believing in its Lord; and the thing is before us—we have the fact in their writings. The argument is, however, a recent affair, drawn out of these last times, because not until now have we seen enough of the laws of nature to conceive of their invariable order and operation. It is well, and blessed be God for the light of science—it has banished chance from the world of matter; but faith had banished it from all worlds at the very moment she believed in God.

True science is light from heaven, and will conduct minds upward, if they will but trace it to its source. But does science, indeed, demonstrate the invariable character of natural laws? Does it prove that all things have continued as they were from the beginning of the creation? The Apostle Peter again gives us a word with which to silence the scoffer:—"*For this they willingly are ignorant of, that by the word of God the heavens were of old, and the earth standing out of the water and in the water.*"* It is semi-science, or rather science by piecemeal and in fragments, that

* See Keith's Demonstration of the Truth of Christianity.

irreligious men, like the giants warring against Jove, have so hastily turned against the word of God; but the very fragments fall back to crush the rebels. The more men examine this earth, the more they find to show that the system of this world has been subjected to change. "Every part of the earth," says Cuvier (Theory of Earth, 5th Ed. p. 7), "every hemisphere, every continent, every island of any extent exhibits the same phenomenon." "It is the sea which has left them (shells, &c.) in the places where they are now found." "The basin of the sea has undergone one change, at least, either in extent or in situation. Such is the result of the very first search, and of the most superficial examination." "The traces of revolutions become still more decisive when we ascend a little higher, and approach near to the great chains. There are still found many beds of shells; some of these are even thicker and more solid; the shells are quite as numerous and as well preserved, but they are no longer of the same species." "The sea, previous to the deposition of the horizontal strata, had formed others, which, by the operation of problematical causes, were broken, raised, and overturned in a thousand ways; and as several of these inclined strata, which it had formed at more remote periods, rise higher than the horizontal strata which have succeeded them, or at least shoals and inequalities; and this must have happened whether they had been raised by one extremity, or whether the depression of the opposite extremity had made the waters subside. Thus is the second result not less clear nor less satisfactorily demonstrated than the first, to every one who will take the trouble of examining the monuments on which it is established."

"A glance at the best geological maps will satisfy an inquirer that a greater part of the present land has been raised from the deep."—Lyell's Geology, vol. i. p. 135

All observers admit that the strata were formed beneath the waters, and have been subsequently converted into dry land."—Buckland's Bridgewater Treatise, p. 44.

So, then, the most superficial observation is sufficient to show that "the calculating the probability of the continuance" of things as they were at first would make a man a very sorry philospher. Any one may satisfy himself, if he will use his eyes, that the earth has undergone a series of vast changes, and that there was a time when it was not fit for human habitation, and another, when, although habitable by man, it yet was submerged. What a series of transitions from zoophytes to man—what changes of nature from a brute world to a world of minds, reasoning concerning their Maker, acknowledging His benevolence, and hoping for an end in keeping with God's character; or else, like Hume, studying history without religion, and despising the forewarnings of Heaven, and viewing humanity in all its pathos only as an accident of the elements, without a purpose but to die.

It would, no doubt, be argued that these changes are themselves the results of the invariable laws which govern the universe. Where is this discovered? There is nothing in the known laws of matter and of motion, as manifest in earth or heaven, to account for changes such as have transpired. Unalterable ordinances can not create new eras. Some hypothesis must be invented, some cosmogony indiscoverable in facts, and unrevealed to man, must be imagined to suit the nice reason of the skeptic. The secret is this—he has an object to serve, some motive for disparaging the claims of the Bible; like Rousseau and Hume, he wishes to prove it false, because he can not bear to believe Christianity. It will not administer to pride, nor suffer a man to hope without holiness: it demands self-denial. It can not be endured—away with it. But how? Can not they direct us to a theory which will dispense with Divine legation and Almighty interference with the workings of worlds? Will not the nebulous notions account for every thing like successive developments, geological and astronomical? and may not man be an expanded monkey, and a monkey an expanded monad? Laplace mathematically sets the heavens in motion, to dispense with the management of their Creator; but he derives his vortices from his own fancies. There are no nebulæ but in our minds and in our defective vision. Wherever man can penetrate with the telescope into open space, he sees only orderly worlds, with nothing among them, in all the planes of all the planets, to warrant the notion that things might not have always been as they now are. And yet this earth takes her place among these planets, with the records of many changes in her bosom. What is the conclusion, but that God has interfered with the regulations of his own world, and may do so again? There is no power but in the hand of the Almighty to alter the aspect of worlds, and what that hand sets in order no other can disturb. The motive with which man regards creation will determine his conclusion; and if he has no reverence for God, he will soon contrive to find that there is no evidence of his superintendence. Newton saw the universe with his soul enlightened by religion; he believed in Christianity, and thus saw heaven opened, and the throne of God: and the devout spirits of olden time looked with the same intelligence; and though they did not measure the spaces between the stars, nor calculate the speed of light, they had yet a sublimer motive for looking up into the skies, for they felt that the Almighty was "*riding on the heaven of heavens by His name, Jah.*"

CHAPTER X.

KNOWLEDGE.

Notional knowledge, or that knowingness which comes to nought, is twin-born with ignorance; and it is that for which mankind naturally entertain an early passion, since it serves to occupy the mind, and divert it from those realities which are of too solemn a nature to allow guilty beings quietly to forget that they have an account to render to the great Judge. It is that, also, which gives rise to all those wordy disputes which cause unmeaning divisions among men, because those disputes, being destitute of definite or real ideas, present nothing for minds to perceive and agree on. It is the opposite of that confident apprehension of something imparted by the Almighty to the mind, and which therefore is worth contending for, as *pro traditâ fide*, and without which we have none but the fool's right to dispute, since, in fact, we have no assured truth to offer, and nothing to testify but that our opinion is superior to our wisdom.

True knowledge is the knowledge of truth, and truth is the parent of faith, hope, and charity. To understand is to perceive the meaning of another mind, and we must perceive the intentions of our Maker before we can adore. Man willingly co-operates with man, from mutual intelligence; and when man discerns the Divine idea in any thing or event, and is personally and affectionately influenced by that idea, then he becomes truly devout—his religion being founded on a felt truth, which so operates on his rational nature, that his motives and actions correspond with the light in his understanding. Thus true knowledge is essential to true religion, for this consists in conformity of mind with the recognized teaching of God, both in natural and in spiritual revelation, for the divinity in Nature requires her seers as well as the divinity in the Bible. Hence every real science contributes to theology, and instructs man concerning the goodness and power of his Maker, and thus far, also, sustains the reliance of the mind upon His providence for intellectual, moral, and physical supply, according to the demand rightfully made upon his bounty as a faithful Creator. But this always implies the use of means, in accordance with the plan of creation, as regards both mind and body. Faith in a falsehood is a false faith, and that will not save us. True faith trusts in what God has done, and therefore what He also will do.

It requires a clear soul to see a truth so as to believe it at first sight, and there is nothing more doubtful than a fact to an ignorant mind. The reason of this is that nothing is understood while standing alone. To separate any idea from its connection is to put it out of its place, and thus to make it a puzzle. It is like presenting a fossil to a man, and asking him what it belonged to when alive, and begging him to describe the nature, property, and fashion of the creature of which it once formed a part. A large and exact extent of knowledge is demanded mentally to allocate any thing, or to form a complete idea of any object before us. Small knowledge has a small vocabulary, and no meanings, or at least few truths, and whatever does not seem to fall in with these few is looked at as a wonder or a lie.

Science is not salvation, and every truth does not confer liberty of spirit; there may be health of soul with very little knowledge. A robust infancy of spirit is indeed often witnessed among comparatively uninformed persons, who evince a strong appetite for truth, and eagerly enjoy it, as the sincere food of the soul.

There are others, however, who have a voracious desire for informotion, who yet, morally speaking, are but atrophies and living skeletons, simply because they are vitally wrong in their intellectual functions, and, like Pharaoh's kine, devour, not that they may digest, grow strong in spirit, and be fit for work, but that they may gratify a depraved disposition, and merely please themselves. These persons are like intellectual cretins, living and moving and chattering among the great wonders of creation; but, not seeing the meanings of things, they do not worship God nor learn any thing of Him. They are too busy with phenomena to look beyond the elements of their amusement; they make knowledge a thing of mere sensation, and thus truth itself deceives them, because their affections are awry.

Self-denial is in no case more requisite than in resisting our appetency for knowledge. The fair tree that flourished in the midst of the lost Paradise shed its seed upon the earth, and the deluge did not destroy it. The tempting fruit is now habitually eaten, but still it is forbidden; and its effects are still to make us feel our nakedness, not with the shame of repentance, but of pride. To indulge our curiosity, irrespective of right ends, is the worst of sensualities. But, of course, the pleasure of indulgence is the sole object with minds not morally enlightened, and if our affections are not trained by association and sympathy with charitable and loving spirits, we must live selfishly.

Yet, how gracious in His tenderness is our God! He constitutes the senses and the soul of the young child to dally with its dangers and its safety with equal delight; and the little creature, ignorant of evil, plays with the crested snake as it would with its mother's tresses. But affection watches over its dalliance, and while it drinks knowledge and finds amusement in every object that does not bear on its front the aspect of anger, it also learns to love and to smile. It needs no law to teach it faith, but it relies, because its selfhood is provided for without inquiry, and the very feebleness of its undoubting life makes its whole existence like a prayer anticipated and answered, ere its utterance. But as it grows in knowledge, it finds both good and evil; it becomes suspicious, and then desire springs up, without a love that may be blessed, and therefore disappointment soon teaches it to mourn, because its will is inconsistent with the universal wisdom that calculates its good in opposition to itself. In this manner we are taught the last lesson that we learn, to submit ourselves to a guiding hand, and to trust our wants, without hurry, to the Mind that furnishes us with knowledge to regulate our affections unto safe indulgence.

This natural tendency, merely to seek gratification for selfish ends, is in no respect more manifest than in our pursuit of knowledge. We are rather disposed to seek a succession of pleasing emotions from ideas as they flit across our brains, than to collect a treasure for eternity, by detaining, analyzing, and arranging them, so as to form a science in our souls. By thus amusing ourselves we frustrate our own aim, and lose the high and holy enjoyment which is ultimately attained by patiently waiting upon truth, from the love inspired by a few glimpses of her vailed beauty. The successful investigation of nature is like that quiet, hopeful wooing which proceeds about its heart-work reverently and religiously; and it finds that recompense which is due only to the fortitude and faith that rely upon God as the author of truth and love, in the possession of which all labor is forever rewarded.

Time is an essential element of our knowledge. Every inquiry into science should be conducted with the assurance, that by observing fact after fact we shall rise beyond the region of doubt, and ascend as by steps to the holy place where God reveals His glory. If, indeed, we enter with the right hope, we advance into a gradual revelation, and feel that the mind of our Maker is meeting us with endless intelligence and joy. God's words, whether established in the elements or written in the Bible, always express the perfection of His character as the parent and the patron of all who seek rest for their spirits in His liberality and wisdom. Thus a man with the temper of Newton will think becomingly about the grandeur of the Creator's physical universe, until by degrees he rises into a clear elevation, from whence, with sublime but sober rapture, he beholds the heavens and the earth as one system of diversified wonders, in which Omnipotence reveals Himself, both as loveliness and love. Thus, too, he perceives, at last, that all that the prophets of Jehovah spake, and all that the apostles of Jesus preached concerning redemption and eternal health, is in beauteous harmony with the teachings of providence, and that the spiritual system of revealed science presents whatever is required to complete and consummate the wisdom inscribed with light upon the world of nature. In short, all inquiry is fruitless and disappointing, unless directed in a divine manner; for there is no science, no beauty, no truth, no loveliness, but in the works of God. Men have ever been able to use their reason to happy and ennobling ends only when they have discarded all fond fancies, and followed the indications mercifully granted to them in nature, when seen in the light that flows from Heaven. God has not left Himself without witness, but men have shown their origin from a fallen father, in their disregard of God's voice. They have not been disposed to retain the thought of Him in their knowledge, nor can they admit His authority over them until they have seen enough of His majesty to humble them in the consciousness that He is the sole source of all power and endowment. In fact, before man can rightly think, he must be so far religious as to be persuaded that wisdom presides over all true knowledge. He otherwise but confirms himself in delusion, and instead of becoming devout, surrounds himself with the palpable darkness of his doubts. But he who seeks wisdom finds it in every department of knowledge. His faculties refresh themselves at the eternal fountain, and, in the perpetual ecstasy of adoration, he interprets the meaning of objects, and finds all things but symbols of the present God. Thus the mind, properly employed, is exquisitely happy. The eagerness of a godly ambition is sustained by immortal hope, and the tree of knowledge, planted by God's own hand, bears ripe fruit as well as beauteous blossoms, to be gathered freely, and freely enjoyed, by all who are entitled to partake, which none can be until arrayed in that robe of light in which the Lord of glory clothed himself to teach us how to wear it—humility.

In the desire for knowledge, as in every other disposition of the mind, we see the distinction between the will belonging to the animal, and that proper to the spiritual man. The animal will is determined only by bodily condition and convenience; but the spiritual will asserts its superiority by desires after intelligence, because, in truth, it enjoys God. The animal mind may have mathematical habits, and be offended at contradictions and deformities; but this is not reason—it is only instinct still. Reason, indeed, prompts men to build beautiful cities, full of splendid palaces, museums and churches, but the reason is not in the materials, but in the ideas thus rendered visible. The policies of an ant-hill or a bee-hive are just as reasonable as the thoughts of those who enjoy mere sights. Not that I would disparage sight-seeing. Every object in creation has in it an idea peculiar to itself, and is worth knowing for its own sake. But the difficulty is to get at it so as to see it. Without purity of purpose, which is the result of a regenerated will, our opinions and prejudices blind us to all beauty, and we can not place ourselves in the right position to behold the divine idea: it is therefore no wonder that people in general are amused with the superficies of things, and know nothing. They do not seek for ideas, because their wills are animal, and desirous only of sensations. Unless there are minds in the beautiful palaces, museums, and churches, capable of abstracting themselves from conveniences, curiosities, and decorations, and of living amidst ideas, and traveling hither and thither in thought, searching after those spiritual realities which objects of sense only very imperfectly intimate—these things might as well not be, as regards spiritual and rational ends. It is the perception of this reason which constitutes what men call genius. It discovers the capabilities of nature, and intuitively proceeds along a path of its own beyond knowledge. Imagination is the pioneer of such minds, opening vistas of vision not to be reached by common eyesight, and crowded with objects, some few of which are now and then imperfectly made palpable and visible by the gifted seers who materialize their thoughts in words, in colors and in marble.

But, alas! evermore there is danger in endowment, without the binding of the soul to its Maker by obedient love—love responding to love commanding. God must speak the Law in keeping with our fellowships, and write it on the heart, or else men will fabricate their own ideas, however foolish, and worship and serve them, however false. All the histories of earth show that unless we are presented with means adequate to our desire for knowledge concerning the world beyond our senses, we must be busy with delusions. But revelation brings the means home to us. In the uncreated Word we have what we want to enlighten thought. We may now learn and love infinitely and everlastingly, because we have objects set before us both appropriate and worthy. The relationships of our humanity to other beings, capable, like us, of expatiating in the productions of Jehovah's mind, when rightly felt, compel us to be religious. Understanding the purpose of our Maker to be our happiness, we can truly delight in His works, and through them sustain our spirits with a perpetual stream of knowledge direct from the fountain of all intelligence; and, imbued with the Divine spirit which communicates life to our affections, the exercise of intellect itself thus becomes essentially worship, and therefore blessedness. Without religion, knowledge is but pomp and vanity; a matter of the earth to die and to be buried. Indeed the love of knowledge is only the love of mere pleasure, unless it is also the love of truth, and truth is never followed for her own sake, except when the mind is guided by those principles which rectify the conscience, and render a man desirous above all things to walk without blame, as in the presence of the Holy One.

As there is no true science but of Divine origin, so there is no morality without religion—nor, in fact, does man possess manly ideas without some apprehension of his position, as the vicegerent of the Almighty on earth, holding his faculties in responsibility to their Bestower. He then feels that obedience is beatitude, and perversity is suffering. There must be some mental association with superior intelligence, some perception of moral relationship to Him whose will is law, before we can entertain a noble thought, or an idea capable of raising our desires above corporeal demand, or elevating our actions out of the impulses of bodily selfhood. But knowledge, united with true love, is religion. There must be sympathy with heaven, as well as an insight of heavenly order, before we can will and work in its spirit; and any motive less than this can be but brutal, if it be not diabolical.

The heavenly feeling or principle is easily distinguished from every other. It is that of a power irresistible, when once admitted—but still of so delicate a nature, that it may at any time be dissipated by a distrustful thought. It is that unselfish spirit which seeks enjoyment only by diffusing it, and knows nothing of violence, offensive or defensive; for it has no pretensions to ownership and authority in knowledge as for itself, because its whole existence is evinced, like that of the peaceful light, by the life, beauty, joy, harmony, and happiness, which it was created to promote and to exhibit. But this spirit operates in the soul by improving our ideas with the addition of heavenly truths to the images of earth. It binds heart to heart, not only by natural affections, but by spiritual thoughts and the interchange of hopes and assurances that spring from the consciousness that God has spoken what it believes, and that faith can not be shaken from its stability of bliss, because it is built upon the knowledge of what Omnipotence has done and said. The witness is within; logic is unnecessary to love, since its life is all demonstration, and it begins as well as ends with *probatum est.*

If education proceed not under the power of this approving spirit, it is better that the soul should be left to the elements to fight its way onward, through darkness and suffering, to light and satisfaction, with the help of God's direct teaching in the mercies of His providence; for the soul is safer in feeling after God in ignorance than in presuming upon knowledge without love. To educate without Christian principle is to educate selfishness, and to refine and intensify the ingenuities of hell: for knowledge, whatever be its kind, must always evince itself in corresponding action. But to be busy about self is not proper to humanity; and even the beasts that perish are better employed than to live only for themselves. Yet this will be the end of knowledge, without the impartation of the principle that excites to action for the extension of social blessedness, in the enlargement of the mind by truths that elevate the affections while strengthening the faculties. These truths are found only in creation, as investigated by true science—and in the Bible, as read by a soul that waits on God. I mean, by science, a system of facts on certain general principles—the classification of the properties of things for the clearer apprehension of God's works. The ideas that do not present us with the true characters of objects are neither scientific nor poetical; and however prevalent they may be, serve no other purpose than to delude the soul by exciting unamiable emotions, to terminate in misery.

Such is the substance of the romance which untried youth, and frivolity at all ages, are apt so greatly to admire. Fancy, when left to her license, unrestrained by a cultivated conscience, has the faculty of a magician, and makes a fool's paradise out of phantoms, and places a glass before the eye of her victim, which distorts every object and decks it with false colors that please those who find it painful to think.

All great and good thoughts are truthful and practical, and true poetry itself is so. But when poetry is realized, slow and shallow minds lose sight of the poetry, as if it were not in the facts before them. They look at the outside of the materials, and forget to look for what is in them. They admire the carved foliage of the chapiters, but see not the shekinah; they are dazzled at the blazing brilliance of the gems upon the high-priest's breast-plate, but discern no divine meaning in their renderings of light; they handle the wires of the electro-telegraph, but perceive not the tractable lightning, and feel not the grandeur of the thought, that man has made the glittering arrows of the Almighty the medium between soul and soul hundreds of miles apart. They acknowledge that the prophet's words are poetical when he says, "for stones they shall have iron;" but they see nothing of this truth in thousands of miles of railway, and the means of bringing this broad, fair world of minds into one compact and sensitive community. The poetry of truth is nothing to those whose business is only a trade, and knowledge is valued only as a saleable commodity by those whose souls live in the market.

There are but two kinds of knowledge—the one of mind, the other of matter. The knowledge of matter and its laws is physical science: the knowledge of mind is self-analysis, which is the highest and most interesting of all sciences, since it includes all we feel as well as think. God reveals Himself in both forms of knowledge. By the material evidences of His power around us, we are taught ideas of time, space, form, color, odor, and every thing that suggests bodily action and presence. By self-consciousness, together with that of external things, we are enabled to reason and associate in spirit with other thinking beings, and even with the Maker of all. The true end or purpose of all science is to inform us concerning the attributes of God, and his relation to ourselves. Whatever fails of indicating this end is error and falsehood. These are sinful, so far as they are willful; they are departures from Divine direction, and therefore also from happiness. As truth is in all respects infinite, so also is its opposite; and hence our chief motive for desiring the constant guidance of truth, as this alone can lead to God, while its opposite conducts to endless darkness. Truth, or the expression of Divine wisdom, alone rectifies the will or instructs the understanding.

The state of the will is tested by the application of

the knowledge we possess, as well as by our endeavors to acquire more. Mind can not exist inactively; it must be busy, in good or evil, as long as we are awake; and he who is not engaged in some useful pursuit, either real or ideal, had better sleep. The feeling of *ennui* is a weariness of soul verging on malignity; and it is peculiar to educated society, because the habit of sleeping, when we have nothing good to think of, is deemed barbarous and impolite. But as surely as a mind is not well employed, nor permitted to withdraw itself in sleep, it will become either imbecile or immoral. There is nothing for educated minds to do but sin, if they will not work. Ceasing to cultivate themselves or their neighbors, and unwilling or unfit to practice the various husbandries of life, they must live on bad books, or qualify themselves for Bedlam. He who is not preparing for the skies, ought to be busy in improving matters on earth, since reason was given to man for no other purpose but to apply knowledge to use, either in this world or some other. As there are but two kinds of knowledge, so there are but two ways of being useful—the one by providing comforts for bodily existence, and the other by providing for the happiness of the soul.

It is useless to educate, unless education itself tend to the employment of man's natural powers, in a natural manner. When knowledge promotes not comfort, it promotes wretchedness and temptation. A man, intellectually cultivated, must be either a patient saint, or a gloomy misanthrope, if placed, by the selfishness of society or his own will, in such a position that he can not profitably or happily apply his knowledge. He may be able to interpret the eloquence of nature, and look out among the stars with a feeling of the infinite glories of heaven, but yet he lies buried in the earth alone with all his burning thoughts. He feels the darkness, the uselessness, and the rotten ness of death, because he lives in the consciousness of all that might have been, and ought to have been for him; but that although awakened into earnestness by the urgencies of his own nature, and by the affected officiousness of artificial teachers, he is still left to shift for himself, though imprisoned in poverty, as if in cold iron, stone, and gloom. Such is the lot of many a classic mind, to whom the plowman "whistling o'er the lea" is a prince. And the reason of this misery is in the fact, that the knowledge which has nothing to do with daily employment, induces pride, false or unnatural taste, and makes this world a wilderness, because the heathen gods are banished, and the vale of Tempé requires tillage, that its inhabitants may eat. And all kinds of education are equally maddening that do not give vigor and liberty to human sympathies, induce a disposition to labor, and make demand for it. There is no happiness without action; and if a man be crippled in every limb, his mind must be right busy, or he must either bemoan himself, or sleep as a brute does when its senses are not acted on. And he who, from the state of his mind and the style of his ideas, or the mismanagement of monopolists, can not get to work, might as well be palsied, or in the penitentiary. Nothing but the stronghold of faith on the right hand of God, as the vindicator of the oppressed, and the omnipotent opener of prisons and graves, can comfort the man who knows and wills, and can not act. Christianity is a business-spirit come from heaven to regenerate the earth, and men are moved by it to exertion, if only to turn the sod with the spade, that the curse which fell upon the ground for Adam's sake, may, by toil, be cured, and the dust of which man was molded might bloom and breathe again of Paradise. But toil must have good hope in it, as well as good knowledge, or it, too, is woe. Work must be done for something—some social purpose, some comfort, some heart-end. In short, as knowledge without love is only vexation, so, unless love and knowledge equally nerve the arm to labor, it is but slavish drudgery; and those who would enforce toil without making it intelligent, and conducive to domestic, social, patriotic, and philanthropic ends, are only Satan's slave-drivers, and receive his wages—living death and inherent condemnation.

The end and purpose of all precept, teaching, providence, and evangelizing, is to make men God-like, that they may endure all contradiction patiently, and persist in forgiving and loving until all faults are lost in the fullness of mercy, and all hearts are either won by the beauty of holiness or forever repelled into their own place by the irresistible force of truth and light.

Happily in this country education always helps to elevate the mind by bringing it into association with useful employment, since there is a commercial demand for knowledge of every kind; but the higher advantage of even secular instruction is shown in its moralizing influence: for by supplying the mind with intellectual objects, it is the better enabled to resist vulgar temptations, and the more so, since education, in a Christian land, involves an acquaintance with much religious and revealed truth. Facts speak strongly on this subject. In the journal of the Statistical Society, (November 1847) Mr. G. A. Porter, states that only one educated person in 76,227 of the male population, and only one in 2,034,133 of the female population, was accused of crime, on the yearly average, from 1836 to 1846, throughout England and Wales. In 1846, only one educated person in Middlesex was rendered amenable to the laws of his country; the annual aggregate of accusations being 25,412. Such facts need no comment.

All true knowledge is divine, since there is no truth but of God's making. But it may be maliciously employed, and the proof of maliciousness is the fact that a soul willfully perverts, to selfish or malignant purpose, the truth that benevolence places before our minds, to rectify our motives, and thus sin turns the truth of God into licentiousness, and takes occasion, from the liberality of Heaven, to render light itself a cloak for disguise and deception. Herein we see the hideousness of a lying spirit: it craftily takes advantage of the gifts of God to deceive honest, unsuspicious, true, credulous souls, and wins upon their affections through their ignorance, in order to obtain some sacrifice on the altar of its cupidity, whether for fame, foı lucre, for lust, or for the satisfaction of whatever disposition or desire may be the dominant principle or motive of its character. Hence the endless variety in the forms of beguiling fiction and of artifice with which men trade with others, and pander to the encourage ment of their own passions. But the most Satanic of all deceptions is the common one of employing one truth for the purpose of concealing another. Thus men believing in the light of nature deny the light of the Spirit, and because God reveals Himself in creation, require Him not to address them in any other way; and thus, too, under the mask of conscientiousness, men cease to exercise charity, and pretend to obey God while they would smite with a curse the brotherhood of Christ, as if they were the rightful monopolists of all wisdom, and as if knowledge dwelt alone with them. Surely, those who lay down laws for consciences, and condemn unheard, must arrogate to themselves the prerogatives of Divine intelligence, and assume such authority only because they believe themselves infallible, while in fact the immensity of their conceit conceals the enormity of their error.

But it is of the nature of knowledge, or an acquaintance with facts and things, to confirm the humility of a truly humbled mind, because it is the quality of such a mind to feel its own ignorance and deficiency, in consequence of its perceiving somewhat of the excellent glory of Him by whose liberal hand all means are administered, and by whose inspiration all minds are endowed with whatever of understanding they may possess. In every mind that is not humble, knowledge is but knowingness, since each new insight into the relation of things only induces such a one to think more of himself, as if he were indeed a gifted seer, to be admired for his consciousness of eyesight. He looks not forth to wonder and to worship. He may, indeed, be well pleased that the universe is so nicely adapted to his individual comfort, but in his self-complacency he never thinks of being thankful to Him who has adapted the sunshine to his sight, and objects to his soul. Though capable of reasoning, concerning the movements of heaven and earth, as fitted to himself, yet, with face opposed to the firmament of Jehovah, he looks up and laughs, without a thought but of himself. The soul, somewhat acquainted with the moral character of his Maker, however, and having respect to His holy law, as the mirror of His perfection, feels that wisdom and love are both infinite, and that the utmost keenness of created vision can but serve the soul to gaze into the profundity before it, so as to discern those rays of light that indicate the glory beyond sight. Like the devout astronomer, peering into space among stars that appear but as points, although they are really centers of revolving and populous worlds, "in number beyond number," the more he beholds the more he feels his incapacity to penetrate the depths of Divine knowledge and goodness. Conscious that he dwells but as an atom of dust on the outskirts of a galaxy of immeasurable glory, moving through eternity in the hand of Omnipotence, he becomes, in his own estimation, as nothing, and he loses all perception of himself in the overwhelming apprehension of the Presence that fills immensity, and crowds the boundless existence He has fashioned with proofs of His power and His wisdom. The Author of beauty and majesty and thought is the object of every rightly-thinking spirit. But what is the vision of the heaven of heavens to a mind that sees not God? It is but as a brilliant chromatropic display, revolving to please a child, that expresses its joy by exclaiming, I see—I see! Thus the undevout natural philosopher, without a spiritual insight, contents himself with regarding the orrery of God but as an invention for his amusement. But there is truly no meaning but moral meaning in the sights and sounds that penetrate to the soul of man; and the Divinity addresses himself personally to each one of us, and demands our hearts, while engaging our intellects. Almightiness is only so far evinced to our understandings, as to teach us to trust Him in His faithfulness for all futurity. Thus every lesson in true knowledge —knowledge of ourselves, of our position, and our Maker—ends in faith, to show us that we are not yet arrived at maturity of life, and shall not know the love that always embraces us until we are born into the atmosphere of a higher and a brighter world, and are able unabashed to meet the eye that guards us. But this fellowship with Heaven is not complete in any partial knowledge, but in that which realizes God so perfectly as to be filled with His own charity, for it is complete love alone that is complete light, and reveals all things without the possibility of error or of doubt. The true idea of any thing is its perfection. Humanity in its completeness has not yet been seen by any of us, but it is that after which every intelligent believer is seeking: when he finds it, he will behold God, and know even as he is known.

CHAPTER XI.

FAITH.

THE duty of doubting is the first consequence of a rational faith, and of our liability to sin. The ignorant and willful have few doubts except of the truth: the false is the most probable to their apprehension, and whatever suits their tempers is apt to become their delusion; for passion is the mightiest of deceivers, and corrupts the reason of every man who has not been instructed to distinguish right from wrong by the test of conscience, rectified by divine law. What we most vividly and selfishly hope or fear is most apt, in this twilight of reason, to deceive our senses and our judgment. If we look into the marvelous history of those deceptions which have deluded the masses of mankind, we shall discover that they have always flourished in proportion as minds have been unblest by the knowledge of natural and revealed realities, and consequently unestablished in any true faith. For however strongly such persons may believe, yet their best convictions amount merely to credulity, since they give credence to something demonstrably inconsistent with some truth clearly evident to all who will use their reason. Whatever is contrary to any known fact is a falsehood. Hence they are forced to set about confirming their folly by persuading themselves out of their senses. It is really a question whether all great impostors are not mad, in consequence of first adopting some notion contrary to moral and physical law, and then reducing all their thoughts into keeping with their chosen absurdity and wickedness. Even a pretense, when pertinaciously defended, readily assumes the appearance of a truth to the mind of the ignorant pretender, partly from the readiness with which a weak intellect assents to a pleasing error, but mainly because the falsehood, being adopted from vanity, administers to the maintenance of pride and so quickly intoxicates the soul and blinds it to all evidence opposed to its delirious indulgence. This is illustrated in a forcible manner by Joanna Southcote's monstrous delusion, which may be referred to, the rather, because its history is recent, undeniable, and well known. Joanna was the daughter of a small farmer in Devonshire, and born in 1750. She lived as a servant, of good character, in Exeter. But observe, though she studied the Scriptures diligently, she did so, not to believe them in the true spirit of religion, since she made her duty depend on outward signs and inward feelings, instead of submission to the plain commands of God. She did not worship, but converted the language of religion itself into her delusion, by the heretical device of detaching herself from others, and interpreting the Bible with a private and particular reference to her own person. As usual in such cases, a strong sense of self, with very deficient natural attachments, and no faith, converted all she knew of the Bible or of the universe into confirmation of her egotistic enthusiasm. Pride was the demon that possessed her, and therefore she soon found that she was especially gifted—she had her commission, and of course her credentials were mysterious enough. She wrote prophecies, which were sealed up from 1794 to 1803, and then being scrutinized during seven days by twenty-three persons appointed by herself, it was henceforth decided by them and some of their friends that her calling was of God. The grand object of her mission was consistent with her state of mind; it was of a very personal nature—she was to bring forth the promised Shiloh. The event was year after year deferred, for very natural reasons. She had reached her sixty-fourth year, without producing any thing but promise. The credulity of her disciples was still stronger in its dotage and so was hers. Mr. Mathias, an upright and intelligent medical practitioner, was at length called to testify to the proximity of the grand event, but he found only a tympany, and, protesting against her blasphemy, was dismissed, to give place to an easier believer who was soon found. Mr. Mathias considered notoriety, and the love of ease and of affluence, the prevailing passions of the prophetess. She passed her time in downy indolence, ate much and often, and never prayed until disease began to cure her of her delusion. Her followers, however, were not to be so readily cured. On her death-bed she thus addressed a number of the most prominent, that is, the most wealthy among them:—"My friends, some of you have known me nearly twenty-five years, and all of you not less than twenty: when you first heard me speak of my prophecies, you sometimes heard me say that I doubted my inspiration; but at the same time you would never let me despair. When I have been alone, it has often appeared delusion; but when the communication was made to me, I did not in the least doubt. Feeling, as I now feel, that my dissolution is drawing near, and that a day or two may terminate my life, it all appears delusion." She wept bitterly. —"Mother," said Mr. Howe, "your feelings are human; we know that you are a favorite of God, and that you will produce the promised child; and whatever you say to the contrary, it shall not diminish our faith." Instead of faith, he should have said madness.

Thousands of educated people deluded themselves in this case, but it is evident that there were no Christians among them. It is also clear that pride and vanity deceived them all; but the deception is just of the same kind as that which is the prevailing epidemic—they all thought that they were especial favorites of heaven, and were appointed to enjoy salvation in a convenient and flattering way, with peculiar privileges, under Joanna's red wax seal, instead of rejoicing in the common redemption, and the testimony of a good conscience both toward God and man. These people had no faith in the truth, and therefore they were prepared to believe a strong delusion. And so it is with all who have not their principles fixed on those moral and religious convictions which induce the instant doubt and denial of every thing which flatters self-love, and contradicts the testimony of truth, as established by Divine Providence, consistently working out its revelations from the beginning to the end—from the fall of Adam to the consummating advent of Christ. A rational faith is proved by rational doubts. In her lucid intervals, Joanna could doubt; for reason believes not by fits, nor according to bodily feelings, but by preserving before the mind's eye clear ideas of those objects which God has revealed. But delusions are always both indefinite and singular. Truth is so decided, that she looks at every step, and tries the ground she treads on, because she knows the enemy would entrap the unwary; and yet she is not suspicious, but wise. As, in scientific respects, a supposed discovery, if not congruous and consistent with the known system of facts, may be quickly pronounced a fallacy by all who are grounded in first principles, so in religion, whatever has not a catholic and uniting tendency must be declared to be assumption, delusion, and imposture; and all who have not that charity which would cover the faults of others but yet bring their own hearts to be tried by the manifesting light, may be assured that, whatever they may think of themselves, they are much in the same predicament as Joanna and her silly flock of followers.

The man of faith has distinct intentions, and he knows what he means by his creed. He has clear and defined ideas of his own wants when he prays, and gives good reasons for his strong hopes to those whom he would persuade. His mental objects are even more distinct than those of his senses, for they are the true things which reason discerns as belonging eternally to the design of God in making man a reasonable and religious being, and in creating an endless series of worlds to exercise and develop his intellect and affections forever. But doubt should not destroy inquiry. Every great truth, when first announced, meets with many antagonists, since that numerous class, the conceited, are not at first disposed to give their fellow-men very much credit for superior scientific, rational, or spiritual discernment, however apt they may be to believe, superstitiously, and to exaggerate the renown of those whom it is the fashion to applaud. "Faith, however, is not our reason's labor, but repose."

As the mathematician has his axioms which he can not doubt, and on which he elaborates his demonstrations, so the man who thinks of morality and religion, or his relations to society and to Heaven, must have his fixed and sure principles of argument and mental regulation. These principles constitute his spiritual faith. Hence true faith is the opposite of fancy, and the negation of fanaticism. It is knowledge made vital, and therefore potential. It is truth, so convincingly perceived by reason, as to be a felt and controlling influence. Like wisdom, faith evinces its intelligence in deeds, or, rather, it is the governing and actuating power of the whole being, like a response of the soul to the impression of realities around it. As the sight of an object of interest, whether abhorrent or amiable, pervades all the body with a feeling of its presence, and every fiber of the frame is roused into appropriate action, so the perception of things as they are in their moral aspect toward us, stirs the whole soul with corresponding emotion. Such is the operation of faith; it pervades with its power all who feel it because it sees the true relationship of souls to their source, and to other beings. It is not dependent on intellectual acuteness, but on the entrance of that light which gives understanding and actuates reason. As all objects of interest appeal to the will, so those truths which are the objects of faith influence our desires and volitions, according to our moral perception rather than our mental acumen. Thus we discriminate between the true and the false, as well as between the good and the evil; and it is the mode of the faithful mind rather to detect the false, by feeling what is evil, than by research after the true, to discover what is good. Trusting in God, the soul bears a talisman which indicates the character of whatever it touches. It has something to confide in, as well as to believe; but it often happens that the wise and prudent fail to discern the beauty and suitableness of those revealed verities which come, like light, bearing its own evidence, and making heaven visible to simple minds that trust in God, because they feel his goodness as well as his wisdom.

We believe many things in a casual way that have no influence on our conduct. We do not feel that they have any direct connection with our well-being; we do not experience real faith with regard to them. Thus we read a grand discourse on astronomy, admire it, consent to its truth, its wonderfulness, and then walk out, amidst the glories of the heavens, in pursuit of our pleasures, without thinking of the sun, moon, and the stars, because they seem to have nothing to do with us, nor we with them. Thus, too, we read the Bible, believe in God indifferently, admire his commandments, deem His anointed One the most sublime of sages and of sufferers, and then go about our little businesses, forgetful alike of heaven and its excellences. The divinity of truth has not entered into our souls to live in us like a love unless it rules us. Such is the manner of true faith ; it realizes the fact, that heaven is really engaged about us, with us, and in us.

Faith has an object and end, and employs the appointed means for its attainment. To use the appointed means for the attainment of ends, desired and foreseen, is the business of faith. Like the mariner, whose hope and safety depend on his steering rightly, if we have faith, we can no more neglect to look outward, onward, and upward, than he can fail to regard the chart, the compass, and the stars, while he breasts the tempest, or takes advantage of the wind that wafts him homeward. Skill, chart, compass, stars, and a good bark, may not save the mariner from wreck, but faith never fails—Providence is always for it.

I am speaking of Christian faith. There is a virtue, and there is a power in this faith, not from the logic by which it may be sustained and defended, but from the love which lives with it, of which love it is well said—Omnia tegit, omnia credit, omnia sperat, omnia sustinet. Reason belongs to it, because it derives its light from the Divine Logos, the source of knowledge and wisdom. Its discernment is far above intellectual keenness, since it perceives—and acts accordingly—that not a desire can be induced in keeping with celestial charity, without a constraint upon Almightiness to fulfill it. The very nature of goodness demands this coincidence. True Christian faith is, therefore, incapable of denial. It works with the power of God; for *he who dwelleth in love, dwelleth in God.* Thus it performs those miracles which are wonders only to the ignorant and unbelieving, such as converting a profane man into a wisely devout being, and filling a wretch with peaceful raptures, by creating a new world of sinless thought and feeling within the soul. It is not afraid amidst the billows. It sees and hears, and holds Him who says to the winds, Peace, and to the waves, Be still. Nothing can resist it but the selfishly busy, hard heart of man—and that it strives to soften and subdue, not so much by upbraiding its obduracy, as by persuading it to trust the outstretched arm of Him whose nature and property it is ever to have mercy. It calls no fire from heaven but that which shall kindle a new life to diffuse itself in everlasting blessedness.

Though this faith comes by hearing, it is not by merely hearing arguments. It comes by hearing the Word of God, which does not ratiocinate, because that word is reason itself, and comes home to the heart that is open to it, and commends itself to the conscience as the address of the creative to the created mind. What it speaks is vital truth—the expression of the Divinity. Can a real Christian be found walking in his new life merely because he has been convinced by documentary evidence? If so, there is a delusion somewhere, and Christianity, instead of proving its origin by its divine consistency, contradicts itself. No, it is God-work—a new existence. The Author of this faith declares that he receives not testimony from man, and that the Spirit bears witness because the Spirit is truth. And we do not see how any other witness can be available toward forming the faith of a disciple of Jesus; since, in order practically to know his doctrines in their living power, it is first of all necessary, according to His own saying, to obey His will and do what He commands.

The secret cause of skepticism is the habit of immorality. Bosom-sins make infidels. If a man have no restraint upon the passions but that of his physical convenience and the desire to avoid the reproach of society, he already denies the right of God to com mand him. He does not honor his Maker by obeying His laws, nor will he, because he seeks honor only from man, so that he can not be approved in his conscience, nor clear in his judgment, concerning any question of duty. In short, how can he, whose principles of acting and thinking are not based upon the Divine authority of the moral law, be capable of concluding rightly concerning the religion that grows out of that law? He must be immoral in the fullest sense, and therefore his understanding must be darkened in all spiritual respects. He can not desire to have Christianity proved to him: it would be madness and despair to him, by convincing him of sin, of righteousness, and of judgment, from which he could have no escape until, thoroughly repentant, and changed in soul, he so believe as to embrace the Saviour, who comes as God, to bestow a new nature and eternal life on all who welcome the salvation, and long for immortal honor after the divine method, or in a manner coincident with the plan of God. To seek immortal benefit in any other way, must be to disregard the perfection of the Deity, and to despise the consistency of His attributes.

But, as before suggested, morality itself is unknown without religion; and the religion that is not divine is false, and so must be the morals derived from it. This is confirmed by all the theism, and mythology, and polite usages of the world, without revelation; for without the expression of the mind of God on the subject of duty, however communicated, there is not sufficient truth manifested to elevate the soul of man above his selfishness, nor sufficient motive to cause him to love his neighbor as himself; because the beauty and the bliss of holiness are never seen until the Holy One reveals Himself, either in the law, which speaks His will, or in the gospel, which livingly illustrates it. The man, therefore, who knows nothing practically of the doctrines of the Bible, so far from being capable of purity of conduct, can not even imagine what the word *sin* means. Hence moral ignorance, or, what is the same thing, irreligious education, is necessarily productive both of hardness of heart and obtuseness of mind, with regard to good and evil, whatever may be the sensitiveness to natural emotion, and whatever the intellectual acuteness. The remedy for this is godly training, not task-work, but Christianity exemplified—the light of life. The child nurtured in the charity of Jesus never doubted his Divinity and never will.

That was better than a mathematical demonstration, which the man felt who stretched out his palsied hand when the Son of God said—Do it. The power was in the will which obeyed, because the act of will was faith. Lazarus, and the son of the widow of Nain, did not want reasons beyond their own consciousness, for believing Him who is the resurrection and the life; nor does the man who, having obeyed the word, comes as impotent, to receive power, need any other evidence in behalf of the Saviour's claims than the fact, that, in having come, he feels full of a new life, and delights in the law of love, because God therein binds Himself to be man's salvation eternally. The suitability of a remedy is proved only by its use, and so the evidence of Christianity is experimental, and not a matter either of logic or of hearsay merely. Though a statement of facts is essential to belief, yet the credential of the statement is in the very nature of the facts, and not in the seeming trustworthiness of the persons who announce them. Therefore, if an angel from heaven declare any other, this gospel alone can be true, because in it God speaks to the conscience of man. Truth, like the light, bears witness for itself, to those who can see it.

But it will be said, What is truth? It is Heaven's answer to the demands of reason. It is whatever is true; and, moreover, it is whatever has been or will be, of God's making, in revelation to a soul, and for its good. Falsehood and delusion are whatever God has not made; and if the New Testament did not meet the necessities of the soul, we should be bound to reject it as an imposition. Faith tells the truth, and has courage to own doubt concerning what is doubtful, because, in this world, darkness is as necessary as light. Faith, however, is always positive in will, but it is good-will. It can not hate any thing but uncharitableness.

The manifestation of moral and religious truth is in the moral consciousness; and the arguments of infidels are altogether beside the mark, unless they have obeyed the gospel, and found it not to answer its professed purposes.

The doctrines of the New Testament are so reasonable, and yet so much superior to our reason that it is impossible that man could have invented them. Men really do not naturally like such truths. There is not one of them to be found among the philosophers of heathenism; and those of infidelity may be defied to show any instance in the history of mankind, in which the nature of evil and its cure was taught, except by revelation. So far from this, the Divine nature was acknowledged, only to be dishonored.

He that is not willing to renounce his sins is not ready to receive the Saviour. What men refuse to believe in the Bible is exactly that without which there is no hope nor godliness. They have no notion of being deemed so deeply iniquitous as to require that Omnipotence Himself should redeem them by adopting their nature in a sinless state, and making atonement in it. They do not desire new principles of thought and holy motives of action; they do not wish to exchange their own spirit for that of Divine love. But mercy will be heard, and when man begins to feel that his necessities are eternal, and yet all things fail, and all friends forsake him, and leave him alone to meet death and darkness, then God makes Himself known, at the first cry for help, as the only and sufficient deliverer.

The heavens reveal man's iniquity, and the earth rises up against him. All things conspire to condemn him, because all things demand faith in God, and yet God is not trusted nor sought. The Dispenser of all blessings must meet the evil-hearted in darkness. Their thoughts exclude the light, they can not see out of the solid grossness of their souls. They must still believe and tremble, from the consciousness that the full revelation of the Righteous One is yet to come. The reply to all questions is—Wait. God owns eternity; futurity, as well as the past, is all His, and in that futurity the reason of the present will appear. Such convictions are inevitable to reason, but reason can not bear them without perceiving some clear proof that God undertakes the cause of all who will trust Him, to remove the curse by removing its cause.

Perfect conformity to the known will of God is the object and aim of Christianity, and any thing less than this is not religion, but notional amusement and ceremonious observance. The test of the truth is open to all who sincerely desire to be satisfied, and philosophers have no right to their adopted name if they disclaim the authority of Jesus Christ, before they have strictly observed the rules of His science.

The experiment he proposes is this:—Yield to the will and see the result. Now, who among the scoffers has fulfilled the conditions which may qualify them to judge Christ? Have any of them worked out in their lives and thoughts the predicates of Divinity in the fruits of its spirit—love, peace, long-suffering, gentleness, goodness, faith, meekness, temperance? There is no law against these qualities. Whoever will practice them will know whether God is the Author of

Christianity or not, for no one can practice them without living and walking in the spirit of Christianity, and then, in fact, the kingdom of heaven is in him, and he can no more deny the divinity of the doctrines than he can the reality of his own life and happiness. The theory of divine morals is no more capable of making us moral, in the godly sense, than the theory of sounds can make us musicians. In order to excel, or even to understand excellence, we must practice what we know. The test is simple and perfect. That must be a bad religion which does not teach charity, and we must be bad at heart if we obey not that which enjoins it. Apply this to Christianity. It, and it alone, stands the test. Its Founder demands faith in its purity, faith working only by love—love to God, as the supreme good, and to man, because he is God's. Evil is to be overcome by good, cursing by blessing, malignant treatment by benevolence and prayer. In short, universal good-will, exemplified in the life, is the only consistent Christianity, for that alone is Christ's spirit; and therefore, intolerance and persecution, in every form, can spring from those only in whom His spirit is not.

We see that the rule is most perfectly fair, because obedience must end in blessedness, and the only objection to the required submission must arise from aversion to all that deserves the name of virtue, or else, why not be patient, good, gentle, faithful, temperate, charitable, in the divine sense? He who would be great in soul must endure all that seems contrary to himself, from some mighty love, which shall enable him, with its unconquerable hopes, to stand unshaken as a rock amid the billows.

Patience is the foundation of all virtue, and includes in it all excellences. The patience of earthly ambition is but pride working on in the obstinacy of its own nature. The patience of godliness is like that which would have borne the cross to Calvary, despite the fainting of the body. The love within it is faithful unto death, despising such shame as mere suffering can bring, while demonstrating the charity of Heaven, even toward those who, in their bitter imbecility, sneer at God thus manifest.

The man of faith is, then, a decided character. The instinct of his reason is a strong will, from a strong motive. He answers the questions, What will you do? what will you be? and says, I will walk worthy of my vocation; I will be a son of God. The Almighty allows and grants what such a mind wishes. A man without a determined final faith, an undoubting trust in the true God, is but as a dry leaf on the wings of the wind, carried about by impulses unresisted and unavoidable. As the leaf can not take root, and it rests but to rot, so the faithless man has no living power in him to draw vigor and beauty from the elements. There is no settled hope without faith, and therefore, no going forth of the prophetic and realizing soul into the future eternal firmament of the true heavens; but fancy, instead, makes dreams of memory, and amuses or terrifies with phantoms uncertain as the dance of moonbeams on the sea. Such a mind has no supreme good, for the sake of which every other object is felt to be inferior and to be held in abeyance, to be enjoyed or endured, merely as it may serve as means to the attainment of the grand end—the unalienable possession of that good. If we meet a man asking for opinions, we meet one incapable of making up his mind; he has not found any object for his faith, he is not in love, he is not living for the Being that demands and deserves his whole devotion. His earth may be like the garden of Eden to him; but he walks in the midst of it, as Adam might have walked in Paradise, without God, and without Eve, without the bosom evidence of Divine love to his large human heart, with its power of multiplying objects of love, infinitely and forever.

Christianity, then, is full of motives for us. It is the religion of experiment, research, knowledge, faith, hope, and love. Hence science follows it. Examine, is its watchword, make manifest, bring all things to the light and see how all truth is conformable to the character of the revealed God, and every real discovery is the expression of His mind. Hence the tendency of true philosophy to ameliorate the fall of man Thus beauty is truth, order is truth, law is truth, love is truth, holiness is truth, happiness is truth, because they originate in the Divine will, and are seen in creatures only as evidences of the Creator. We can not account for them without faith in His perfections; noi can we behold their contraries without a conviction that an opposing agency has been permitted, only that Goodness may be manifestly Almighty. Antagonism is universal, that created intelligence might every where know that the Infinite One holds the balance of existence in eternity. Good and evil are positive conditions of God's own existence, as made known to creatures, for He can not be known but as the Author of law, thus constituting obedience—good, disobedience—evil. Created mind must grow by exercise, inquiry must be carried to the utmost, and this it can not be without the permission of evil. It can not doubt enough without this contradiction. Do you say daringly, What is the use of sin? If you feel afraid of its horrible nature, as well as of its consequences, God himself will answer you—it is to prove the love and power of him who cures it, and yet condemns it Penitence is always met by mercy. But, if you would be happy in unholiness, God will yet reveal himself to you—but in fire, for the Divinity is to be seen also as the terribleness of righteousness. Herein is the reason of faith; souls are required to rely upon their Maker as the reconciler of all things to Himself. He must reconcile them by His own acts, because all things are possible with Him. Thus Christianity bids us look to the contrariety within us and around us, in creation, in history, in our own experience, for the purpose of teaching us whose is the power, and to force us upon Jehovah's help, as the only sufficiency of a deathless spirit.

All mystery begins and ends in one word—God. Every mind must be stopped in its progress by pain, unless it turn toward the Almighty. He has imparted to us rational consciousness, that we might feel our need of His guidance, and enjoy it by apprehending that His purpose is love, and that He is our everlasting Providence. We would ignorantly satisfy ourselves, from ourselves and from creatures, but our wants refer us back to Him from whom we wander. He is the competency of our reason, and, whether we know it or not, our spiritual nature demands exactly what the New Testament reveals as the birthright of our regenerated being—to be heirs of God, and to be actuated by an inhabiting spirit that shall respond to the benevolence of the Father who makes the Son of man the inheritor of His kingdom and glory. This is not a mere sounding sentiment, but the necessary result of Divine and human being.

The love that conquers all things is the love of truth. This is the living principle of faith. But absolute truth is the will of God. It can not be a creature's, but faith is given, that is, spiritual strength, to struggle for self-mastery. This power is called into action by insights into the vastness of Divine love, for conformity with which it causes a man to hunger and thirst, because the soul, instructed by Heaven, sees that the happiness fit for man is completed only in fellowship with God. The true believer always connects the moral attributes of Deity with his conceptions of Divine power, and with him, therefore, Providence is but another name for the Creator's faithfulness to His creatures. Throughout the wide universe, Faith beholds evidence that Goodness regulates Might, so that all her expectations are raptures, because all futurity, all eternity, can be nothing but the unfolding of love. Hence Death is no longer the King of Terrors, with uplifted hand ready to strike the trembling heart, but like an angel at the bed of a slumbering child, fanning it to sleep with a lily plucked in Paradise, and filling the soul with visions of Heaven, by blending in brightness before its eyes the sweetest images of earthly beauty and affection.

Charity, in its full acceptation, is nothing but faith in God, applied to one's own necessities, and proved by practice. From this loving faculty of faith it enters into the heart of a man to understand that the doctrine of forgiveness is divine, and shows us how the love of the Father obliterates iniquity, just as the light removes darkness, by destroying it and taking its place. By faith, we learn all things pertaining to the ways of the Almighty, in creation and in regeneration, in the life that now is, and in that which is to come. It sees that the ground of our standing in the *anastasis* is that on which we stand now—the redemption of our nature, and its perfect restoration, through the going forth of salvation from the heart of Immanuel, to all who are drawn to God by trusting to the immensity of love seen in that heart. When our Lord said, "Whosesoever sins ye remit, they are remitted," did he not teach the same truth as when he instructed his disciples to pray—"Forgive us our debts as we forgive our debtors?" If we forgive not those who trespass against us, our Heavenly Father will not forgive us. What must it be to remain unrepentant and unforgiven, with eternity upon us? The terrors of the infinite abyss and of utter darkness may express it—words can not. The devils that believe and tremble may conceive it, but no unbeliever can conceive it *yet*, nor can he until he believes without hope, and has in his heart that faith of fear which excludes love, a state of mind sometimes witnessed here. What if it should last eternally? To be unforgiving and unforgiven, to dwell forever in the burnings of our enmity against the Almighty, must be the fruition of faithlessness, for, without the hearty reception of mercy, sin must grow in its malignity forever.

Good will is one with good faith. We can not show the real spirit of forgiveness without being in a fit state to ask and obtain pardon from Heaven. Although universal charity is the universal law, and all sins abhorred by the sinner are covered by the hand of God, yet forgiveness is the proper business of the Son of man. It is the creature alone that is injured by sin, and the Holy One removes it, because He is the lover of His creatures. He gave the law because He could not but love what He had made, and He gloriously illustrated the nature of His law when He made full provision for curing the consequences of its breach. And it is because the Almighty is the Father and the Saviour, that He insists on a temper in man fully ready to forgive all offense when fully repented of, and this forgiveness is demanded by Him as an evidence of our estimation of His own mercy toward ourselves. But God can be merciful only as the Holy One, and those who would blaspheme His Spirit, by expecting mercy without holiness, have never forgiveness.

We can not overlook or put out of our sight the idea of another's scandal and offense against ourselves, as long as we desire to keep at a distance from him; and what is needed to make a true evangelical alliance is mutual repentance and forgiveness, or a fuller feeling of Divine love, for surely all sectarianism among Christians is a sin against Christians and against Christ. The separation of Christians and their dislike of each other, in consequence of opinions or of forms, seem to intimate that those forms and opinions, of however little importance in themselves, are made to appear of great magnitude by the mist through which they are seen. The true faith doubtless possesses warmth enough in its charity to melt and remove all mere superficial distinctions, not, indeed, by reducing them to a dull uniformity of aspect, but as if into that sea of glass where the full beauty of heavenly light is seen in the variety of its harmonious refractions.

Now we have probably perceived that man is very defective, without finding in his heart and his circumstances strong motives for desiring an increase of faith. So there are motives *for* faith as well as *in* faith, because it is the submission of the soul to reason from the felt fitness of truth to our understandings, and because truth and reason are created for each other, and are one in the All-wise. Hence faith is evinced in obedience to the Divine will, because that will is the best, and alone to be infinitely trusted. God's will, indeed, is the real essence or life of any being, for what He wills it to be, that is its perfection; and we know what His will is toward us—sanctification, devotedness to Himself—a life of light like His. We know the wisdom of heaven, by seeing what it has done, and, if we believe it livingly, it will be manifested in us, either by doing or suffering, with the light and bloom of immortality upon us.

The same power of mind by which we understand that the worlds were formed by the word of God, and that things that are seen were not made of things that appear, is that by which we also believe whatever is consistent with the character of the Creator. The man who, with a pure conscience, is brought into any trial, hopes for deliverance by the Almighty, and therefore will not accept of any compromise with sin or Satan, tyrants or death. He aims according to his hope, and trusts in him who shall abolish whatever is opposed to himself. Men of whom the world is not worthy, and who are rejected by it, are the trusters in God. Having become persuaded and possessed by the truth, or by a distinct consciousness of some Divine attribute in relation to themselves, they are incapable of doubting the existence of whatever may be necessary to the full manifestation of that attribute in their own souls; and, knowing that contradictions exist only in created intellect, they look for the harmonizing of all Jehovah's appointments and permissions. Any act of God, felt in an especial manner by the man of faith, is therefore like a direct promise to his soul, the fulfillment of which is expected without faltering or fear. His reliance is on the Omnipotent. There is no faith but that which endures, as seeing Him who is invisible. But then it is not incongruous and unreasonable. It infers from facts to facts, and judges what to hope from what is and has been. Thus faith looks for life through death, because both life and death are but parts of one purpose in God. It keeps the end in view, and knowing nothing of chance-work, it looks for future things but as the results of things present, since the Divine Being is evolving all events in the revelation of himself as the rewarder of those who diligently seek him. And, as surely as a man yielding to nature, and trusting to feeling and experience, calmly closes his weary eyes at night, with an assurance, rather than a hope, that there will be a sunrise to-morrow; so undoubtingly does the man of spiritual life and consciousness, when the shadows of death fall upon his eyelids, compose himself to sleep, with the certainty of a coming morning and a glory above the clouds.

Such belief is essential to reason, for reason is nothing without religion, since she can not question the perfection of Deity, nor suppose that the design of things is left incomplete, or can fail in execution. But this must be the case if man be made with hopes that end in nothing—with capacities for life and knowledge, and the beatitudes of adoration, to be dashed to the ground like a beautiful vase, either in anger or by accident, from the trembling hand of its maker! There is not any accident with Omnipotence, and the wrath of Love must praise him. What he wills is what we want—and when our wills are coincident with holiness, we can not believe what shall not be.

We have many motives why we should pray for an increase of faith, and not the least is the desirableness of being prepared to meet death peacefully. Christian life, when vigorous, always exemplifies this power of quietly triumphing over the last enemy, because faith realizes the fact of being already risen with him who died for us. But this peace precludes expression. When Dr. Hope was asked by Dr. Latham, shortly before his death, whether he felt quite happy, he replied, "Perfectly so—I could not have imagined the joy I now feel; my only wish is to convey it to the minds of others, but that is impossible. It is such as I could not have conceived possible." Now this was not a false peace, for he afterward said, "Christ is all in all to me."

Faith is the necessity of the creature, without which there is no true idea of existence—for we can not bear to look into eternity without it. There is nothing possible in the trackless future, save to faith; but faith always sees its way, and can not miss it. Though, like Columbus on the waves of an untried Atlantic, it find no guide nor guerdon below, yet heaven above directs it in a right course to the riches of a new world, where all who arrive may exclaim, with the sublime navigator, "It was Thou, O great God, who inspired me and conducted me!"

CHAPTER XII.

HOPE AND FEAR.

HOPE and fear are the great ministers, masters, prophets, and seers of our life. But they are great deceivers as well as great seers, and always prophesy falsely to those who are ill-disposed. They connect the past and the present with the future in their visions, and impart a power to our spirits by which we experience whatever degree of pleasure or of pain may arise from the prospect of the fulfillment or the disappointment of our desires. Hope governs us by promises—and fear, by threats. They have, consequently, an influence on all our motives, and constitute the sole persuasives to voluntary action, with a view to coming events. They are, therefore, involved in the consideration of every part of our subject, and might, perhaps, with propriety have been disposed of without distinct investigation, but that a clearer notion of these emotions may enable us more fully to discern the nature of moral government, and the manner in which anticipated punishment or reward operates on the mind to improve its volitions. Here a world-wide expanse of metaphysical speculation opens before us—the lights and shadows of interminable mysteries are there; but we will not enter, lest both writer and reader should find no end amidst those mazes in which angels have lost their way. There is sufficient of a plain and practical nature to be seen, while we stand on safe ground, and observe what is doing among the denizens of this world, under the persuasions of these eloquent, but also most delusive teachers.

There are three modes in which both hope and fear influence our nature,—by appealing to our instincts, to our natural affections, and to our reason. Our instincts are moved by those impressions on our senses which convey ideas of pain or pleasure, irrespective of moral considerations: thus certain properties of things, being the natural provocatives of appetite, are associated with desire for indulgerce; and, as far as those appetites are concerned, we may hope for the possession of their appropriate object, or we may fear their loss. These instincts imperatively demand attention, since they are the groundwork of our social existence, as creatures dependent on bodily adaptation and supply; and however philosophic may be our habits of contemplation when well furnished with bodily appliances, our reasonings will avail nothing in appeasing the pangs of hunger or of thirst. It is doubtless the prerogative of reason to control the instincts by religious and moral motives, by hopes and fears, in relation to our Maker, our fellow-man, and our family affinities; the body must be so far kept in subjection, as that appetite may be appeased, as a necessity toward higher purposes, rather than indulged, as an end in itself; but yet the physical demands of our existence are so immediately imperative, and so regular in their recurrence, that to reason against their dominion, without providing for their moderate indulgence, is as vain as to bid the ordinances of nature to obey your voice, because the alternation of light and darkness happens not to suit your notions of propriety. Holiness is obedience to law for divine purposes, and God is obeyed, by using the body under the blessed restrictions of Christian temperance; for thus the whole life becomes eucharistic, being dedicated to the Holy One in prayer and thanksgiving. If then, even the devoutest saint must yield, and that in faith, to the instinctive cravings which arise from the state of the body, how shall we suppose that men whose minds are moved for the most part by appetite alone, shall be able to resist them. He must have a strong spiritual faith of some kind who is not a rebel at heart, when called upon by authority to starve, while he sees that the plenty of his neighbor is so protected that even charity can not touch it.

Although reason has no morality but in governing the instincts, yet if the instincts be not suitably provided for, nature is outraged. To offer a book to a man who wants bread, or to promise the advantages of intellectual advancement to one who sees no prospect of obtaining another meal, is to insult the God of providence in the person of his needy creature; and to inform a man of religious duty who has never seen a family virtue, is to tell him of something beyond his faculties. Feed the hungry, clothe the naked, are as binding and as divine as any commands in the decalogue; and the way in which the Almighty teaches the hopes of heaven, is daily to supply the wants which belong to earth; and those who place themselves willingly in the way, so as by the craft of covetousness to divert the gifts of God's bounty from the homes of their fellow-men, are hateful at heart now, and are to be hereafter especially marked as the accursed. To do good, is to communicate to the needy, and to administer comfort to the distressed. This word *comfort* means so much of present accommodation as will allow hope to sit smiling with us in our homes, and prevent the intrusion of any dispiriting apprehensions of coming want. But if hope and comfort be wanting in any dwelling, what can be the motive most prevalent there? Ask what is the temper of a tiger hunted into his lair, and there torn by dogs; and then ask what a sinful man feels, withh is capacity of loving, hating, hoping, and fearing aggravated to the utmost, and having persuaded himself that the selfishness of his potent neighbor has rendered his home a hell. It is true, he may experience even a more intolerable and a more common torment; he may feel that he has brought desolation and misery upon himself and his family by his own guilt. But in either case, how is he to be helped? I say by encouragement to hope, and by his reasons to fear. Let him feel that the condemnation of his neighbor does not deliver himself from judgment. As a rational being, let him be persuaded to exert himself. But how can that be, without hope? Instinct prompts to seek death, rather than to live on in a world without hope; and it will be no wonder, if one who knows nothing of the Divine method of doing justice, should imagine he is fulfilling the law of Heaven, by wreaking his own vengeance according to the blindness of his fury and his ignorance. That man can have no idea of hope, but in relation to his instincts. First, show him plainly how to satisfy his appetites safely, comfortably, and with a sense of home and fellowship and responsibility, and then you may be able to convey to him the idea of a nobler enjoyment and a diviner hope. Give him means; give him something to do for himself; and then instruct him as to what the Saviour has done for him. He will scarcely be convinced of sin by his sufferings; he must be able to look at the reason for his hopes and his fears; he must be softened and soothed by the sacred spirit of kindness bringing proofs before his eyes, that Heaven has not forsaken him, but rather has sent angels to minister unto him, before he can feel afraid of his own sins. The thief on the cross was not converted by his own crucifixion, but because he saw that the Son of God was crucified. *This man hath done nothing amiss*, was his reason for calling him Lord, since his own conscience informed him that, if the righteous suffer, there must be a kingdom beyond this world. The Saviour's good deeds had been such mighty witnesses for him, that his Divinity was plainly seen by the man who felt that he needed salvation;

and thus God ever reveals Himself through those who are obedient to His will; and if we expect to teach the divine character of Christianity without embodying its spirit in ourselves, in deeds of kindness, we are but verbal Christians, ready, perhaps, to give our bodies to be burned in proof of the sincerity of our opinions, and all our goods to feed the poor, for the magnification of our bubble merits; while charity, in the true sense, never moved a thought in our minds or a muscle in our limbs. But there is nothing so terrible as the unresisting gentleness of a soul governed only by truth, and determined to prove it by dying, if necessary, to declare it. It is this that appeals to the Almighty, as the vindicator of the oppressed, the innocent, the obedient; and it proves that Jesus, the Lamb led to the slaughter, was really the Son of God, and that his blood was on his murderers only to save them, if they repented in His name.

We can not, however, make men comfortable any more than we can make them conscientious, in spite of themselves—they must themselves be improved—their souls must be set right before their circumstances can be permanently benefited. Those can not be helped who can not be caused to feel their own responsibility, and be induced to use the means that Providence supplies for the purposes of social intercourse and comfort. The grand difficulty with criminals, in all grades of depravity is to convince them that they are so very faulty as you seem to think them. If their feelings were as sensitive as those who pity them, they would die of remorse; but this is a state of mind rarely known in our prisons, except by those who, under some sudden provocation, have committed violence against those whom they really loved. Hence it is that inspectors of prisons have declared so many of their inmates to be incurable. There is no power in manacles and misery to convince of sin—but a few soft words and gentle looks from Sarah Martin or Elizabeth Fry, or some such firm, fine soul, possessed by God's charity, can bring tears from the heart of any man who is not mad, and even from the mad too. Remorse can have no place in a mind that has no desire for amendment, and that desire can not spring from fear, since fear knows nothing of desire but to avoid suffering. Something morally beautiful must be apprehended, some lovely spirit of encouragement must come, some hope with regard to a better standing for the poor wretch himself must be induced, and then there will be some foundation on which to build. But public justice, in the estimation of criminals in general, is but a cunning trap contrived to catch them, and preserve others from their depredations and violence They commonly no more associate ideas of sin with their sufferings than they would with those of a wild beast caught in a gin. They only think themselves unfortunate in not having their own way, while, at the same time, they grant that you have a perfect right to protect yourself from them. Hope or fear, in a moral sense, they scarcely understand. Such a state of mind may be traced to three causes.—First, a habit of discomfort; secondly, total ignorance of religious, and therefore of moral obligation, thirdly, positive defect of understanding, from some degree of insanity or idiotism. The majority of criminals spring at first from a class that are born and bred in crowded wretchedness, to whom it is an object of ambition and honor to become members of a swell-mob, or to act in the capacity of a meretricious decoy to perdition. Nor can this be very surprising, when we find medical men reporting to the Poor-Law Commissioners thus:—"I attended a family of thirteen, twelve of whom had typhus fever, without a bed, in a cellar—without straw or timber shavings, frequent substitutes. In another house I attended fourteen patients: all lay on the boards, and during their illness never had their clothes off. I met with many cases in similar conditions. Yet, amidst the greatest destitution and want of domestic comfort, *I have never heard, during twelve years' practice, a complaint of inconvenient accommodation.*" This was at Derby, in 1836, *without a famine.* We see that this habit of discomfort and wretchedness exists till it actually destroys humanity, by so blunting the mental faculties, and depressing the sensibilities both of soul and body, as to render men and women incapable of reasoning and acting for themselves. I have referred to a comparatively comfortable place and people; but if we look into the abodes of wretchedness in Ireland, for instance, or only peruse the record scattered to the world in newspapers, we shall find whole families consisting of scores—fathers and mothers, and their parents and their children, sleeping, starving, and dying together, on the same floor, with scarcely a sheet or a blanket among them, amidst indescribable accumulations of dirt from the cattle under the same roof. Thus the malaria accompanying ignorance and want poisons the mind as well as the blood. In this prevalence of inhuman destitution, we see at once the impossibility of moral training, since those decencies of life which form the basis of virtue must be unknown among such herds of unhappy beings. That a state of brain amounting to irresponsible incapacity must certainly often result from this degradation, need scarcely be shown, especially when we remember that raw spirits are the common stimulants of parents in such states (at least in our large manufacturing towns), and that their children consume immense quantities of opium. The business of people under such circumstances, is to place themselves as nearly as possible in a state of mind that knows neither hope nor fear in connection with things around them; and by listless vacancy, or by intoxication, to indulge themselves with dreams in which the soul, unfettered by cold and rigid facts, may vindicate her attributes, and bring into being a world where the wildest affections may riot as they list. The absence of physical comfort, while forbidding its proper enjoyments, and diminishing the probability of its continuance, tends to destroy the hope of life, and of course, also, in every respect, to lessen its value. Death becomes so familiar as to be no longer fearful; the fostering of life is then but a weak instinct, and natural affection only an excitant of desperation. Where half the children die before reaching the fifth year, and seventy-six out of one hundred of these die before they reach nine months, as is the case in those dense places populated by the poor, as in Liverpool and Manchester, we can not wonder that domestic hopes and fears soon die, or live only in confusion.

It is not to be questioned that immorality constantly tends in all respects to degrade human nature, and that the more strikingly from contrast, in highly civilized society; and the strongest proof of this debasing tendency is found in the fact, that neither hope nor fear will rouse those who are once brought down to its depths to make any effort to elevate themselves, unless constantly encouraged and directed and assisted by those who are sustained by Christian motives to work with all their might, as for the salvation of immortal souls.

Those who have no consideration for the comfort of others are in danger of losing their own, just as the man without objects of affection soon becomes a burden to himself as well as to others. This state of indifference to others never occurs without the subjection of the man to some sensual vice that obscures his moral perception, and so far causes him to approach to the state of an idiot. The social decencies gradually disappear, and, as in the awful case of the habitual drunkard, so, in all selfish abandonment, the horrible derangement of the heart daily grows stronger, until reason is at length led captive by the tyrannous fiend. Habitual drunkenness is the type of all vice, and it is that form of madness which is not only the most disgusting, but also the most difficult to manage. Hope and fear lose their hold upon the soul, or have no power to persuade to better conduct. The man can not refuse to destroy himself as long as he can reach the stimulus that shall hurry him to destruction. Imprisonment for a long period is useful to such persons, because it forces on them the necessary abstinence, and allows reason to awake from her frightful trance. But yet, unless a pledge bind the conscience, and the man feel socially engaged to improve, with the consciousness of many eyes being on him, and many hearts interested in his success and watching for his welfare, his hopes and fears will die away, and he will fall again into the slough.

We must raise men's ideas of good and evil, and give them God's estimate of right and wrong, if we would induce them to make effectual efforts to save themselves. The noble hope and the worthy fear of the Christian can alone animate society in the divine manner. The fear that is the principle of wisdom, and the hope that can not be confounded, do not spring out of the ground, but they are communicated from soul to soul, under that ministry of the Spirit in which men taught of Heaven speak faithfully of their knowledge and expectancies. But the child that is informed of no duty but to help itself, and knows no object of interest for his soul, beyond the means of obtaining the meals of the day or a shelter from the weather, hopes and fears only in relation to the bitter pains and savage pleasures of his miserable necessities, nor throughout his stinted lifetime can he riso out of this entire pauperism of existence, unless, lifted by some kind spirit above the direct dead weight of his fleshly wants, he become sensible of his spiritual being and necessities, and, through the teachings and the sympathy of an awakened soul, taste the true privilege of an undying humanity. Immorality and its misery must be great hardeners, indeed, to produce such indifference to life and immortality as we constantly witness among the ignorant and ungodly. But if we look into the facts of such cases, what do we learn? Is it true that the haggard wretch in the condemned cell now argues with the chaplain, that, as he expresses himself, to be hanged is the end of it? Is it true that a life of guilt has been so hard and horrible, that the sinner's only consolation is an endeavor to persuade himself, with a scornful smile, that in a few hours he is to be as if he had never been? It is true. And is it true that that miserable being was once hushed to sleep upon a bosom warmed by a love intensified with the remembrance of Him who drew mysterious life from a woman's breast, and called her mother? Is it true that the culprit is he who was nurtured in heavenly reverence and love, and who, as a child, heard gentle whisperings of prayer for him, from the lips that kissed his pleasant cheek? and did that child's own mother teach him to kneel, with hands upraised in hers, and eyes like hers turned toward heaven, and lisp, Our Father? It is not true. Such a case we can not find. These words of prayer have never been the earliest to form themselves in an infant's language and understanding, without being the last to leave the heart of the man. Many a child trained in godly admonition, has indeed turned prodigal, and been selfish and miserable enough in his waywardness; but in coming to himself, he has remembered his father's house, and with the remembrance came humility and hope; but the unhappy man, who, because he knows not why he should hope, is determined not to fear, has really never been vitally, practically, instructed to believe in God as the author of life and immortality to the guilty and condemned. That is a valid plea with Jehovah, which David utters, "*Thou didst cause me to hope upon my mother's breast.*" Yes, God is the God of hope and patience, and every soul that He has made has a right to depend upon his hand for every help, as long as the claim is made in the name and for the sake of the Divine humanity. Human beings are to be treated in a humane manner. But it requires immense faith to be kind enough to those who seem to have nothing to recommend them to our hearts, but their depravity and their danger. We can not conquer them but with a godlike spirit. We, at least, must have no fear in our love, that we may show them the terrible nature of disobedience, and prove that it is an advantage to die in resisting sin, because there is a life to come. Our life must be the expression of our faith in the eternal decision. "I will continually hope, and yet praise Thee more and more," must be the temper of our spirits, because we hope in the Almighty, in despite of all appearances. This devotedness to God's service and manifest joy in it can alone demonstrate the fearfulness of offending the Discerner of hearts. The most obtuse of criminals, in this manner, can not but see that the pleasure of doing good is a fact; and as there is no power of seeing God without benevolence in one's own heart, so there is no way of manifesting the demands of God upon the conscience without "the visible rhetoric of a holy life," and depraved men never tremble but when they witness this vital mode of preaching righteousness and judgment to come. When Mrs. Fry first addressed the female prisoners in Newgate, she spoke of Christ having come to save sinners, even those who might be said to have wasted the greater part of their time in estrangement from their Maker. What was the consequence? "Some asked who Christ was; others feared that their day of salvation was passed." Ignorance had done its work, but it was not because those abandoned creatures had no taste for truth, but because no one had cared for their souls. With tears of joy they welcomed the formation of schools for their children. Mrs. Fry succeeded in making prisons places of reformation, simply because she set about the work with faith enough for the mighty occasion. The sheriffs, the ordinary, and the governor of Newgate, thought her experiments hopeless. But the humble and meek are always to be exalted, for they rely on something above themselves; faith takes hold on the hand of the Almighty, and passes over difficulties without seeing them. Mrs. Fry, at first, indeed, "felt as if going into a den of wild beasts, such was the yelling and struggling;" but, trusting in Heaven, she labored calmly in love, and great was the change that came over the outcasts—"They soon became harmless and kind;" or, in other words, the kindness shown to them was reflected in their own characters; fear fulfilled its right office, in connection with hope, when opportunity and encouragement were afforded to industry and attention. What they needed was right occupation for their minds and hands—something to accomplish, with a reasonable expectation of pleasure to themselves, and to those whom they could still love; for reformation is impossible without employment and without hope. The wants of the mind being thus supplied, many of those outcasts had reason, as one of them afterward wrote, "to bless the day that brought them inside the walls of Newgate." This was written by one who appeared hardened beyond recall, only because the angel Hope, with her stories of love and devotion, had never entered her miserable home. And who is there among the best of men and women that might not have been equally incorrigible in vice, if those motives had not been presented to their hearts, without which humanity so readily gives place to ferocity, desperation, and madness.

Hanging has been invented as a convenient substitute for Christian kindness; and it has even been thought by grave men who read the Bible, that society has been improved by reflecting on the fact, that the wife of a forger has been hanged for helping her husband ; and it has been deemed to be obedience to God and the Saviour, to take the wailing babe, not a week old, from the bosom of its mother, that she might be pinioned for the scaffold. The criminal code, imprisonment, banishment, stripes, and the gallows, are inventions contrived in vain to cure or prevent those evils which grow in the heart of man. Under the artificial fostering of society, vices of the darkest dye luxuriate to the full. Law can not check them, because acts of parliament do not enter into the affections, and make no provision for their natural exercise and protection, development and prosperity. They provide only for the security of money, and those who have it to spend, or possess a craft by which they may get it. There is nothing in the law to encourage faith, hope, and charity, or to cheer the sensitive soul in its hunger after something it may, in the true sense, call its home and its own. The heart is not instructed by statutes, nor can its rights be defined and defended by folios. It is the Bible alone that presents religion as the refiner of our hopes and our fears; the truths contained in that book are those which alone have force enough to render morality a business of the life, by claiming and controlling the thoughts and feelings, with respect to our eternal relationships, rather than from considerations of any passing convenience. It is God's truth that causes a man to feel that he belongs to God, and is to be judged impartially.

The courts, either ecclesiastical or civil, are alike incapable of vindicating the oppressed and delivering the weak from the wicked. God must do that, and He does. But He has given into the hands of men the means of rendering all that is proper in human emotion promotive of social happiness, and woe be to those who possess those means and will not use them. Every child in the land should feel that he is loved both by God and man; and in love it should be trained with something for its heart to work with. Give it Bible-truths, with all their terribleness of beauty, not in mere letters, but in spirit, by mixing its interests with the interests of those who live out those truths in their daily activities. We want schools, not for tasks of book-work and stitching, but for fellowships in affection, industry, and thought, and wholesome fears. Without heart-work and the morality of homes on the plan of heaven, there is no remedy against the propagandism of hell, with its subtleties of misery, nursing infernal fire in the dark, till it bursts into flames that devour its irrecoverable victims, while society looks on and delicately shudders. Philanthropists, go on—your business must prosper; you work for those who laugh, but you work that they may reason and be saved. By the terror of iniquity, by the terror of the love that can not save the impenitent, by the holiness of Heaven, by the worth of souls, Christian philanthropists go about, like your Master in His work, for by the certainty of death and of life you shall conquer.

But while advocating the authority of kindness and hope, we would not forget that fear is the parent of prudence and the teacher of wisdom; since the anticipation of danger is often its avoidance, and without foresight there can be no preparation. Fear is essential to systematic perseverance in well-doing. There must always be a woe in not doing what is known to be a duty, and the extent of this woe can not be too plainly declared. Even St. Paul felt that he would be but a castaway, if he relaxed in his faithfulness as an apostle and evangelist; but yet fear was not his motive: he was constrained by love and affection and gratitude and hope, though he could have experienced nothing of these feelings, without a sense of the evils from which, through mercy, he was delivered. He felt the fearfulness of falling into the hands of the living God, without a propitiation; and when he understood how justice was satisfied by the just atoning for the unjust, he saw that both reason and affection required the entire submission of the redeemed life to the service of the Saviour. If we feel the terror of being eternally lost, it must be in the fact, that love itself must condemn us, because we are incapable, in our chosen maliciousness, of appreciating the love that would save us. There can be no hope for those who will not accept of mercy; but, of course, with them remains a fearful looking forward to the fiery indignation that must consume every adversary of God. But the energizing fear has always hope to help it. There must be the felt possibility of escape from the object dreaded, or fear at once deadens the soul in despair. Desire is the spring of all action and hope; and therefore, to leave a man without something to desire, which may also be hoped for, is to chain him to death itself. But have men, under the Christian dispensation, a right to deprive criminals of life, except to save life, as in case of deliberate murder? Are we to commend men to the mercy of God and entreat them to trust to it, and at the same time tell them that God in structs us not to show them any mercy ourselves, in any other way than by depriving them of the possibility of showing the sincerity of their repentance and amendment; We must acknowledge the question difficult to answer.

Mrs. Fry in her evidence before the committee of the House of Commons, well expressed the secret of successful government: "I think I may say we have full power among them (the female prisoners), for one of them said that it was more terrible to be brought up before me than before the judge, though we used nothing but kindness. I have never punished a woman, nor proposed a punishment." It is the holiness of this charity that subdues the heart. It would bring peace and order into the home of devils, if it could enter there, for it would bring reverence and hope along with it, like a revelation, as it is, of God himself. Yet fear is necessary; it is the only restraint upon those who have no regard for the interests of others. It is the only counter force to the hopes of the wicked—the only mastery over minds uninformed, uncharitable, selfish; and therefore without the power of punishment there can be no government.

Threatening and violence are the only arguments of those who obey not the law of God. It is but the depraved policy of cowards and hypocrites to resort to such means. Every generous mind can feel the force of generous motives, and therefore the best policy of government is to foster all that is generous, so that men may dread the dishonor of crime rather than its punishment. The opposite system excites a pride and hardihood in vice, and gives crime a coloring of heroism, since it seems to set the villain at defiance, through his fears. But sin soon learns to be courageous, and a conscience that knows nothing of righteousness counts it honorable to brave death.

Those who fear nothing are in the most fearful state; all the danger of carelessness or a false confidence is theirs, and they rush on destruction like the horse in the battle, crying, Ha, ha! There is a natural daring in some minds that seek enjoyment only in the face of danger. Their fiber is so insensible, that they find the common aliment of souls insipid, and as with the rhinoceros, thorns, so to say, are but the condiments that increase their relish; yet they may be led by a child's hand.

The only persons saved from the deluge were those who feared the threatened judgment, for God gives warning, and with it hope, that fear may work salvation, and not despair. Fear is the proper state of guilt, and Cain would have had no protective mark set upon him if, in his terror he had not cried unto God; for he who fears the wrath of Heaven is in a condition of mind to bear being preserved from the vengence of man. As long as there exists in the mind a dread of the just consequences to accrue from evil actions, the man is not incorrigible, as there yet remains a power of amendment, by presenting to him an object worthy of trust, and a means by which he may hope to escape. But if he be saved, it is by hope—by something that inspires a reasonable expectation, something that nerves the arm and animates the heart. Fear may drive a man to the city of refuge, but hope imparts her strength to his limbs by her encouragements, and she runs before to open the gate of salvation, that he may quickly enter.

The love of life is the desire of happiness, a desire not here fulfilled—our hearts being set on wrong objects, since our hopes and our fears equally deceive us. Every conscious creature desires to live as long as it finds it possible to hope and to enjoy, but we are apt to give our hearts to things that can neither be enjoyed nor trusted. If there are more suicides in the world than those believe who call the breath of the body the sole life of man, it is because there are so many men mad enough not to perceive that their Maker has provided a remedy for all evil, and that He will supply abundance and peace to those minds that proceed in obedient confidence, trusting for provision to the hand that guides us on the way. If at any time we feel dissatisfied with the prospect of existence, it can only be from distrust of God or entire ignorance of His nature and property. We fail to look toward the light that flows down upon us from heaven: we have fixed the eyesight of our souls, with all the delirious love of our willful hearts, upon things that neither transmit nor reflect that light; and when our imaginations cease to clothe them with delusive brightness, it seems as if the sun were quenched, and we were left alone with darkness and with death. We then feel the palpable gloom of that hell which is created within the heart, by fear constantly uttering a denial that the dominion of God is love. The faith that then actuates us is but as the trembling terror of a soul filled with the idea of the power that seems to encircle existence with the shackles and scourges of an eternal tyranny. Guilt, that is self willfully seeking gratification without love, must despair when left without a desire that can be gratified but by aggravating its own misery. This doom of darkness appears to be impossible, but from the ignorance and insanity of believing life to consist of what we now possess rather than in what we are, as related to our Creator, both by our hopes and by our exigencies. The passion for death always springs from disappointment, and this arises alike from unwarrantable hope and panic fears. Thus we find that persons who live without religious feeling or a sense that life is the perpetuated gift of God, and who are unconscious of the Eternal's claim upon their souls, think of self-destruction whenever their headlong passions are thwarted by Providence. There are others who are driven to despair by false notions of religion. If they think of God, it is with no knowledge of His grace, imagining that He can forsake and forget them, just like those creatures whom we unduly trust. They take the evidence of their own emotions in testimony of the character of the changeless One, and therefore they can not know Him who is really seen only as the Saviour. They mistake the weariness of their own nerves for a sign of being appointed to perdition, while at the very moment they are invited by all the tenderness of Jesus to partake of his rest. Oh, that we always believed the words and deeds of God! Our own evil will would then no longer conjure up a relentless avenger to pursue us beyond refuge, but we should see that He who is the Just is also the Justifier. There may be, and, indeed, often is such a vision of sin in the heart, as to induce self-abhorrence and consequent despair; but it is an error, or rather an entire confusion of things that differ, not to see that sin is hateful because it is inhuman, and that man should not so regard his own nature as to forget that the Lord of life has created and redeemed it for his own glory.

We must not overlook the physical connections of despair. A brain that can not rest will be apt to cause hopelessness, from the bare irritation of restlessness, because the mind must feel destitute of all remedy when the nervous system can not sleep. The state of the body then becomes like that which accompanies the most painful emotion, and the muscular actions resorted to for the relief of the undefined uneasiness, together with the central disturbance of the brain, produce a reflex operation on the mind, and fix upon it an accumulation of despondent ideas which frequently result in a madness so complete, that moral discernment is lost in the hurry of confused emotion, and the destruction of the body seems the only mode of escape from the misery that is in it. The earliest appearance of this state should be met by the fullest sympathy, entire exemption from all demand, with change of occupation and of scene, with opportunity to use the muscles rather than the mind; but, above all, the calm of religious hope is the medicine for the troubled heart and the weary brain.

Religious despair is never witnessed except where revealed truth is either partially known, while some essential part of it is practically concealed, or else where the conduct contradicts the faith. A change of heart is demanded, but the free gift of the Spirit to that end, for all that ask it, is perhaps not positively announced or accepted. The heinousness of transgressing against a righteous God is fully and properly exhibited, and then, perhaps, so far from showing that He is waiting to be gracious to all that come, the terrors of an unknown reprobation are proclaimed, instead of the reconciling efficacy of the cross. Thus sensitive spirits are driven to despair. They feel the serpent sin coiling around them, and crushing them with tortuous embraces. The poison works within them mightily, but the antidote they can not reach. The prevention of this awful malady is to be found only in the loving education of the faculties, and in reliance upon Him who surely will impart the blessing he has promised to all who seek it. From the earliest dawning of light upon the mind let it be busy with appropriate objects, and be taught from the first that the proof that God hates sin is the fact that He loves every body. That blindness of soul which does not permit a man to know the fitness of the provision made for our nature in all its needs, can be cured only by the finger of God. With Him all things are possible, and therefore we dare not to talk of despair while professing to trust in Him. He carries on the training of our spirits beyond the grave, and causes the minutest seed of living faith to germinate and unfold into the fruition of eternity.

"*Timor fundamentum salutis.*" Yet fear itself is proportioned to our hopes, and our dread is rather to lose what we love than of meeting an indefinite evil.

Terror can not persuade those who have no hope, and desperation is beyond the influence of fear. The doctrines of the New Covenant are terrible to impenitence, but inviting as light to the repentant. Eternity offers nothing to be hoped without faith, and therefore there is no room for presuming on a salvation if not sought now; for hope is a present and praying principle. He who fears God is afraid of nothing but sin, because he knows that nothing else can injure him. Thus Luther said, "Let them threaten me with death, with torture and the stake—what is all this to me? It makes no impression on me. It is the merest trifle to the agony I endured in my religious life before I found a Saviour."

CHAPTER XIII.

LOVE.

Faith is the test of love, and love is the test of faith. We can not believe and love, but because faithfulness and love are manifest in deed. Thus our Father in heaven never calls upon us to endure, as seeing him who is invisible, until he has demonstrated his claim upon our hearts. He gives us occasion to trust when he has taught us to love; but only that faith and love, growing together, may find a fuller bliss in further evidence of His favor.

If then you would train a child aright, imitate Heaven. Above all things make him believe you, because he has reason to love you. Let him feel and hear and fear your authority, because you obey and are bound to obey—God. Let him know who holds the absolute right to rule without being doubted; and that as Christ has commanded you to train the child for Him, you do so because the source of power is the source of good. A child needs not much reasoning; he is convinced intuitively. Let him feel that you *have* right, by feeling that you *are* right. But when that child begins to say, "why?" know that fallen reason is urging it to further exercise of faith and love; therefore answer it in the language given you by God, for if that child's soul be not thus met with admonition, godly nurture, and instruction, it will speedily obtain delusive answers for itself in false desire and fearful credency. Good education is the training of the mind to good feeling—the communication of intelligence in love and faithfulness—in short, religion: but bad education is whatever induces a mind to distrust others rather than itself, and sets it selfishly at work to find satisfaction in knowledge without love, in facts without faith, in dependence on the senses for sufficiency rather than on God.

Love, itself may abuse power. Howard was, as a philanthropist, a blessing to the world, but, as a father, however affectionate, he seems to have been unwise; a mistaken sense of duty caused him to pierce his own heart. He thought it his duty to insist on obedience merely on the authority of parental power, instead of enforcing it by the attractiveness of fatherly feeling and consistency. Natural faith and affection are not blind, but well able to distinguish their proper objects. He taught his child, while still an infant, not to cry, and never in all its childhood permitted it to have what it demanded with tears! God forbid that our Father in heaven should thus treat us. He expects us to be in earnest. But, said Howard, the government of a being that can not reason a bout the fitness of things should be only coercive and in fear. He overlooked the discernment that is keener than reason he forgot that the heart has to be educated as well as the head, and that it is ruled aright only as long as love is visible in power. A child that must always govern its feelings, from fear of others, will soon be a hypocrite and a tyrant. When the fetters upon it are removed, the soul will rush into selfish extravagance. and, perhaps, perish; like a bird from a cage, unfit to use its wings, and aiming only at pleasure, while incapable of providing for its own wants. Thus Howard's son was in infancy coerced, without fondness; in youth, *commanded* to be moral; in manhood, became debauched, and then mad.

If a man's heart be governed by love for God, he may trust to its naturalness for the proper expression of that love in all his relationships. It is, however, very easy to say that we love God, and yet deceive ourselves.

We can not love Him without loving holiness and hating evil. But we know neither what is evil nor what is holy, until taught of God to estimate the loveliness of his own character. We must see the beauty of holiness, before we can desire to be holy; and this we learn from the fact, that every doctrine that is divine begins and ends in love. If God were not Love, how should we have thought that was His name? An evil spirit never suggested that word. God must have revealed Himself ere we could have believed it. There is no Almighty Love among the worshipers of evil spirits—they tremble in their idolatries, and know nothing of a power to cast out fear. Nor should we have found a way out of torment, had not God himself come to dwell in humanity among us. To know the true God and eternal life, is to know Him whom God has sent. If, then, we would govern rightly either the passions of others or our own, we must evince the divine life as a power utterly opposed to all evil, and bound to resist it even unto death, and make ourselves a sacrifice rather than resign that which alone is really life.

The law of love is the law of liberty. Supposing we were at liberty to choose our own pleasures, should we decide on self-denial, as the beginning of bliss? If the care of oneself is virtue, as we are taught by some who treat largely of our moral constitution on physical principles, then, of course, self-denial is foolishness. But mere self is not the main motive any where in nature. Love is stronger than death; and love is the law of Heaven, written in the hearts of all creatures. From the lowest impulse of natural instinct up to that of the highest angel, the sense of others absorbs that of self; and all happiness is found in that intensity of feeling that blends self-consciousness so completely with the sense of some beloved being, as to render them but one. Even among the lower animals, the love of offspring is mightier than that of self-preservation. That is a beautiful but yet common kind of fact which Hogg, the Ettrick Shepherd, relates.—"We had one very bad winter, so that our sheep grew lean, and disease carried off many. Often have I seen these poor victims, when fallen down to rise no more, and even when unable to lift their heads from the ground, holding up the leg, to invite the starving lamb to the miserable pittance that the udder could still supply." How many a human parent endures the bitterness of this world with heroic front for the sake of his little ones, but for whom he would prefer to hide himself and die! Thus, by love, our Maker provides for our spiritual progress, amidst the trials of our affections, and if we know Him, enables us, in their very agony, to approach most nearly to Himself, in the apprehension of *His* charity who heads the army of faithful sufferers, and will ultimately lead them, triumphant over self, to that home of rest where excellence shall no more need denial, but where intelligence, effort, and experience, shall completely, and forever, harmonize with love. "Endure, as seeing Him who is invisible." Tribulation is the channel of blessing. Love mingles its virtue with the troubled waters, and a weak man, who enters them with faith, grows strong in soul as he struggles with the wave that would otherwise overwhelm him. He breasts it, and rises above it, and returns to the work of life no longer impotent. But it is He who asked the man if he would be healed, and who touched him, and said, "Go—sin no more," that must be still the healer. It is only from a consciousness of what He is to us, as the Saviour, that we can fulfill the duty of bearing trouble, and walk in the dignity of a citizen of heaven. "*Endure as seeing Him who is invisible.*" Where is the man with a heart that would call that woman unhappy who should lose her own life in rescuing her child from the flames? or who is there among men, who would love him who could never do a good action without calculating how it might be accomplished without hurting himself? The infidel system of morals knows nothing of love in its Divine forms, and its abettors would have scoffed, as those like them did, at the Man of Sorrows, who bowed His head as He hung upon the cross; they could not have seen what faith learns from love—that the Son of God suffered Himself to be immolated merely to demonstrate what love can do to win hearts and to teach men to understand the nature of the mercy they would trust.

We can not, if we would, live only to ourselves; heaven and our hearts forbid it; the eternal future of weal or woe forbids it; the revelation of God in providence and grace forbids it; and Christianity is, in its spirit and its deeds, a total denial of this self. But the law of Heaven is not incongruous; it enjoins love, and so orders causes and consequences, that the obedience of love enlarges the power of loving, and with it the capacity of obeying and enjoying. And there is no substitute for love: when this is wanting, its opposite is present—those who obey not love, submit to fear, and fear is the most cruel passion in the world; since it will commit any crime to calm itself, if only for a moment, although the more wickedness it commits, the more is its torment. Now this must be the government of infidelity; and what are its modes of action and rewards, the outrages of the reign of terror may, without comment, suffice to show. Where a righteous God is not acknowledged, there the very love that is divine *must* form a hell, and rule in fire.

Love can not be partial, but, nevertheless, it must be according to faith. Most persons will own that the law of love is a beautiful law for the government of spirits in general; but, unfortunately, the majority of persons condemn themselves as often as they make this acknowledgment. They well approve of being treated according to the rule of a considerate and charitable regard for all their own interests, but some blinding conceit, or selfish deception, hinders them from acting on this rule with regard to others. "Love thy neighbor as thyself," is mentally applied as a Divine direction for the regeneration of society; but we are apt to forget that the renewal of our own minds in the spirit of this law is the only proof that we feel its value. It is possible to make ourselves so completely our own objects, as really to look at nothing else with any degree of love, and then to render it the business of life to be adulated and admired. The passion for human approbation scruples at nothing that may serve to win applause; and men can imitate demons from a desire to be idolized. But the true hero is not ambitious of distinction. He wishes, indeed, to rise to the height of excellence, but he aims not at being alone in heaven; he loves others as himself, and believing in God as the source of blessings to the innumerable company that walk alike in light, desires all the families of mankind to be as the children of one Father. His idea of love is the love of Him who would have all men to be saved and to come to the knowledge of the truth; of Him who laid down his life for his friends, that they might *be made perfect in love*, and be with Him in glory. The love that can not bear all contradiction and injustice, in order to remove the curse upon prejudice, is a love that can not stand the test; it lives not in the faith of God, and therefore will endeavor to excuse itself from obeying the command that requires the manifestation of love to others in spite of their hatred. Love is due to none, if not to all—and if to all, it is not because we have any especial right in it, but as the common gift of God, like the sunshine that falls equally upon the just and the unjust, although none rightly enjoy it but those who feel that light is love, for without faith in the Giver we find no spirit of goodness in the gift.

Love makes the character of a man, and the selfish are the miserly, who, in their eagerness to possess, lose the power to enjoy, and set themselves at their right value, as worth only so much in pounds sterling, to be used by their heirs and undertakers.

Unhappy man—most wretched of all disconsolate lovers—in love with thyself! Most unworthy is the object of thy affection; but, alas! it will incessantly obtrude itself, and utterly shut out even the capacity of enjoying a pleasant thought. How can *he* rest upon his heart's love, who is forced to show himself so much attention as to exclude all other objects, as if God had not another creature worthy of his care?

Even Narcissus saw something to admire: though but the reflection of himself, it returned his smile; but he who thinks only of himself, sees nothing that can permanently please him. The world of light is a blank creation to such a soul, and compared with it an oyster at the bottom of the sea is a princely being, since it voluntarily opens its shell that life may play about its heart; and when the sunshine reaches down to its home it feels that it is alive with its neighbors; for even the creeping things in the great deep have senses, and rejoice in the use of them.

The Maker of man designed him to be unhappy, except when his heart is engaged in making others happy. This is the only way in which man can imitate God; and though man can create nothing for himself, yet his proper satisfaction is not otherwise than divine when rightly using divine gifts. We are to behold that God's works are very good, and we are so to feel the goodness that they manifest, as livingly to express the benevolence of their Maker. He gives us senses to put us in relation to all outward sources of delight: He gives us reason and affection, that we may think and love; He gives us will and muscle that we may hope and act. Thus we are called on to attend to every thing rather than ourselves; and not to live in the enlargement of our souls as unequaled and unmatched but by minds in communion with each other, with God and His universe, is to frustrate the purpose of our being. We are to be happy, but only in living activity and in sympathy with happiness. We are to produce joy, in order fully to perceive it. We are to look for smiles, and so act that those about us may always meet us with a cheerful face and a confiding heart.

Love judges righteously. If we judge our friends before we judge ourselves, we condemn *them* for the evils that are in *us*, and are thus in danger of feeling hatred, and entering into the fire unquenchable. *That* charity begins at home and ends there, which does not act with a clear conscience. *If you love those only that love you, what thanks have you?* That is the love of men, who think they can find nothing in themselves to be hated and avoided. Christian charity is of a holier order; it repents of the evil at home first, and then, finding the pleasantness of the light that shines into the soul from heaven, sets about awakening other hearts to a sense of their own evils, only that they may reap at length the joys of goodness. God being on the side of this love, it fears the power of no adversary, and feels indeed, that enmity is destroyed so far as concerns itself. This Love has, in fact, no enemies, except in the will of those who oppose it; but, as they can do it no harm, and it can do them great good, it embraces them with prayer, and would teach them the secrets of a new nature. As charity thinks no evil, so it speaks none. It meets even Satan himself with becoming dignity, and would not ignorantly abuse a power it understands not, but says, "The Lord rebuke thee." And how did the Lord rebuke the Prince of darkness? Not by accusing him, but by meekly telling him the truth, and so defying him. To accuse and to calumniate is the fallen spirits' own business, and they are his advocates who imitate his doings.

How great must be our proneness to evil, and how vast our demand upon long-suffering mercy, since, though good and evil have been equally before us all our lives, yet, in spite of our convictions, the evil most readily cleaves to our mind. The ideas that most prevalently haunt our souls, in solitude or in society, the readiest associations of our memories, either in profane places or in sacred, are still of a kind that should make us ashamed of ourselves. But we scarcely blush so deeply as we ought, even though they present themselves and come in the way when we would bow in spirit before our Maker. Indeed, so little do we faithfully realize the perversity of our affections, that our very prayers, whether in godly words before our eyes, or in God's own language on our lips, are offered rather as carnal wishes, to be gratified for our pleasure; than as the real wants of a guilty spirit needing to be purified. O thou holy searcher of hearts, cleanse thou our thoughts by the inspiration of thy Spirit, that our love and our desires may be fit for heaven.

Love is antagonist to self-will. Self-will in man is self-love, and this is always murderous, because it is lawless: seeking only the gratification of impulses as the only reason for action, it necessarily becomes enraged at any will opposed to its own. It aims only at destroying what it dislikes. It can not submit, because it can not trust nor give credit to any authority that would regulate its violence. It can not tolerate any order but its own, and that is seen only as a desire for the destruction of every impediment to the reign of its own growing tyranny. It may exhaust its means of action, but itself is still the same, and it can neither be expended nor be made to repent. This self-will slew Abel and slew Christ, merely because they were willing to obey, and, as sons of God, worshiped and served in a way appointed by Divine wisdom rather than human will. It converts natural attachment itself into occasion for its worst exercise. Thus, when James and John knew Jesus only in the light of a natural affection, as a good man in his earthly appearance, they would have called down fire from heaven to consume those Samaritans that would not receive him. Now God in Christ is constantly opposing this spirit. Those, therefore, who think they worship him aright, and yet with a pious self-will set up their own authority, deceive themselves with a notion that they are serving the Holy One and the Just, while they are only pleasing themselves. They know not their own spirit, nor that the spirit of truth is the spirit of love, or they would not vilify their brethren and devote them to perdition, because they walk not with them. The only cure for this Satanic disposition for exclusiveness and vengeance is to know God as Love, and submit to Him. Thus we shall find the highest motives and the highest bliss in renouncing the natural impulsive self, and partaking of the very selfhood of the Divine nature, be wholly governed by Jehovah's spirit, with a consciousness that his will is holiness itself and happiness.

The innumerable conflicting elements of human passion are ordinarily set in motion by this unsanctified self-will, and therefore we see throughout history and on every hand, lawlessness at work to obtain forbidden ends, and struggling with a burning zeal to reduce society to clanships under opposing heads, by systematizing religion itself on the principles of hell. The remedy is plain—obey God. But we may pray and sing praises in the name of obedience, while yet adoring only our own blind wills. The spirit of Heaven must be in us before we shall really obey, and this spirit does not so much command us as constrain us to act with the charity that never fails, because it absorbs our hearts in devotedness to our Maker and Redeemer, and therefore induces us in truth to love our neighbors as well as ourselves, because they equally with us are loved of our Father in heaven. Thus the only sufficient motive for self-denial is that which our Saviour felt—a benevolence that knows no will but the love of God.

Christianity proposes an excellent way for the settlement of all disputes; it sets up love as superior to all other authority, and as the only interpreter of God's mind. If any teaching tend to encourage an overbearing temper, or the assumption of a right to dictate to consciences, except by preaching the charity of God's word, it evidently comes not from above. Whoever endeavors to secure advantage to himself, or his party, to the prejudice of others, is not moved by the spirit of Heaven, and the only proof we can afford of our believing the truth must be seen in our practice of charity. This is the only spirit that is infallible: it works with the hand of the Almighty, and trusts to the decisions of the All-wise, and presents God himself as the salvation of all who submit to Him in faith, hope, and love. The church must fail to persuade the world until it is visibly one in the light of its love, for it is not the temple of God unless His glory manifestly dwell in it. The word of life is the lamp of light. It is utterly vain and vexatious for men to dispute about the significance of this or that doctrine, creed, form, or ceremony, until they feel the love that thinketh no evil; for until then God is not with them, and therefore their discussions must end, as they began, in darkness, distrust, and ill-will.

Love is the mainspring of all action and enjoyment

but its might is revealed only by its trials, and that is a mockery of love that is not faithful unto death, because all things perishable must terminate in that. But it is in the nature of love to live on with growing strength to the end, and it brings a man up to the very entrance of Hades, with his whole soul transformed into the likeness of his prominent love, as if to intimate that he must thus appear before the Judge of spirits; and according to the character stamped by his affections upon his life, be appointed to his everlasting place and fellowships. We become like what we love—the will is the man himself, as regards desire, action, thought; and to know the state of a man's will is therefore to know his spiritual standing as God sees it. In order, then, to become godlike, we must love God. But how can a creature of such conflicting passions, and with a mind debased by attachment to the meanest objects, be capable of turning his attention from the attractions of forms and colors and voices, which he calls beautiful, to contemplate invisible perfections? How can we cease to seek satisfaction through the senses, that we may possess it in our souls? This change implies the presence of a transforming spirit; it is equivalent to a new creation; every faculty must change its place as well as its employment. It is effected by a word, but it is a word that not only creates light but also the power of seeing, and is itself dwelling in all that it produces. God speaks and it is done; the man who lived in the world of sensation begins to breathe in the world of spirit; the heart that was agitated by earthly emotions is awakened to the consciousness of heavenly affections; the mind that deemed the play of shadows and the impressions of the elements on his nerves to be truth, now exercises a discernment that reaches far beyond the region of the senses, and is impressed by objects worthy of an eternal love. The soul of the true believer like the [illegible] at deep, may be agitated on its surface by passing winds, and be partially darkened by clouds and eclipse, but while earth influences its currents, it is still penetrated throughout by the attractions of heaven, and the light of other worlds is always on its bosom.

By faith man sees God. He recognizes Divinity in all that the universe utters of excellence, and he loves with a true adoration, because he feels that the united attributes of his Maker constitute the one perfection of beauty. He no longer perceives Jehovah in divided properties, but in his personal majesty and goodness, not as an abstraction, but in relationships, and that not simply to existence as a whole, but to himself as a member of His family; and feeling the gentleness of His gracious hand, the new man responds to the touch of his Maker, and, like a son, from the heart exclaims, not only "My Lord and my God," but also "Thou art our Father."

But we can not thus love our Creator without sympathy with Him. We need not merely to believe in the Almighty, but also in Immanuel. God must be *with* us. We can not sympathize with an unrevealed Deity, and he can not be revealed to us but in our own nature, since there is no other way in which we can have communion. Love must be humanized in order to be known by us, since the principles of Divine and human existence in fellowship of spirit, knowledge, love, and truth, require us to see exactly, and in demonstration, what obedience signifies—even the fulfilling of the law to its most perfect illustration, as the expression of Divine love to reasonable and yet sinful creatures. Hence the beauty of God is seen in Jesus, since no other being ever gave us an idea of perfect love, or a love without a motive beyond itself. Heroes have been worshiped because of their exploits, but there is not one among the host of the great doers that a little child could love for his deeds. Earthly heroes are all helmeted, and the nodding plume bears terror in it to every simple heart; but the majesty on the brow of the Lord Jesus was that meekness that would invite a little child to smile in his face, and cause all heaven to bow down in love, while smilingly He whispered of happy things to the trustful being in His arms. He took them in His arms, and blessed them. That is the place of blessing. May we be as His children—believing, sustaining, blessed.

O Lord Jesus, all miracles are performed in thy name! Impart thy spirit to us, that we may so use thy words as to feel ourselves passed from death, and able to call the dead to behold thy life, and live like thee and with thee, in the glory everlasting of thy love. "The true morality is love of thee." It requires that all the demands of the soul should be satisfied from thy fullness. Complete salvation is what we need—a well-being that can not be disturbed. But this can only be obtained by union with Him who is one with God; and this is possible only because our individual welfare is one with the glory of the Redeemer. In Him we have sympathy with Heaven, because love is infinite; in Him we learn the significance of duty to the Deity, because He has fulfilled all righteousness, and shown us how obedience is love. Thus we gain the highest good, since thus the peace of God is brought by love to our consciences. This delight of the soul in the law of God is opposed to all disorderly and mean desires, and, in fact, the warfare of the Christian consists in maintaining a struggle against all inferior motives, from the transcendent excellence of this love. Hence it is manifest, that as man possesses no sufficient motive for self-denial without a Divine communication, so it is impossible for a man to be truly moral without being religious. He can not feel bound to consider the happiness of his fellow-beings unless he feel bound to obey God, and he can not faithfully acknowledge his obligation to God until he knows somewhat of the love of God. There is an especial adaptation of the necessities of intelligent creatures to the spiritual bountifulness of the Creator, and we are capable of attaining to His love, because He has made provision in the new covenant to meet every demand upon His mercy, without denying that of justice, since, in conferring his favor as obtained through Christ, He imparts his own spirit. Therefore, we can not ask too freely from the giver of all good gifts, since in proportion as we ask we receive, and in proportion as we receive we are made like God, and therefore meet for the inheritance of the kingdom where love reigns, in all its manifestations, as God revealed in man.

Human love can not reach content until it rests in God. We shall surely find, that the affection and the friendship that lead us not to the fountain of life, will deceive and afflict us, and leave us amidst the shadows of death, seeking rest and finding none. The soul of man must, in all its attachments, tend either to heaven or to hell. The spirit within us is either holy or profane, and either opens the heart to admit the reproving and rectifying light, or wraps it up in darkness to brood over sin. Every character is known by its affinities, and reason is distinguished by its relationship to the Divinity. Hence rational love is always religious; it realizes a sacramental meaning in all its engagements; it feels full of eternal life.

As Adam received the companion of his nature and being from the hand of Jehovah, as an everlasting evidence of Divine love accommodated to himself, and as that love constituted man and woman one in all the purposes of existence, so all real love unites those who feel it as heirs together of the same life. Any thing in the name of love beneath this is mere passion, either instinctive or Satanic.

Since all true love is so far Divine in its nature as

always to conduct the soul to God, for safety and satisfaction both for its object and for itself, whatever has the opposite effect, has in it the spirit of idolatry There are three kinds of passion especially idolatrous which yet are designated loves—the love of wealth, avarice; the love of praise, ambition; the love of bodily pleasure, voluptuousness. They all set up something to be worshiped, not to symbolize, but to conceal the claims of God. The most dangerous is the most fascinating,—that incontinent love of mere beauty of person and pleasure of sense, which, when suffered to possess the soul, holds it in captivity, like the demon which the disciples of our Lord could not cast out; it needs an Omnipotent interference, as well as fasting and prayer. This unloving spirit of false pleasure, impiously absorbing the soul in the flesh, is the type and the reality of all God-forsaking. Every thing that has true love in it is lawful because love can neither tempt nor yield to temptation without denying itself, since it seeks pleasure only by being blessed in blessing, and therefore can not deviate from the path of obedience, faith, and honor. A man can not love an object that he would injure, for it is of the nature of love to constrain to any self-sacrifice for the sake of its object; it always speaks and acts after this manner: "What ye shall say unto me, I will give. Ask me never so much dowry and gift, and I will give according as ye shall say unto me; but give me the damsel to wife."

The worst of all mockeries is a marriage without love, a yoking together, but not a union, bondage without a bond, a multiplication of all the burthens of life for both parties, without a mutual life-interest, and like the offering of a whole family to false gods, whose demands are never satisfied, because, whatever the sacrifice, there is still no atonement. Too many matches are made in a confusion—they have no faith in their composition, and therefore an abundance of sin. There may be sincerity enough in them, but too often it is sincere selfishness; a sense of God's favor has nothing to do with it; the compact is a merely civil affair, as if the Lord of life had not instituted nuptials to evince His own love and dominion, His own union in power with submissive humanity, so that command and obedience should be the expression of one spirit, and that spirit, love. The chief concern of this life is least understood—the science of union is not studied, the principles of peace and of happiness are lost in commercial relations, or left to the discernment of minds blinded by passion. In this artificial state of society, nature attempts sometimes to vindicate her own majesty, but, being thwarted in every direction, the heart usually becomes attached to inappropriate objects, and either cherishes its own maudlin romance, or resigns itself to some ignoble decision, that plants a thorn in every step of life. Those who do not think that their hearts need any instruction from their Maker, will, of course, be indifferent about the doctrines of revelation on the subject of love, but they will learn, perhaps too late, that in this, as in all other matters that belong to the soul, there is no security but in following Divine guidance. Where the spirit of Jesus is, there is liberty, and there only, and he who chooses to act without submission to the mind of Christ is so far not a Christian. The ethics and true philosophy of every form of love are found in the New Testament, and it will be quite enough for all practical purposes if young men and women will study and apply the philosophy there taught, for then they will find no danger in each other's society. They will there see what sobriety means, and if, under the laws of nature and of providence, they should be drawn into closer association, it will be in all respects a sacred adaptation for the help of each other's faith, in mutual confessions of faults, and in mutual encouragements to trust their God, as the source of hope, faith, love, and joy. Far be it from us to deny that almost every heart has something of sincerity in its love. This would be to assert that mankind are more generally governed by the intellect than the heart. But the love that is most sincere is almost always the most impolitic, and therefore society protests against, condemns, and punishes it, or else some passion of a more hardening and ambitious character is in the mean time roused up in the bosom and banishes the true love from the thoughts, or forces it to give way to the prouder tyranny. There are but few who have not felt the potent and transforming touch of a real, generous, unselfish love, if not in their own hearts, yet in appeals of other hearts to theirs. It is this apprehension of love, as a thoroughly unselfish spirit, that lights up the conscience, and whispers, with a mighty voice, commanding us to confess that love had rightful claims upon us, which have been awfully resisted, and must hereafter be vindicated even in our woe. It is love that inspires hope, and makes salvation possible. It is love that redeems the lost, and preserves the blessed; it is love that brings a man to judgment and condemns him; it is love that calls true hearts to inherit the kingdom of the Father; it is love that stamps perdition upon faithless spirits.

All who have felt the purity and power of unselfish affection, with an acknowledgment that to be just or to be happy they should obey it, must feel self-condemned in the remembrance of those motives that have induced them to act in defiance of its dictates. It was probably thus that the mind of Napoleon, when, under disease and weakness, he approached the verge of the spiritual world, was brought to reflection. Then the one whom he had most injured came to him in vision, as if to reprove in order to encourage him, by intimating the undying nature of love, and to call up, in the fallen and desponding man, a consciousness of the wrong he had wrought, and to prove that the best hopes of the heart are associated with quiet, relying, and domestic affections, and that life is worth nothing without a love that endures all things, and survives death.

"It was on the 26th of April, after a calm night, he said to Montholon, with extraordinary emotion, 'I have seen my good Josephine, but she would not embrace me; she disappeared at the moment when I was about to take her in my arms; she was seated *there;* it seemed to me that I had seen her yesterday evening; she is not changed—still the same, full of devotion to me; she told me that we were about to see each other again, never more to part. She assured me of that. Did you see her?' Whether it were a feverish dream or a real and actual vision, its purpose was equally experienced. It impressed its moral on the few melancholy hours which now lay between him and the grave."—*History of the Captivity of Napoleon at St. Helena, by General Count Montholon.*

What is it to have resisted the claims of natural affection and the appeals of a true love but to have resisted the Almighty? He speaks to us by all that would invite us to the active fellowships of benevolence and peace, and it must be the felt contrariety of will to the love that constitutes the brightness and bliss of heaven, which kindles the flames unquenchable, and gives its life and venom to the gnawing worm that can not die. But the suffering of guilt is not the final object of reason and of faith—it is deliverance. The lessons of love are those of adversity dealing in no falsehoods, but promising true happiness by right means, and assuring us that God afflicts not tyrannically, but only for our good. Love must be tried, and purified even as by fire; it alone is worth the crucible. But why, throughout this checkered world, do the inoffensive and undefended become the prey of the rapacious? Why is death the origin and end of life? Human philosophy would say it signifies nothing more than that a greater number should enjoy themselves through successive destruction. But O Thou Maker of man, is that thy teaching? Is it for this that the whole creation groaneth together until now? There is a restitution, a liberty, a redemption, for the glorious coming of which the creature waits in hope that can not be confounded, since it is the expectation of the sons of God, in whose hearts Omnipotence diffuses a sense of His own love.

But yet, O my God, why dost thou permit the innocent to suffer? Why was the sweet child whom thou didst give me to love as my life, why was its smiling beauty made hideous with agony before my eyes, and then lulled to sleep with new loveliness in the arms of death? Love must live by faith. That was the vision of my own sin, reigning unto death; I must look beyond.

"*Eloi, Eloi, lama sabachthani.*" God hath for saken his only begotten Son; the holy child of the Highest bows his head upon the cross, and it is finished. But why does it behove Jehovah to bring sons unto glory, by making Jesus perfect through sufferings? It was because he was holy that he did suffer, and that for us. We bless thee, O manifest God, that we are not left to infer from our fears how we must be brought to thee, but to learn from thy love; and though reason can not create a single star to gleam upon our midnight, yet thou hast given us the faith that operates with love, by which we penetrate the gloom, and look into the infinite light beyond our prison-house. We are therefore entitled thus to challenge the Almighty, and say, "*Though thou slay me, yet will I trust thee,*" for by the abundance of thy love, righteousness reigns in life everlasting, since through the risen Saviour we enter into the glory of his own resurrection, and find our own perfect humanity one with God's.

Love is a motive for immortal hope and advancement. It may be said that our natural affections present us with sufficient motives for moral conduct, since they can not prosper without reciprocal restraints. If we love an object, we shall undoubtedly seek to adminster to the happiness of that object. Pure love always blesses where it can, and it is never disappointed as long as it is met by a corresponding heart; yet misery most assuredly comes upon it either because it is not duly appreciated, or because it witnesses pain and sorrow where it would fain speak peace and joy. And then, supposing it to have ripened into its best maturity between the most friendly hearts, disease and death must arrest it there, so that earthly love itself terminates in darkness, to be felt the more palpably in proportion to the strength and the intensity and devotedness of that love. Sad ultimatum of that which alone promised happiness, and alone could feel it! If in this life only we have hope, so far from inducing us to cultivate the family and friendly charities up to their highest refinement, it would seem that the less we knew of them the better, since despair must be their end. Surely this deadly view of love can not be of that order which casts out fear, for torment is the only fruit which it prepares for death to lay in the dust, without a living seed within it to spring into new life.

The stoic philosophy is becoming for mortals. To refine the feelings by lessons of benevolence is but a cruel mode of education, if the young spirits, thus trained to diffuse their charity in smiles and gentle sympathies, are only at last to encounter pangs and then to perish. If we have suffered our intellects to be thus schooled by the doctrines of skepticism, it has been against the teachings of our hearts, for they are wiser

We feel that our affections are comfortless without hope—but what hope? Hope that dies, if it dare to look forward a few years? That, indeed, is godless, and does not deserve the name of hope. It is desolation and despair, when it comes out from its creeping and crawling state. When it gets its wings, it finds no food, and perishes. We do not, we dare not, sit down deliberately, with all the brightness of the world about us, and teach our children that death is to be the end of hope and of love. They know better, and will not believe us in our reasoning against reason. Human nature wants motive to take it beyond the grave, or it must grovel, and grub, and sink into brutality, and hideous, hateful, hating fleshliness. It can not go onward, it can not climb, it can not look toward heaven, if the glory from afar do not draw it upward. It must bound itself like an earthworm in the clay—it needs no eyes—the light is useless, but to stir it into life, which serves no purpose except to gather grossness, that it may nourish the soil in which it crawls. Human nature nowhere decently submits to this deadly philosophy, and wherever kindly affections have room to flourish, they assert their origin, and point to immortality. Even the laws that man imposes upon society found their force upon divine authority and order; and they would be without sanction, if without acknowledgment of God. And those closed hearts, that try to accommodate their affections without religion, must also do so without reason, without hope, and without morality; for whatever their feelings may be, their instincts alone guide them, and the love of a lioness to her cubs is quite as amiable as that of a human mother, if she press not her baby to her bosom with the consciousness that God warms her soul with parental fondness, as an intimation that He loves forever. She can not breathe the proper breath of love, as she looks upon the cheek of her dependent child, unless she sigh a prayer for eternal blessings on it. Thus she comes in faith to Heaven, and finds in God that quiet for her heart which He inspires with affection, only to instruct her how largely to trust Him with demands upon His providence and favor.

Love is not an accident of matter—a casualty in creation—a phosphorescence from a dead fungus; there is meaning and motive in it, devised in the Eternal Mind from which it flows, to indicate to every soul that feels it truly that God is not far from any one of us. It is a ray from the source that never sets—a line of light connecting us with the Everlasting, among which we may live in correspondence with the Father in the assurance that we never shall be forsaken here or hereafter. It is to this human love and its necessities that the divine love of Christianity addresses itself. For this the Lord Jesus was a child of woman; and the maternal love is imperfect, peaceless, almost profitless and destitute, without the fulfillment and satisfaction of its wants—without the spiritual and celestial spirit that appeals to it and completes it, by expanding it into full life by submission to God, as its everlasting source and sustentation. All love must end where it began—with impulse, if it be not principled in the soul; for without faith it does not realize its relationship to the Creative Being. But thus conscious of its true existence in Deity being sanctified, it becomes immortal. It longs to be eternal, and believes that all its proper objects will be provided, purified, and preserved for it in heaven.

Love is the basis of repentance and forgiveness.—The normal influences of both natural and spiritual existence are to no other end but to evince the benignity of God. But the will of man is not forced into conformity to this universal law, but on rational conviction, otherwise it would be impossible he should be conscious of willing. Yet man feels, whenever he reasons, that if he do not thus rightly use the means with which he is endowed, he is positively opposed in his inten tions and actions, to the constitution of the universe, and therefore, to the Almighty, whom he must meet only as a constant antagonist,unless, by the entrance of moral light into his understanding, a change of mind be effected, and his motives and desires take the direction which God has appointed. This can occur from no other cause than a persuasive knowledge and feeling of the Divine character, as entirely worthy of the highest affection and confidence of an intelligent creature. Thus reason becomes religion. It is felt to be iniquitous and malevolent willingly to do any thing inconsistent with the kindness and charity of the Godhead, or irrespective of the majesty and government of Goodness. But a man thus convinced in his conscience of having set himself against the purposes of his Creator, and knowing, from this intuitive admonisher, that the will of God must be utterly resistent and destructive to every thing that is not conformable to good-will, per ceives no escape from the righteousness of the Divine decision against himself; for love itself would be resolved into an empty sentiment unless it were one with justice. Thus the man self-condemned must breathe in terror, until he discovers the way of forgiveness, without derogating from the glory of *His* diadem whose decree against a perverse will is unalterable. This he can not find, until he perceives that the faithfulness and righteousness of Jehovah are required to absolve the truly penitent, and to purify him from guilt, because true penitence itself can arise only from God's own spirit in the man. In fact, the doctrines of that wondrous book, the Bible, so much quoted, and so little appreciated, are the only doctrines among men which elucidate the enormity of moral evil and at the same time illustrate the manner of its removal; for no other truths than those therein revealed, tend in any measure to demonstrate the necessity of repentance, and a new mode of spirit and of life.

Since without love we feel no sorrow for having offended, so we cordially seek forgiveness only from those in whose love we have reason to believe. It is the apprehension of the forgiving heart of true love that brings tears into our eyes, on remembering our sins against it. Could Judas have met the eye of Jesus, and felt His love as Peter did, instead of going to his own place, through despair and suicide in the field of blood, his soul would have been drawn more closely to his Lord, while in some secret place he wept bitterly, because the sense of his own treachery would have deepened in proportion as he felt the greatness of his dying Saviour's love.

The most unhappy are the most amiable, if they but know the worth of love. Not those who spitefully make themselves wretched; but those who find themselves out of place, undone, and in despair, and ashamed to look up, because of self-reproach, and because no kindly eye speaks to them. These are they that the Son of God prefers to converse with alone, and to touch with His burning words of love, until their hearts leap up in the light of heaven. Such are fit to feel the divinity of compassion, and respond with a life to the smile of God seen in the Saviour's face, when He says, "*Be of good cheer, thy sins are forgiven thee.*"

CHAPTER XIV.

THE LOVE OF ACTION AND POWER.

The infant no sooner moves its limbs, and feels that they are moved at its will, than it begins to enjoy itself in the use of its own power, for power is evinced only in action, and every action is a certainty—an advance in positive knowledge. The infantine motive is the motive of all. It is the love of power, or rather the pleasure of self-consciousness in the use of means, by which we obtain outward evidence of our own inward life and of the reality of things, in relation to ourselves. Every voluntary bodily act is an action of mind, in which there are both attention and intention, and, therefore, the very essence of all that constitutes actual enjoyment. This love of action in the use of power is shown in a great variety of manners, but in all its manifestations it appears only either as a desire to influence others or to employ ourselves. Every new exertion of power being so far an extension of our faculties, or a larger realization of our own existence, it is no more wonderful that we love to exercise this power than that we should wish to use our eyes, and help them with the telescope to look further into the heavens. All advancement is due to this love of power. When rightly exercised, it serves to prove that God does not deceive us with appearances, but that by His very nature there is truth in all he has made. Whatever a man contrives to accomplish by new means, or to a greater extent, brings his own spirit more into vital connection with the moving universe, and more out of the region of death. He who first traveled, without fear, sixty miles an hour on a railway, was conscious of a new kind of life; but the man who invented the steam locomotive that drew the train, containing himself as the mind of the moving mass, was the man who most enjoyed the love of power and of action.

All the delights of discovery arise from our admiration of power, as evinced in the divine disposal of the elements for given purposes; and it is in the nature of the mind, according to its prominent disposition, always to aim at making a practical use of knowledge, by rendering science the minister of pleasure, by presenting new combinations to the senses, and by enabling man to extend and establish his dominion over the earth. Were Napoleon now in his former place, he would summon the lightning to his aid, cause it to open passages through the mountains, and transport his armies on its wings, and the world would admire, while trembling at the power that converts savants into slaves.

So great is our sympathy with the bare exercise of power, that the ambition of tyrants and conquerors inspires a feeling of sublimity, when, with commanding skill, they wield the energies of millions, and so enchant the nations as to make them submit to their caprices. And indeed, it is wonderful that he who led so many thousands to inglorious destruction in Russia, should, at a word, call armies to the slaughter at Waterloo.

Those who do not habitually contemplate the demonstrations of Omnipotence, as seen in creation and in providence, are always ready to be captivated by daring spirits; and those who do not addict themselves to the quiet activities of science and of social commerce, are ever the first to talk of glory, and, under the pretense of defending their own rights, to trample on those of mankind. In short, those who do not worship God, will worship themselves, in the form of some ostensible hero; and, whether it be such a one as Napoleon, or even "that spirit unfortunate" that reigns in hell, they care not, so that he is active and ingenious enough to keep their pride astir, while employing them for his own purposes.

Some men work with their own means, others take advantage of those of their neighbors. Society is maintained by this love of power, but in one class of minds it takes the direction of activity, and in another the desire for possession; the co-operation of these constitutes commerce, and introduces those arts of industry which supply the means of luxury and comfort. But as it is more blessed to give than to receive, so it is happier to be active than passive. It is better to be busy in devising and employing the means of turning nature to advantage, though seemingly reluctant, than to be supplied like a plant without personal effort. All the free creatures of earth, air, and sea, are constrained to exert themselves for the supply of their own wants, and the feeling of necessity which causes exertion is the means of all their happiness. Thus it is also with man; and therefore, if he who is provided with a daily sufficiency without toil, turn not his mind to the consideration of his spiritual progress and usefulness, he must be running riot in iniquity, and studying how he may please himself in the indulgence of whatever taste may happen to predominate, since it is impossible for the soul to cease from action as long as the nerves will obey it. Activity without faith, or a feeling of duty, is the turmoil of hell, and to seek the power of being idle is to court the company of demons, with their torments. The mind will, while in the body, become subject to the body, unless struggling on in the pursuit of truth, it holds dominion over appetite. Unholy, unsocial, and brutal pleasure will debase all man's faculties into bodily passions, if, in the leisure of exemption from labor, his heart and mind are not busied about those nobler objects which the worlds of nature and of providence offer so freely to our souls. It is not surprising, therefore, that when men of sober and industrious habits succeed in acquiring the means of retirement, and withdraw, it is too often neither with ease nor with dignity; but in fact, they leave all their pleasure in town, with their business, and, not being mentally provided for, they sigh, amid their paradise, for the loss of that cordial with which Mammon sweetened toil; and, finding nothing at hand in which they are fit to be employed, become either hypochondriacal, dreamy, or dangerous in their miserly irritations.

The love of power takes as many forms as there are minds, since every mind possesses something in some measure peculiar to itself, either in its motive or its means. But the aims of men are generally directed according to their social feelings; for whether we seek knowledge, eloquence, or wealth, we usually acquire and employ them only that we may attain a station in society, or an influence among our friends or in our families, that will enable us to enjoy an extension of our individual endowments, by fellowship with others, or by inducing them to act in keeping with our own wishes.

There are, however, misers of all complexions, whose only business is to wrap up their acquirements, and hide them away, as the Indians do their choice gods; and well may they conceal them, for they are but paltry idols at the best. The desire of possession of any kind, like that of gold, merely as money, is a monomania of the hoarding disposition, which gets its own punishment, if not its cure, by depriving itself of the means of enjoyment in the very act of increasing the store.

Thought must precede, accompany, and follow experiment, or industry will be wasted, and we shall make no advance in true observation. Many enjoy their senses for a lifetime, and die without being the wiser for their experience.

Want is the parent of industry and research; but the wants of man arise partly from his bodily demands, and partly from those of his mind. Reason has desires of its own, which lead to action. The apprehension of a possible advantage induces an effort for its attainment in proportion as we feel its desirableness; but we judge between the degree of difficulty in an enterprise and the benefit to be derived from it; and prudence decides whether it would be better to undertake the task, with the means we possess, or forego the advantage. We say—Is the object worth the labor? Some kinds of labor bring only sorrow. Industry expended on that which helps not to satisfy some proper desire of the mind, is only productive of greater discontent, since the intention is always to happiness, and this intention must of course be disappointed as often as our aims are not directed to the attainment of right ends. It is, therefore, essential to the prosperity of the mind, that a man should first of all determine that what he seeks is compatible with the Divine appointment, as regards the means by which man shall really obtain good. The inquiry—Is it lawful? should precede every undertaking. Conscience will reply correctly, or at least suggest a test for self-determination, by recalling to the mind the royal law—Do as thou wouldst be done unto. This applies to all affairs—handicraft, or head-work, for both are worthless if the heart be not in them to good purpose. Now, whatever will contribute to the benefit of society is a good employment. Industry, simply considered, is a benefit in itself, and idleness a curse, because he who has no duty to engage him is a hindrance to others. Of course, those who can not work—as from disease, for instance—may yet be blessings, by giving others occasions to work for the best wages, the reward of active Christian charity. But those who will not toil for themselves and their own house are not worthy even of their food.

There was business on earth for man before sin entered it. The spirit that animated man, before the breath of Satan blighted the blooming Paradise, was the spirit of industry, that went cheerfully and right-heartedly to work, and wisely directed all the aptitudes of nature to the noblest ends, by engaging every gift of God, so as to develop the growing fund of goodness contained within it. The happiness of every creature consists in its appropriate action, and if we would feel that God, in mercy to man, uttered a malediction on the ground, we must learn that the way to the highest, holiest, most sabbatical rest, is through patience, and toil, and death, and burial in the dust, for thus we secure that fullness of earthly blessing which is poured upon the soul like a flood of light, and animates to duteous activity, not as a mere contented obedience, but as a feeling that God himself has called a man to walk in the path he occupies, as the way that shall end in the unutterable joys of heaven.

The first employment of man, even in Paradise, was to increase the comforts of earth to every creature in it; therefore no one can be wrong who, with a right motive, sets about improving the facilities, or increasing the productiveness, of agriculture and commerce. He is obeying God, he is helping to supply the natural demands of human kind, and promoting the establishment of universal peace. He is blessed. And the man who searches after truth, and diffuses it when he has found it, is also industrious in the right way, and he also is blessed in his labor. Whatever calls to action in a right cause opposes discontent, by exciting a hope that has the property of happiness, in itself, because it engages the soul in a pursuit that ends only in finding some higher and happier employment. The man duteously busy is heavenly in hope, in action, in habit, and in end, because he is using divine means for divine purposes, and for the advancement of himself in the good of his neighbors.

There are no good works without faith.—We must believe in the reward and the Rewarder, before we can possess a right spirit for labor; since, otherwise, our employment will amount to no more than the drudgery of seeking vain amusement, or of slaving on in greater degradation than a muzzled ox under the sharp stimulus of the goad. But patience, too, has perfect work, and it is blessed, indeed, for its life is faith; therefore plod on, weary workers, and your souls shall yet be free.

Youth is especially the period of activity, and if the habit of mental economy be not then formed, it can rarely be afterward acquired. Without the active vitality of spring, we look in vain for the blooming vigor of summer and the rich fruits of autumn. How weighty, then, the responsibility of youth, and how urgent the duty of every individual who possesses influence on the young, to cause all means in their power to bear upon the formation of the characters of those to whom society must look for new impulses and power. Young men, stir up your strength; your country looks to you, not merely for the maintenance of its greatness, but for the fuller development of its majesty, as the mistress of the world. Think, that you may act, and act worthily of your high vocation, as the transmitters and improvers of all that is noble in institution or intention. Remember, the means are in your hands of changing the aspect of the whole world, and causing it to reflect the glory of heaven in its face. The machinery by which states and all their societies are to move onward is to be kept at work, and governed by your management and strength. It is not placed in your power for yourselves, nor by yourselves: you serve God, or you are called to serve. If you refuse, you serve God's everlasting antagonist, and you know his wages. The Almighty has brought you into being, and made you men, that the business of human ity may be yours, as it is His. He demands your hearts and your hands, to co-operate with omnipotence in the service of the Son of man and of God, that you may inherit together the glory that is coming. The world must be set in motion, both mechanically and religiously; therefore He gives you the steam-engine and the Bible, with which to regenerate mankind. Truth and engineering, science natural and science spiritual, are the only civilizers and reformers; the one for the body, the other for the soul. If you would succeed, you must use both, with a consciousness that all power is God's. He bids you deposit the lightning, that it may conduct your thoughts, as rapidly as they arise, from land to land, and He requires you to take the light from heaven into your hearts, and speak it every where. Thus the wide earth shall be as if condensed into a chrysolite, with radiance streaming through it, and all its inhabitants shall be united in soul by divine knowledge, and feel that their homes are hanging upon heaven by bands of glory. All nature shall be spiritualized to the apprehension of mankind, and they shall see, like angels, that the meaning of all things is the mind of God.

All God's universe is in motion under His hand—move with it. Let the harmony of His purpose be yours. Let power be ruled by love; let the activities of that animating spirit govern you, for if it do not, all the elements that are so inscrutably active about you and within you will war against you, and whirl you into outer darkness. But your minds being regulated by obedience to the Divine Word, you will find all things working together for your good, and you will, in fact, be obedient to the very thought that, being spoken, brought light into existence, and thence all things; and thus you will act at last as if constituted like it, by being really, and in spirit, united with the Word, that was God, and dwelt among us, and whose glory we beheld as full of grace and truth. Minds not thus submissive to Heaven become more miserable in proportion to their efforts. They may strive to be idle, but they will only be wretched.

The indolent disposition is not punishable by British laws, as it was by those of Athens and Rome, yet it surely meets the misery it merits, and, like every other indulgence in iniquity, bears within itself the elements of torment. Neglect of means will substantiate the final condemnation—"Inasmuch as ye did it *not*" will be the damning decision. *Not* to serve Him, before whose judgment-seat all must stand, is to serve the enemy of God and man. It is not a mere *waste* of spirit and of power, but it is the employment of gifts against the Giver.

Would it not be strange, if in countries professing to deem God's word the only moral directory, that there should be less of public devotedness than among people who did not like to retain God in their knowledge? The youthful Hannibal dedicated himself to vengeance for his country's sake; but you, Christian young men, devote yourselves to the good of man for God's sake. You gird yourselves to battle, not against earthly foes merely, but against spiritual principalities and powers, that the enemy may be driven from the home of your neighbor, as well as from your own heart. You fight under the banner of Heaven; the sun is your shield; you conquer with light, which is both your defense and your weapon. Go on, from conquering to conquer. The Christian, thus armed,

> "Can hold no parley with unmanly fears—
> Where duty bids, he confidently steers;
> Faces a thousand dangers, at her call,
> And, trusting in his God, surmounts them all."

The triumph will be glorious, if only you are sure that you are battling in a right cause and with the right weapons.

Young men who believe in Jesus, "*I write unto you, because ye are strong, and have overcome the Wicked One.*" Consult the living oracles in all your movements. So surely as Providence endows you with vigor and social impetuosity and power, so surely are you responsible for the use of those means by which society might be blessed by you. The energy and life-blood of society are in your veins, and if the body politic be stagnant or disordered, it is from some defect in you—some unwillingness to work as God would have you work. Whether a feverish delirium distract, or a perverted energy convulse the hearts of law-makers and laborers, whether the land languish like a swamp, or thrive like a well cultivated field, will mainly depend upon the manner in which you think and act. Therefore look into history for wise examples, and into your own relations to God and man for motives, for means. Your time is embryo eternity. Whether your activity shall be blessed or baneful, rests with your will—on your moral intelligence and conscience. What do you mean to do? Trust not your own judgments; but let the experience of age and staid reflection regulate your energies, and then advancement will be safe as well as certain. A glowing disposition, a sunny enthusiasm, a hearty devotedness, will only aggravate ruin and disappointment, without a good cause and a sound discretion. Therefore, let youth never think itself safe and in the right way, until it has at least felt enough doubt concerning its own power of discernment to induce inquiry, and the right estimate of reverend and tried men. There is no escape from the consequences of misconduct, and their condemnation is the deepest who abuse advantages in the presumption of self-confidence. The Lofty One inhabiting eternity blesses none but the humble, and blesses them because they are in earnest in seeking and working out their salvation. They receive power from on high, and consume not the bounties of Heaven upon their lusts in the pride of a lying life.

Since man fell, toil has been a necessity, and therefore so far a sorrow. The same amount of exertion which, when voluntary, is a pleasure, under compulsion becomes a pain. Yet, by setting the thoughts on the end and object of labor, rather than on the thing itself, we find the necessary exertion to be the direct means of tranquilizing both mind and body, while, at the same time, it increases and accomplishes our hopes. Thus, having fulfilled our daily toil in the act of meditating on the sunshine of to-morrow, we peacefully close our eyes on to-day, without a doubt or a dream, the darkness passes over us, and we awake in light with new life in our limbs. By making labor an exchange for commodities, God has taken away much of the curse from the ground. He might have enslaved us all without redemption, but that He is love. We might have been driven as convicts, as we are, in chains to toil, without wages or reward, but that when he enjoined labor, He also promised rest, and giving us six days for neighborly co-operation in our common weal, demands that we all meet Him together on the seventh. He has made the Sabbath for man, to teach him that the soul that comes to God ceases from his labors, as to all trust in them; and that, though his works follow him, it is into rest; for the business of a worshiping spirit is performed without effort, and is but as the activity of life infused into the body by the breath of the Creator. Wherever this spirit of freedom and of power, from the consciousness that God inspires us, is not felt, there is bondage, and the debasement of the drudge, even in attempts at worship. The Lord of the Sabbath is the Lord of life, and of liberty; and wherever his authority is denied or not known, there the curse of slavery is felt, and the whole creation groans. No people can be blessed without keeping a holy day—a day sacred to God; for the animal nature will tyrannize and suffer, unless both the soul and the body enjoy their sabbaths. All the functions of a man's life are ordered with respect to weekly periods, and the habit of observing a seventh day, as an entire respite from toil, favors the regular distribution of vital power; and the repose of a spirit retiring from worldly employment to the inner sanctuary, is like drawing a fresh supply from the fountain of health and salvation. It will be vain for philanthropists to endeavor to teach gorgeous barbarians and tyrannical savages their own value and the value of their fellow men, at any thing more than a marketable estimate, unless they first demonstrate the fact, that the Almighty has put a price upon each soul, and values it as that of His own Son. Let men know and feel the meaning of the Lord's day, as the promise and pledge of the glorious rest of regeneration into spiritual activity and life, to which all are called to aspire, and then, and not till then, will humanity be developed as the spirit of true industry and neighborhood and joy.

But work on earth is the business of man. Each in his sphere has something to do, and happy is he who does it with all his heart, as unto God, and not to man. The only care essential to a right industry is to see that one is doing his duty. The encouragement to exertion is to feel that we are not working under a task-master, to make bricks without straw, but that each of us is at liberty, or should be, to do the best with the ability that God gives us, under the conviction that we shall not be condemned for deficiency, unless we willingly and indolently abuse the abundance of means bestowed on us. There is a ministry for every man; we must all serve; and all that is necessary to render our service acceptable to God, and really serviceable to man, is a right spirit in our place. Any one who has the power of acting, or, I may say, even of willing, has the power of acting, speaking, or praying, in such a way as shall do some good to some body. Every one exerts an influence by his very thoughts. By right thinking, we shall use every opportunity of so working as necessarily to do the best under the circumstances, for the good of society and ourselves. Therefore let us say with Augustine, Insiste, anime meus, et adtende fortiter.

Industry is essentially social. No man can improve either himself or his neighbor without neighborly help and to better the world is to set the world to work together. Every useful invention has been carried out and perfected by the co-operation of many minds, or by the successive applications of varied genius to the same objects, age after age. The mechanic must aid the philosopher, or he must stand still in his demonstrations; and the philosopher must aid the mechanic, or he will work and work without wisdom. The astronomer needs his telescope, and the chemist his materials and apparatus. The sciences hang on the arts, and the arts on the sciences. But without the philosophy from Heaven, neither art nor science would look off the earth, and industry would die a natural death and rise no more, for religion alone is the living spirit of human sociality and power.

> 'If any strength we have, it is to ill;
> But all the good is God's, both power and also will."
>
> SPENSER'S *Fairy Queen.*

Even those who can do nothing but receive help, can receive it in such a manner as to bless the helper, if only by causing him to feel that it is indeed more blessed to give than to receive. A soul sensible of realities always sets itself and others to work to some purpose. There is always hope in true activity; the will works in the brain and muscles of a man who works because he wills and knows what he is about, and why he is busy. But what kind of willingness that is which animates a man under the lash, the coward conscience of the slave-driver, when God speaks to him silently and alone in the stillness of death, can best say.

Most persons have an activity of impulse, a sort of childish playfulness, in wasting energy. Such persons please themselves and benefit others only by accident, and because they can not help it. There is no steadiness without an aim, and unless the aim, be a worthy one, the spirit does not fully nerve the arm. All evil disposition is impulsive, and therefore fitful, foolish, wayward. It may be obstinate, but it can not be truly persevering, since it does not look to the end, but merely goes on pleasing itself to the best of its ability, as suitable objects may happen to offer excitement and inducement. It can not be hopeful in a rational sense, because no man can discover a reason for hoping that ultimate success, in a satisfactory sense, can crown a bad action, much less a habit of such action. Hence it follows that healthy and hopeful activity is impossible, without an approvable motive; in short, there is no blessing for a bad will. A good and honest intention is blessed already, and works with increasing blessing, since what is consistent with the real welfare of one's neighbor is in keeping with one's own safety, because it is according to the law of God which is the law of blessing to all who will obey it. Good intentions, then, set men properly to work with what means they possess. Therefore be strong, O man of poverty. Believe in the Giver of strength and opportunity, and you shall feel the seeds of an immortal vigor growing in your veins. See that you pray and live, desiring exactly what the All-wise knows to be best, and then you will bear your burden with a light heart, and sometimes look up into heaven so joyously as to forget that the earth must be dug into, even to make a grave. It is not real good intent but hypocrisy that paves the pit of darkness, while sincere, love-born purpose lays the golden pavement of the city of God.

Every individual should feel that he has some business that must be blessed, if he use his means for the best, since the God of providence calls for exertion only because He grants the ability and intends a happy result, which must arrive. We should therefore act as integral members of a whole company, where God is overseer, and then we shall find also a time for rest as well as for labor, and the soul will indeed enjoy a perpetual sabbath of its own, in the peace of that faith which animates it with Divine energy, and with hopes that terminate only in the eternal happiness to which they point.

CHAPTER XV.

CONSCIENCE.

HOWEVER diversified may be the estimates which men in general form of virtue, and however widely they deviate in their conduct from the line they deem right, they are always so far self-complacent, as very adroitly to supply excuses to satisfy their own consciences. They measure themselves one by another and see so many faults in their neighbors, that they feel entitled to be lenient to their own. This kind of conscience is uncharitableness, and belongs to those who are most scrupulous in demanding license for themselves, while most punctiliously rigid in refusing all liberty to others. Nevertheless, even these men of most unconscionable consciences are open to some sort of conviction: for when the law of God is manifested to their understandings, they at once acknowledge its goodness, justness, holiness, and thus they bear witness against themselves and in favor of Divine purity; but then they are very apt to infer that this holy, just, and good law has nothing to do in regulating the duties of their own lives, not because it ought not, but rather, perhaps, because they see not how it can. They can not endure their own legal condemnation, and therefore imagine they are to be saved by a faith that does not work by rule, but trusts in a righteousness that it will not adopt, forgetful that though man is saved by God, yet it is not in spite of himself. Happy indeed is it to have a soul freed from terror by a vision of grace reigning through righteousness unto life; but this is not seen in its heavenly manner until we love the Father, because he first loved us. Then, indeed, a sublimer motive penetrates the spirit, like the angels' strain stirring the hearts of the shepherds on the plains at Bethlehem—"Glory to God in the highest, peace on earth, good will to man." But this glory, peace, and love are most visible to man when the Lawgiver illustrates the beauty of holiness, in human submission to the Divine will, for then we see how the agony that breaks the heart is triumphantly endured by love, and then the bowing down of the head, in obedience unto death, shows us how the God-life of humanity enlightens Hades, and enters into Heaven. Conscience lies dark and dormant until the light of the Divine character shines into man's understanding. We can not be conscientious until we believe in Love. The testimony of moral perception is never clearly elicited from our hearts until reason is illuminated by a manifestation of truth as the will of God. Until then we only speculate on ethics, like the heathen who knew not God, and therefore could not see the ground of moral excellence. As Dr. Thaer pertinently says:—"The ancient philosophers have much disputed whether there be one virtue only, or many; one vice, or many. It depends, as it appears to me, on what our notion of virtue or vice is; for him who strives after a steady perfection in soul, there is but one virtue. He who, on the contrary, looks upon virtue, in relation to civil society, and calls that virtue which advances public and private happiness, and that vice which disturbs it, he may have many virtues and many vices. I believe that these opinions are not merely speculative, but have a real influence on practice. He who adopts the first notion, not in word merely, but embraces it as warmly and sincerely as I did—he, if he sinks in one respect, sinks in all. Christ says, 'Whosoever shall keep the whole law, and yet offend in one point, he is guilty of all.' I feel, Lord, thy truth!"* A consciousness of sin is an experimental and personal matter.

We may perceive that many things are really good or really evil, but we do not discern truth in its nature until we perceive that every truth involves the idea of perfect righteousness, and implies the entire intolerance of all injustice by the Author of all truth, and that therefore every evil disposition must be essentially hateful to any mind that is in accordance with perfect love. Truth and love are united, as the necessary expression of the divinity to all intelligences, and they that separate them, in their thoughts and actions, have an evil and unhappy state of spirit and a growing tendency to darkness and doubt. If they follow truth without love, in the divine sense, it is also without moral feeling, and therefore merely to gratify some proud or debased passion; for if they possess any kind of love, without the love of truth it can only be either sensually or diabolically. When they believe they must also tremble; since, in either case, the revelation of Deity must be surprising, hateful, and condemning to them. In the light their consciences may and must awake, but only like a wounded man that has slumbered dreamily with opiates, to be roused to the realities of agony. When truth, as a ray of the Sun of Righteousness, shines into the secret depths of a man's soul, he must acknowledge the Holy One. Then he ceases to speculate about sin; he feels it, not merely as an evil, because it is apt to produce inconvenient effects, but as essentially iniquitous and horrible, because against the will and ordinances of pure love. The heart of Him who lamented over Jerusalem, and was pierced on Calvary, is the place in which to see sin in its hatefulness; since there we see how a man that

* From a biographical notice of Albert Thaer, in the Moral Aspects of Medical Life, by Dr. Mackness.

could not sin must suffer, in sympathizing both with God, as the Father, and with man, as the prodigal.

Many writers have learnedly and elaborately discoursed to prove that it is the natural right and office of conscience to condemn the wrong-doer. If it be meant, as it appears to be, that conscience thus acts, although no divine enlightenment reach it extraneously —then, surely, more is asserted than either experience or revelation will warrant. *Faith comes by hearing, and hearing by the Word of God.* It is the office of the Holy Spirit *to convince of sin, of righteousness, and of judgment to come.* How could a man like St. Paul have persecuted the early Christians with so ready a spirit, and think all the while that he was doing God good service, if his natural conscience had been a sufficient guide and governance for his conduct, in the difficult affair of choosing to resign all his old prejudices, while obstinately bent upon proving his zeal, by imprisoning and stoning those who preached against them? "Father, forgive them, for they *know not* what they do," was the Saviour's dying prayer. The evil conscience of unbelief is blind as well as impious. The law of God must be felt as God's charity in the soul before it can conscientiously do its duty; and we may as well look for a world of beauty without the sun, as for any right discernment or moral excellence in man, without the light which flows into his mind from revealed truth and the revealing Spirit. Whatever be man's discernment, he is not in a state prepared to do unto others as he would be done by, until the law of love enters into all his desires and actions like a new life; for, without this how can he avoid thrusting his own selfish claims in the way of his neighbors, instead of making his neighbors' interest one with his own?

It is true that certain heathens eloquently discourse concerning the *vera lex* and the *recta ratio, naturâ congruens, diffusa in omnes, sempiterna et immortalibus;* but alas! he who wrote these words said, also, that he was entirely faultless. Thus, amidst their prevalent superstitions, and their worshipings of deified lusts, how obscure were their notions of the Divine law. Their conscience never condemned their creed, nor does any man's. The *lex vera* of their minds was not divine, and did not reach the thoughts and intents of the heart. If it condemned the man who willfully injured his neighbor, or broke the laws of his country, retaliation or retribution could expiate the offense, for guilt was not understood to be, as it is, a pollution cleaving to the spirit, to be removed only by that repentance which accompanies an entire change in the state of the will and conscience. There was no forgiveness in their law, because there was no charity; and if their fabled gods were ever to be appeased, it was by cruelty and vengeance.

The atonement made by love attracting men to God, by subduing their hearts, was God's own method, which men untaught could never have discovered; and not knowing and feeling this, their consciences could not recognize either the law of life or of liberty. Even the slight glimmering of the *recta ratio*, which the heathen recognized as from Heaven, was probably conveyed to them through tradition from a period when the only God was worshiped, or else they derived it directly from the Hebrew bards and prophets, for the chosen people were a testimony to all nations. But truth did not suit man's disposition; he did not like to retain God in his knowledge, and eternal life had no abidence in him—nor has it ever, but by the inhabiting of the Holy Spirit imparted to all believers in the redemption. Hence it is that, among the ignorant and faithless, the law of God has no felt authority, and charity is at best but a family virtue. A law that could regard every human being as equally entitled to be loved with a man's own self, is altogether beyond their apprehension; so that the words, *just* and *good* are terms expressive of unknown qualities, or only narrowly applied to the very partial relationships of kindred and of clans.

A society of philanthropists endeavored to encourage deeds of charity and virtue among the Pawnee Indians. They found a young man of that tribe who had daringly signalized himself by rescuing a young woman from an awful death: while she was surrounded by her intended executioners, he rushed into the midst of them and bearing her away to a spot where he had placed a fleet horse, he escaped with her before they had time to recover from their surprise. It might be supposed that a sense of that injustice with which a number of warriors were about to expiate some small offense in their helpless victim, moved him to this noble deed; but when the philanthropists presented this young warrior with a silver medal for his reward, he exclaimed, *I did not know that I did right!* In short, his conscience had only condemned him for interfering with the cruel usages of his savage countrymen, and the only excuse he had to offer for his daring deed, was the sufficiently manly one, that he wanted a wife.

So far is it indeed from being true, that conscience holds supremacy over the soul, that the facility with which we naturally excuse our own acts is a demonstration of the need for a rectifying and enlightening power from above, in order that man should perceive his duty, and fulfill it. Without this, men yield to whatever passion may happen to predominate, and exhibit no more conception of moral rectitude, in the workings of their affections, than any gregarious tribe of animals. Witness the degradation of woman, where the Christian spirit does not assert her dignity; witness the universal subjection of the weak to the willful, where God does not speak. Without the rectitifying spirit of truth, men always seek their own pleasure, and their love is as lawless as their hate. Their ideas of righteousness extend no further than to expediency and convenience, and they interpret even the word of God by the principles of the market, counting that loss which another gains, and that fair profit which aggrandizes selfishness, by taking advantage of ignorance and trust.

In order to study to have a conscience without offense, we must know the Divine will, and willingly obey it.

Those without the written law are a law unto themselves, and they are judged according to the light that is in them. Did the Hindoos deem Suttee sinful? No. Neither their gods nor their consciences taught them any thing of the real nature of sin. They would have thought it sin not to burn the widow with the dead body of her husband, because such gods as they knew were likely enough to be pleased with such sacrifices. Thus the understanding of every nation and every man is darkened by some deluding demon, so that conscience can not see, until the true light shines upon the soul, by giving it the knowledge of the true God in Jesus Christ, who is the Judge of all. In Him alone the authority of conscience is asserted and vindicated, and no spirit but His can clear the earth or the heart from that darkness in which cruelty delights to dwell, and cause faith, hope and charity to take its place. The condemnation, however, comes with the true light that flows from heaven, and awakens the conscience while convincing the understanding; and if men will not bring their deeds to be reproved, it is because they prefer darkness to light, and would rather perish than part from the sins they love.

Before we can approve what is right, there must be the *entrance* of that light which brings with it the *feeling* of Divine purity. The cultivation of conscience, even in a Christian requires something more than intellectual apprehension. A cordial faith in God's goodness must actuate the life, and produce in the conduct a reflex manifestation of the love which is revealed in the believer's mind; for as warmth is mingled with radiance in the vivifying sunbeam, so the light of a true and heavenly faith never enters a human soul divinely to quicken it, without a corresponding love.

Christianity is not a system of ethical philosophy, merely to make us acquainted with the names of the virtues, but a system of means by which we are brought to God, and caused to resemble Him. The truths embodied in Christian doctrines minister their own spirit to those who obey them in love, for this is obedience to God, and therefore the union of the human with the Divine will. The reception and enjoyment of Christian truth must, therefore, prove the value of the soul, by expanding its affections, desires, and capacity, in a manner coincident with the beauty, sublimity, and vastness of the objects thus presented to the mind, as fit for its love. Truth supplies the spirit with true hopes, because, being obeyed, it renders the conscience void of offense. It promises only what it must fulfill, since we thus enter on the enjoyment of our eternal patrimony, as heirs of the Almighty.

Plato truly says, that the conscience is the god within the soul. But then a holy state of conscience can spring only from faith in a holy God, and the soul's possession of a false god must be a false faith, a false conscience, and a life of delusions. With a right apprehension of the Divine character, as revealed in the sacred Scriptures, we shall always be able to discriminate between moral good and evil, and shall not be deceived by facts, as unbelievers constantly are, since in reality they reject the master or key-truths, simply because these truths do not please them, and they subject themselves, by choice, to those errors which confirm theu condemnation.

They excuse themselves from serving God, even though they can not deny his right to their obedience. But if they were utterly ignorant of God and His demands, we should not be surprised at their having no conscience in respect to God, and therefore no sense of having sinned against Him. They believe in some other than the true God—some undefined power, some energia, some mathematical principle, some omnipotent agency without personality, against which there can be no such thing as sinning. A Copper Indian, who worships a personal god, though wrapped up in his mystery-bag, has some check upon his conscience; but a man who is neither a heathen nor a Christian worships nothing, and has a conscience that can not be cultivated, but on the principle of pleasing himself, as his own supreme.

There is no duty where there is no law, and no true law where there is no love, for no being has authority to control the actions of another, but for his advantage. Resistance to mere despotism is not disobedience, except in case some authority, superior to that which would tyrannize over us, commands submission to the tyranny for the sake of the superior authority. But, even then, we recognize in that superior authority a right to command, only because some ultimate good is to result to ourselves and to others. Hence Christians are content to suffer wrong rather than resist the ap pointed power, so long as, by so doing, they are exercising faith upon the good-will of Him who thus commands them to submit. Yet if the appointed power assume a right to compel our submission in a manner that clearly contravenes the superior law, we are, in fact, called upon to refuse obedience. Thus, when the Apostles were commanded to cease speaking in the name of Jesus, they preferred to suffer the consequences of resisting this command, because they had received distinct instructions from Heaven to preach in that name:—" *Whether we ought to obey men rather than God, judge ye.*" They were conscientious, they acted from a sense of duty, and felt where the authority resided, and on what that authority rested—even the benevolence of God.

Conscience, then, is the principle which perceives duty, and prompts to its fulfillment. Duty itself is altogether dependent on relationship. Thus every rational member of society owes a duty to the rest, as far as they become connected with each other, in maintaining the well-being of that society. Our domestic relationships are regulated by laws written on our hearts, and fathers and mothers feel the claims of their offspring upon their affections and vigilant care, to protect and to do them good, and every child feels, as soon as it can reason, that reverence and obedience are due to that parental love. But we all instinctively perceive that the claim ceases, unless enforced by affection; for in fact, the right to govern is founded entirely on love, and he is disobedient to the law of God who endeavors to hold dominion on any other principle. This is the bond of all Divine appointment, in the relationships of humanity, and nothing can be tolerated by God which may be hurtful, for His law means only—Thou shalt do no ill, but love thy fellow-being as thyself. And whosoever, apprehends this law, and does otherwise, acts against his conscience, and is condemned by his own heart.

But where there is no law there is no transgression. The Almighty, however, has not left himself without witness, for wherever reason exists, there are to be seen evidences innumerable of His wisdom and goodness But reason itself grows blind, and without discernment, when mankind are driven by each other's cruelty and neglect to depend upon their animal cunning and instinct for sustenance and protection. Physical comfort and mental enjoyment, amidst appropriate objects of affection, and with a knowledge of those grand truths most interesting to humanity, are essential to the right development of reason, and without them man's sublimer faculties of foresight and reflection, and his power of inferring the future from the past, and the invisible from the evident, are all surrounded by a cloud, through which the light of heaven fails to pierce. The truth of this observation is demonstrable by reference to examples, which are found wherever hunger and ignorance, the two great brutalizers of the human race, have done their worst, in reducing men to physical and mental degradation, as among those inhabitants of Sligo and northern Mayo who were driven out from their homes in 1641 and 1689, and forced to live almost like wild beasts surrounded by their foes. Thus, also, is it with the Bushmans, in their depth of miserable abasement, absolutely burrowing in holes of the earth, and supporting a low, dwarfish, and monstrous existence, with a loathsome industry by which they scarcely live.

Ignorance and hunger, as before stated, are indeed the grand brutalizers of mankind. If we take a child from among the most degraded of the human family, and treat him as we would be treated—by kindness, and kindly associations, and suitable instruction—he becomes gradually elevated into a style of man altogether above his progenitors; and with the enlargement of his mind begins the enlightenment of his conscience. But such is the inveteracy of inbred evil, that it requires as many generations to pass under advantages as had passed in degradation, before physical and mental improvement can reach any considerable excellence. With these advantages, however, the savage features, both of body and mind, disappear, and instead of bearing the disgusting signs of barbarism upon the face, human beauty then mingles in the expression of all that is amiable and intelligent. Although, even in the lowest, most destitute, and miserable state of human beings, some traces of kindly sociality are still visible among tribes and families, yet it is indisputable that conscience must be as degraded as their condition, for, in fact, such wretched depression precludes all but the merest animal claims upon the intellect. When men are without God they are also destitute of ennobling and elevating hopes; a sense of moral deficiency is unknown, and conscience, therefore. finds no occasion for exercise beyond the low accusings and excusings that spring from the acknowledged propriety, in some mean degree, of those affections without which kindred and kindness would be unknown.

We perceive that argument agrees with fact, in assuring us that human reason possesses but small ability to discover moral and spiritual truth, abstractedly considered, or in the principles that are the foundation of correct thinking and acting. This inaptitude of our reason to reflect on spiritual motives, as the right ground of sociality and of religious feeling, arises not from inadequate endowment or from too limited a power of perception, but from the perversion of our affections. The faculties are usually engaged in a manner so far below their proper functions, that those ideas can not be excited in the soul by which it might be prompted and induced to look back, to meditate on its origin, or to penetrate the future, in search of its final appointment and the end and purpose of its being.

Although, while without a knowledge of God's claims upon our spirits, we necessarily move like wandering stars without definite orbits, and subject to laws and attractions beyond calculation, yet His attributes are not naturally and spontaneously the objects of our thoughts, and, indeed, when left to ourselves, we really do not acknowledge Him in any of our ways. But herein the prerogative of reason is manifested. When we are instructed concerning the being of God, either by inference from His handiworks, or from the dictation of His word, we at once, and as if intuitively, confess that He is truly Almighty and All-wise, the Author of all, and therefore the proper object of adoration and of trust, *in whom we live, and move, and have our being*, and everlastingly possess the springs and energies of all our capacity of action and of existence. And whosoever has received intelligence enough to discern this degree of truth, must either, in a corresponding faith, commit himself in obedient reliance unto his God, or else feel conscious of struggling on in a darkened path, according to the miserable waywardness of selfish habitude, believing, trembling, and defying, because, like an apostate spirit, the will is not at one with revealed Wisdom. The man who is in a state of will to receive revelation from the God of all wisdom, perceives the necessity and the blessedness of living in conscious dependence upon the instruction, strength, and love of Him who is the faithful and unfailing Creator, because revelation itself is God's appeal to the heart and to the intellect of a being, that can make no progress in moral and spiritual improvement but as he is taught and attracted by the Divine character, as if speaking to him in the demonstration of deeds done in his own nature, that truth might be felt in human consciousness as the reflex of God's will, and that thus true worship might be verily founded eternally upon sympathy between man and his Maker.

Thus Muller, the great historian, says, "The Gospel is the fulfillment of all hopes, the perfection of all philosophy, the interpreter of all revolutions, the key to all seeming contradictions in the physical and moral world. It is life; it is immortality. Since I have known the Saviour, every thing is clear; with Him there is nothing that I can not solve."

When conscience speaks the truth, she declares that the Bible is the book of God. They both condemn us on the very same principles—the breach of known law; and they both assure us that there can be no safety or blessedness but in such a change in the state of the will as will not suffer us to rest in soul without a conformity of our desires and actions to the standard that we feel to be holy, just, and true. In short, enlightened reason tells us that we need a restoration of the moral image of God, in order to salvation, and the Bible tells us the same thing, but with the important additional truth by which we are instructed how that resemblance to the Holy One is obtained and perpetuated. Neither conscience nor the Bible will countenance any known evil, whether among nominal Christians or professed Infidels. By their condemning power they alike declare the voice of God. He speaks in both. To the heart he speaks. He will not tolerate any habit that opposes charity. He declares that every spirit that submits not to kindness is utterly reprobate, ungodly, unchristian, and in itself anathematized and hopeless, until convinced that Omnipotence is Love. Then repentant, it clings to the Almighty, and will not let Him go. Then its plea is valid. It claims eternal blessing from The Everlasting Father, and can not fail, because it hangs upon the bounty of that heart so freely opened to bestow its immense benevolence on all who seek the fellowship of the faithful Creator. To trust God, is to honor Him; to believe Him as our Parent, is to find Him so. To feel assured that He can not forsake us, is to know that He more freely gives than we can ask. To cast off selfish anxiety, is to rest upon the Father's bosom; and to look forward without fear, is practically to own and to enjoy the love that is perfect, and therefore always prepared to sympathize with us in our trials, to rectify our souls, to anticipate our exigence, and eternally to provide for us.

THE END

Miss Sedgwick's Works.

Miss Sedgwick has marked individuality; she writes with a higher aim than merely to amuse. Indeed, the rare endowments of her mind depend in an unusual degree upon the moral qualities with which they are united for their value. Animated by a cheerful philosophy, and anxious to pour its sunshine into every place where there is lurking care or suffering, she selects for illustration the scenes of every-day experience, paints them with exact fidelity, and seeks to diffuse over the mind a delicious serenity, and in the heart kind feelings and sympathies, and wise ambition, and steady hope. Her style is colloquial, picturesque, and marked by a facile grace, which is evidently a gift of nature. Her characters are nicely drawn and delicately contrasted; her delineation of manners decidedly the best that have appeared.—*Prose Writers of America.*

MEMOIR OF JOSEPH CURTIS. A Model Man. By the Author of "Married or Single?" "Means and Ends," "The Linwoods," "Hope Leslie," "Live and Let Live," &c., &c. 16mo, Muslin, 50 cents.

MARRIED OR SINGLE? By Miss Catharine M. Sedgwick, Author of "Hope Leslie," "The Linwoods," "Means and Ends," "Live and Let Live," &c., &c. 2 vols. 12mo, Muslin, $1 75.

LIVE AND LET LIVE; or, Domestic Service Illustrated. By Miss C. M. SEDGWICK. 18mo, Muslin, 45 cents.

MEANS AND ENDS; or, Self-training. By Miss C. M. SEDGWICK. 18mo, Muslin, 45 cents.

A LOVE TOKEN FOR CHILDREN. Designed for Sunday-School Libraries. By Miss C. M. SEDGWICK. 18mo, Muslin, 45 cents.

THE POOR RICH MAN AND THE RICH POOR MAN. By Miss C. M. SEDGWICK. 18mo, Muslin, 45 cents.

STORIES FOR YOUNG PERSONS. By Miss C. M. SEDGWICK. 18mo, Muslin, 45 cents.

WILTON HARVEY, AND OTHER TALES. By Miss C. M. SEDGWICK. 18mo, Muslin, 45 cents.

www.ingramcontent.com/pod-product-compliance
Lightning Source LLC
LaVergne TN
LVHW020242110826
845151LV00003B/1009

* 9 7 8 1 4 2 5 5 2 8 7 3 7 *